—1—
A King's Heritage

In a prominent place on the mezzanine floor of The Regent, regularly honored with offerings by members of the hotel staff, stands a bust of His Majesty King Vajiravudh, sixth ruler of the Chakri Dynasty. It serves not only as a memorial to one of Thailand's most versatile kings but also as a reminder that the land on which the building stands is Crown Property and that the surrounding area was the scene of several significant events during his eventful reign.

Born in the Grand Palace on January 1, 1881, King Vajiravudh was the son of King Chulalongkorn (Rama V) and Queen Saowabha. A half-brother, Prince Vajirunhis, had been appointed the first official Thai Crown Prince; when he died at the age of 17, the title was given to Prince Vajiravudh, then the eldest son of the highest princely rank.

His preparation for the throne was exceptional. He was the first Thai king to be educated abroad, going to England in 1893 and studying there for nine years, first with private tutors, later at Christ Church, Oxford (where he read history and law), then at the Royal Military Academy at Sandhurst. He also travelled extensively through Europe, meeting foreign rulers and heads of state, and on his way back to Thailand visited the United States and Japan.

During his studies he also received regular instruction in the customs and traditions of his native country. King Chulalongkorn explained the importance of this in one of many letters he wrote his son: "I would at this point impress upon you the fact that in sending you abroad for a European education, it is not my object to have you useful solely through your knowledge of foreign languages and European methods of work. Your own language and literature must ever be in constant use..."

After a reign of 42 years – the longest in Thai history until it was exceeded by the present monarch in 1988 – King Chulalongkorn died in 1910 and King Vajiravudh succeeded to the throne. There were two coronation ceremonies, a traditional one held shortly after the king's death and a much grander affair held toward the end of the following year. Foreign royalty and other representatives of fourteen governments came to the second – England, France, Russia, Germany, the United States, and Japan were all represented – and lavish entertainments went on for several weeks, bringing Thailand and its new ruler an unprecedented amount of international attention.

PRECEDING PAGE:
BUST OF KING
VAJIRAVUDH
ON THE MEZZANINE
FLOOR.
FACING PAGE:
PHOTOGRAPHS OF
CHULALONGKORN
UNIVERSITY, THAILAND'S
FIRST UNIVERSITY.

His succeeding reign of fifteen years saw a number of notable achievements, many inspired by Western models. In 1913, he introduced surnames for all Thais (personally devising many of them himself), an immense aid in personal identification and the keeping of official records. He designed the present Thai flag of red, white, and blue stripes, replacing the older one showing a white elephant on a red background which, in the words of one writer, the King found "too exotic, too quaint for a young nation that wanted respect, honor, and esteem for its progressiveness". A national scheme of public education was proclaimed, leading to an act in 1921 requiring compulsory education for both boys and girls from the age of seven to fourteen, the first such initiative taken by any government on the Asian mainland.

Though Thailand declared itself neutral at the outbreak of World War I, King Vajiravudh's pro-British sympathies eventually led him to enter the conflict on the side of the Allies, sending an Expeditionary Force of 1,200 volunteers and earning his country the right to attend the 1919 Versailles Peace Conference. This in turn promoted a willingness on the part of Western governments to renegotiate unequal treaties that had existed between them and Thailand since the mid-19th century and replace them with fairer agreements.

In addition, King Vajiravudh founded the Thai Boy Scouts, introduced Western sports to the country, improved the status of women in several ways (one was by openly attacking the traditional practice of polygamy), and stimulated patriotism by constantly stressing those qualities that made Thai culture unique. Devoted to literature, he wrote numerous original plays, poetry and prose works as well as translations of Shakespeare (*The Merchant of Venice* and *As You Like It* among them) and new versions of classic Thai works.

From the upper floors of The Regent, guests with rooms in the front can glimpse an impressive collection of multi-tiered roofs with colored tiles rising against the sky beyond the race track and golf links of the Royal Bangkok Sports Club across Rajadamri Road. Some take these to be part of a Buddhist temple complex, not surprisingly in view of similar architectural features. In fact they belong to the oldest buildings of Chulalongkorn University, Thailand's first institution of higher learning and one of the most enduring memorials of the sixth reign.

King Chulalongkorn had founded a college under the Ministry of Interior to train civil servants needed for the growing needs of government administration. King Vajiravudh decided to expand this to serve all ministries, naming it after his father, and later to transform it into a proper university on a large piece of land donated from his own private holdings. A modified Khmer-Thai style was used for the two original structures, which have steep soaring roofs and guardian *nagas*, or sacred serpents, at the base of each entrance stairway.

When the institution was officially opened in 1917 it offered eight courses of study – Agriculture, Commerce, Education, Engineering, Foreign Service, Law, Medicine, and Public Administration – and all classes were taught in these buildings; at present they house only the Faculty of Arts, while thirteen other faculties are scattered over a vast surrounding campus.

The Royal Bangkok Sports Club, of which King Vajiravudh served as honorary president, also witnessed at least two historic events during the same period. One occurred on January 31, 1911, when Prince Chakrabongse, Chief of the Army General Staff, and Prince Purachatra, Commander of the Army Engineers – both brothers of the newly-crowned king – assembled at the club along with hundreds of less illustrious spectators, so many that fifteen new entrances had to be added and four bridges constructed across neighboring canals.

The great attraction was a Belgian visitor named Van den Born, who proceeded to climb into a flimsy-looking contraption (actually a Henri Farman biplane from France), sped down the length of the race track, and, in the words of a contemporary newspaper report, "simply drifted off into the air". The machine made a graceful pass over the surrounding fields, including the site of The Regent hotel, and then landed with admirable ease. Barely eight years after William and Orville Wright had first demonstrated the possibility of flight in a "heavier than air craft" on a beach near Kitty Hawk, North Carolina, aviation had come to Thailand.

King Vajiravudh made several personal visits to the club during the week-long demonstrations, inspecting the plane carefully and conversing with Van den Born. Commented the *Bangkok Times*: "No attempt has been made to break records but the aviator has certainly demonstrated that aeroplaning is a practical thing, and nothing could have been more graceful than the way the machine was made to salute the King on the occasion of His Majesty's first visit to the ground."

With the King's enthusiastic support, three Thais went to France the following year to receive flying certificates and the Ministry of War authorized purchase of seven aircraft. When the pilots returned toward the end of 1913, they displayed their own skills at the Sports Club. "At half past seven the motor of the first monoplane was started," reported the *Times*, "and the machine shot forward. A cheer went up from the assembled spectators as it rose into the air and sped across the golf links. Turning at the Sala Daeng end, the aviator made a circle of the course and then went over the links again to land. Bunkers seemed terribly prominent, but the aviator chose his spot, and the hum of the motor died as he glided gently to earth."

In his diary for that day, of that momentous event, King Vajiravudh noted, "I am delighted to see that we Thais are not bested by the Westerner; truly we can do whatever they can do."

Subsequently the newly-formed Air Service moved its operations to Don Muang, north of Bangkok, a site selected because it was less subject to floods though it was then connected to the city only by railway. (Don Muang, incidentally, is the oldest airport in the world still being used in its original location.) By 1917, the service had grown to the point where an aviation contingent numbering 340 was included in the Expeditionary Force sent to France. By 1922, it was operating a regular airmail service between Bangkok and the northeastern part of the country, the first such service in Southeast Asia.

Somewhat less spectacularly, but also with lasting future results, in September of 1915 the Sports Club was the scene of Bangkok's first football game. The King had seen matches earlier that year on a trip to southern Thailand, where, perhaps because of the British in nearby Malaysia, the sport was enjoying a regional popularity. "I am happy with this English game," he wrote soon afterwards, "and wish that it would spread widely. Perhaps this is because I was educated in England, but I hope you won't think this is the only reason. I hope you who are of the same race and generation as myself will agree that football will be useful to the Thai people."

On September 5 a match was held between British members of the club and Thai players from the Wild Tigers, a para-military organization that had been created by King Vajiravudh. The British won, but this by no means cooled Thai enthusiasm for the sport. A gold cup competition for Thai teams was started that same month and in November the Football Association of Thailand was founded. In a final round of games held from December 24, 1915 to January 6, 1916, the Thais won against the Westerners, to the joy of a large crowd of spectactors, including the King.

In 1925, King Vajiravudh began plans for what he saw as one of the major events of his reign, the Siamese Kingdom Exhibition, designed as a showcase for Thai products as well as for Western goods that could aid in the country's modernization. He donated a large tract of his personal land at the corner of Rajadamri and Rama IV Roads, which he named Lumpini Park and on which various facilities began to rise, among them a Chinese clock tower that still stands, an exhibition hall, and facilities for assorted games and entertainments. A brochure for visitors and fair-goers was also prepared and teams invited from neighboring countries to compete in "the first great Asiatic Football Competition." Afterwards, the grounds would become a permanent park for residents of an area that was rapidly being developed, as well as a site for future fairs.

The exhibition was scheduled to open toward the end of the year, close to the King's birthday. On November 25, after a brief illness, he died suddenly; and one of the first acts of his successor, King Prajadhipok, was to cancel the event. Lumpini Park remains, however, a welcome expanse of green amid the high-rise buildings of modern Bangkok and a popular place for morning exercises. At its gate stands an imposing statue to the man who made it possible, erected in 1940 by a government that had replaced the absolute monarchy of King Vajiravudh's ancestors but that recognized his many valuable contributions to the nation.

FOLLOWING PAGES: MEMORABILIA OF EARLY AVIATION IN THAILAND, INCLUDING THE FIRST FLIGHT DEMONSTRATION AT THE ROYAL BANGKOK SPORTS CLUB IN 1911.

—2—
THE ART OF THAI MURALS

Covering an entire wall at the head of the stairs leading from the lobby to the mezzanine is a dazzling example of Thai mural painting, an art form most commonly seen adorning major Buddhist temples. Other similar works are prominent in the decorations of the Pimarnman reception room on the mezzanine level and The Regent Ballroom. Before discussing the creators and subject matter of these contemporary works, it might be worthwhile to look back at certain ancient traditions which provided their inspiration.

The product of cultural influences that began in India and spread through Sri Lanka and Burma, Thai murals evolved over the centuries into something highly distinctive, with their own artistic conventions and style. The earliest surviving examples have been found in a cave at Yala, in the far south, and in a temple near the first Thai capital of Sukhothai. Both date from the 13th century and are painted in dark, obscure places, not as decorations to be admired but as pious offerings to make merit.

These murals show horizontal rows of stylized Buddhas and attendants, separated by such symbols as multi-tiered umbrellas, ceremonial fans and stupas (spired Buddhist monuments), and are believed to be typical of most religious wall paintings in Thailand until around the middle of the 17th century or possibly later. Earth-tone colors – red, yellow, and white – were predominant, derived from powdered riverbed clays bound with strained tree gum and animal glue, while green was obtained from crushed plant stems and black from soot.

Such paintings experienced a dramatic change during the 17th century in the great capital of Ayutthaya. The decorative but rather monotonous rows of figures gave way to spectacles of complex action incorporating inspirational legends, celestial beings who paid homage to the Buddha, Hindu deities and even mundane scenes from everyday life of the time. With the introduction of paints in powdered form from China, the colors became richer and more varied; and master painters with individual styles began to emerge from the ranks of nameless artisans employed to adorn the increasing number of temples.

Almost all the great Ayutthaya-period murals were lost when the city was captured and destroyed by the Burmese in 1767. A little over a decade later, however, following the establishment of Bangkok as the new capital, one of the chief aims of the new Chakri Dynasty was to

PRECEDING PAGE: PART OF THE LOBBY CEILING MURAL, WITH CLASSICAL THAI MOTIFS.

FACING PAGE: CENTRAL PART OF THE LOBBY'S STAIRCASE MURAL, SHOWING THE FIRST BANGKOK KING ON HIS THRONE WITH THE GRAND PALACE BEHIND.

recreate the splendor of the past. Painting was an important part of this endeavor, and over the next seventy years the art reached new heights, with fine examples appearing not only in Bangkok and Thonburi but also as far south as Songkhla and as far north as Chiang Mai.

The primary purpose of the temple murals was to instruct and inspire by illustrated example. (Their creators, significantly, were not regarded as "artists" in the Western sense of the term; they were known instead as *chang khien*, (craftsmen who paint), and none of the works was signed.) The subject matter was predominantly religious – scenes from the life of the Buddha and episodes from the moralistic Jataka tales which deal with the Buddha's previous incarnations and show how he mastered various virtues – though vignettes of daily life also appear in many, especially in lower (i.e., less important) sections.

To the Western eye, such paintings may at first glance seem confused, a bewildering, tapestry-like swirl of color and two-dimensional figures with few, if any, evident clues to organization or story line. A closer study, however, reveals certain classic conventions that aid in comprehension. The various scenes of a particular story may or may not be chronological, but in general they are separated and distinguished by architectural or landscape features (or, in the earliest ones, by jagged lines). Moreover, the human and semi-divine figures are painted in several styles, each strictly defined by the type or status of the character being portrayed.

The most stylized are the highest-ranking: the Buddhas, the bodhisattvas or Buddhas-to-be, the noble ascetics, the kings and queens and their royal attendants. These have the same mask-like faces, often displaying a faint smile and depicted in profile or occasionally in a three-quarters view. The noble figures express themselves through a standardized collection of gestures and postures still used in classical Thai dance, what one scholar has called a "a type of 'pictorial dictionary' for the identification of the character  and the action portrayed". Grief, for instance, is manifested by tilting the head toward one bent arm while the other hand is held against the heart; arrogance is shown by placing one hand on the hip and brandishing the other in a threatening manner.

Stylized, too, though to a lesser degree, are such mythical creatures as the fierce Garuda, the graceful, half-bird half-woman Kinnari, and the grotesque ogres who act as guardians. Various animals that play important roles in the legends – elephants, horses, deer, and rabbits – are painted according to idealized models as well, but often with a free-flowing charm that sets apart the work of certain artists.

The most realistic scenes are those showing details of daily life. Here, the painter – or, more often, painters, for teams of *chang khien* worked on larger murals – was freed from rigid conven-tions and could indulge his imagination and, frequently, his sense of humor as well. Here, we see ordinary Thais with individual characteristics engaged in a wide range of homely activities, such as hunting and weaving, gambling and preparing food, paddling boats and spanking naughty children, making merit and enjoying open-air theatrical performances, and even involved in romantic dalliance.

Domestic and religious architecture is rendered in careful detail, as are fish traps, cooking pots, charcoal braziers, and farming implements, making the paintings a valuable record of life styles that have all but vanished in most of contemporary Thailand. Similar care is taken in the depiction of domestic animals, fruit trees and flowering plants.

Classic Thai painting began to lose its vigor around the middle of the 19th century, as both artists and their royal patrons increasingly felt the impact of Western culture; a particular painter named Khrua In Khong is credited with introducing three-dimensional perspective to the flat murals during the reign of King Rama IV, and figures in foreign dress even began to appear in some works.

The traditional techniques and disciplines by no means disappeared, however; they continued to be taught in such institutions as the Fine Arts University and assorted vocational schools; and when the art form enjoyed a revival of interest in recent years skilled painters were available to meet the demand for new works.

An acknowledged master was the late Professor Paiboon Suwanakudt, popularly known as "Tan Kudt". In his younger years, Professor Paiboon studied at the Fine Arts University under an Italian, Corrado Feroci, founder of the university, and, like many Thai artists of his generation, at first experimented with European styles. He felt more at ease with his own native forms, however, and eventually began to concentrate on traditional works, finding inspiration in the murals painted during the early years of Bangkok. Because of his fame, he was

called on to create the original murals in The Regent lobby: a large one at the top of the stairs, measuring twenty by five meters, as well as ceiling decorations, both painted in tempera on silk stretched over plywood panels. Assisting him in the job were some twenty of his best students, along with three of his own children. When he became seriously ill halfway through, his daughter Phapthawan took over and saw the work to completion.

Planning of the hotel, in 1982, coincided with the celebration of Bangkok's Bicentennial, which led Professor Paiboon to choose as his subject for the main painting not a conventional Buddhist theme but the establishment of the capital and the Chakri Dynasty which has ruled the country ever since. This enabled him to include a wide range of activities, from a splendid royal coronation to intimate scenes of daily life, as well as assorted symbols, both secular and religious.

As in all classic murals, the most sacred figures are to be found in the upper portion, separated from the rest by flowing lines. Here, among numerous divinities flying about the heavens, can be seen two representations of previous Buddhas, each seated on an elegant chariot surmounted by graceful spired roofs, flanked by traditional multi-tiered offerings. These reflect the close relationship between kingship and religion that was a prominent aspect of Thai society in both Ayutthaya and early Bangkok.

Just below this enlightened realm, viewed from left to right, are a number of significant figures and scenes. On the far left is a richly caparisoned white horse, an animal often associated with royalty and suggesting purity as well as wealth. Nearby can be found a festive scene of soldiers, courtiers, and common people and a glimpse of the massive walls that surrounded the original city of Bangkok, built (like Ayutthaya before) on an artificial island created by digging a canal at a point where the Chao Phraya River bent sharply.

A gracefully curved royal barge forms the next prominent feature in the painting, a reminder of the magnificent craft that carried kings and other high-ranking residents of the capital along the river in the days when the Chao Phraya was the principal avenue of communication. It also symbolizes the growing trade that brought prosperity to the young capital and soon forced it to expand far beyond its walled heart. Just over fifty years after it was established, an English

PRECEDING PAGES:
THE LOBBY
STAIRCASE MURAL,
DEPICTING THE
ESTABLISHMENT OF
BANGKOK AS THE
CAPITAL.

visitor found an estimated 70,000 floating houses and shops along both banks, as well as numerous Chinese junks and ships, which had come from far-off Europe, anchored in the stream.

The center of the mural shows the King seated on his ceremonial throne, homage being paid to him by his subjects, and, on the right, a stylized representation of the Grand Palace. This dazzling collection of structures, which still contains the greatest concentration of classic Thai arts to be seen anywhere in the world, covers an area of nearly one square mile, and was started shortly after King Rama I came to the throne in 1782. Artisans were brought from all over the country to adorn its various royal residences and audience halls, as well as the adjacent Wat Phra Keo, a temple complex in the Grand Palace compound which enshrines the sacred Emerald Buddha.

The work took three years; official consecration of the palace took place in 1785, marked by a three-day celebration during which monks chanted prayers from the battlements that studded the city walls, the Emerald Buddha was ceremoniously brought across the river from its temporary home at Wat Arun, and the King bestowed a lengthy, honorific-filled title on his capital city. (Thais shorten this to Krung Thep, City of Angels, while most foreigners have continued to call it Bangkok, the name of a busy trading center that formerly stood on the site.)

Below the spires and traditional layered roofs of the palace is an ornate chariot, another emblem of royalty. This is decorated with *hongs*, known in Sanskrit as *hamsas*, mythical swan-like birds that served as a mount for the god Brahma; one of these, gilded and flashing with inlaid mirrors, also adorns the prow of the 46-meter Suphanahong, greatest of the royal barges.

On the far right, balancing the horse figure, is a royal elephant, ceremonially garbed for a procession. Elephants played a major role in Thai life of the past, not only for transportation and forest work but also for use in war, when hundreds might be used in a single battle. A celebrated event of the Ayutthaya period, taught in every Thai school, took place when King Naresuan defeated a Burmese Crown Prince in a heroic elephant-back duel and thus saved his kingdom. Although the military importance of the animals had declined by the mid-19th century, they were still regarded as sufficiently useful for King Rama IV to write a formal letter to U.S. President James Buchanan in 1861, offering

A WHITE HORSE,
OFTEN ASSOCIATED
WITH THAI
ROYALTY,
FEATURED
IN THE LOBBY'S
STAIRCASE MURAL.

FROM THE SAME
MURAL, AN
ELEPHANT, WHICH
PLAYED A
PROMINENT ROLE IN
WARFARE AND
ROYAL
PROCESSIONS.

to send a number that might be released and produce future wild herds in the warmer states. (By the time the letter reached Washington, Abraham Lincoln was President and the Civil War had started; Lincoln wrote and thanked him but noted that "our political jurisdiction...does not reach a latitude so low as to favor the multiplication of the elephants, and steam on land as well as on water has been our best and most efficient agent of transportation in internal commerce".)

Across the bottom section of the mural, uniting the various elements of the huge composition, moves a gala royal procession rich in colorful detail: marching soldiers and commoners in traditional dress, war elephants, elaborate barges rowed by teams of chanting oarsmen, palanquins, and an auspicious white dove. Close examination also reveals carefully rendered buildings and assorted activities characteristic of the city in its early days.

The lobby ceiling designed by Professor Paiboon is divided into nineteen major sections and incorporates motifs inspired by classic Thai patterns, many of which also appear on items associated with royalty, as well as Buddhist symbols. At the corners are faces of the mythical beast Rahu, who tries to devour the moon during eclipses and must be frightened away with firecrackers and other noise-makers, while in between can be discerned graceful *kinarees*, legendary creatures that are half bird, half human.

More murals can be seen in the Pimarnman Room on the mezzanine floor. Pimarnman was the name of the Palace of the Gods, and here Preecha Taothong, the artist in charge, has created two separate paintings that suggest celestial abodes. One shows Devas, or divinities, from Hindu mythology drifting through a serene setting of clouds and mountains, while the other represents the ethereal life on and around Mount Khaokrairat, the Thai version of the Hindu Mount Meru, symbolizing the 33 levels of heaven. The delicate colors and light-hearted mood harmonize with the Pimarnman Room's vaulted ceiling, gilded columns and general feeling of airy elegance.

Given the hotel's close association with traditional Thai painting from its conception, it was only natural that murals would also figure prominently in the design for a new ballroom, officially opened in May of 1990. Measuring 120 by 60 meters and covering the four sides of the ballroom's frieze, these are the work of Professor Paiboon's daughter

Phapthawan, who assisted on the lobby paintings and later went on to achieve reknown as an artist in her own right. She and eight associates who specialize in Thai-style works founded the Tan Kudt Group in memory of her father and have held a number of exhibitions, both in Thailand and abroad, as well as working on murals for several temples and other buildings.

The ballroom paintings, also in tempera on silk with designs of gold leaf, depict scenes from an upper sphere of the Buddhist cosmology, a Suwanphumi or "heaven" just below the one in which the ultimate happiness of Nirvana is achieved. Widthwise, one side portrays the royal chariots of the Sun God and Moon Goddess moving away from the two lower corners, thus symbolizing the passage of day and night; in the center is the Vimarn, or palace, of Heaven.

The opposite frieze shows the palaces of the guardian angels of the four parts of the compass: Tao Kuwane of the north, Tao Thatarote of the east, Tao Wirupak of the west, and Tao Wiroonhok of the south. The painting along one side of the ballroom's length shows aspects of Dao-Dueng, ruled by the God Indra, among them such architectural features as a *chedi*, or spired religious monument, a pavilion, and a royal edifice known as a *prasad*; in addition there are various trees, shrubs and garden scenes.

On the opposite wall are different celestial spheres and planets both large and small, scattered in multi-colored rays. At once classic and modern, The Regent murals reveal the continuing vitality of an ancient art, one that remains an important part of Thailand's rich spiritual and cultural heritage.

DETAILS FROM THE BALLROOM FRIEZE. TOP: THE KING PRESIDES IN THE *VIMARN* (HEAVEN), FLANKED BY COURT ATTENDANTS. CENTER: CIRCULAR *BOKKHORANEE* OR LOTUS POND IN THE GARDEN OF HEAVEN. BOTTOM: THE DIFFERENT CELESTIAL SPHERES, WITH MUSICIANS.

FROM THE SAME
FRIEZE, TOP: THE
KEEPER OF
CELESTIAL TIME
LOOKING DOWN ON
HEAVEN, WITH THE
GODS OF THE FOUR
COMPASS POINTS
SEATED IN THE
PAVILION.
CENTER: CELESTIAL
PALACE FLANKED BY
WHITE RELIQUARY,
WITH GUARDIAN
ANGEL OF THE EAST
AND PLANET IN
THE BACKGROUND.
BOTTOM: THE
CELESTIAL PALACE
RULED BY GOD
INDRA,
WITH COURTIERS.

–3–
TRADITIONAL
LIFE

E ach room in the hotel displays a painting in the classic Thai style seen in the lobby murals. Apart from their decorative appeal, these paintings reveal aspects of traditional Thai daily life. Most of these Thai activities still survive, despite the changes Thai society has experienced over past decades, and despite the influence of Western culture.

KITE-FIGHTING

Kite-flying in Thailand is by no means limited to children and the young at heart. It takes teams of skilled adults to maneuver the huge specimens sent aloft between February and April at Sanam Luang, across from the Grand Palace, when dependable late-afternoon winds sweep over the oval field and break the summer heat.

Actually symbolic battles of the sexes, the matches involve two kinds of kites. One, called the *pukpao*, represents the female, and is a small conventional diamond-shaped affair with a long tail; this is flown by only one person and has the advantage of being able to move swiftly if handled properly. The other is the *chula*, or "male," which is star-shaped and enormous, often measuring several meters across and requiring a team of up to twenty strong men to manipulate.

The match starts when the huge *chulas* sail across their boundary line and enter *pukpao* territory. The big kites are armed with a bamboo hook, and the object is to ensnare one of the *pukpaos* and bring her down in the male domain. This might seem easy enough to an outsider, but in fact the dainty, darting females are an elusive prey and as often as not manage to loop their lines around an invader and bring it crashing to earth.

All this is governed by strict rules, mostly established during the reign of King Chulalongkorn (Rama V); there are umpires, registered teams (often sponsored by business firms), and a championship cup for winners at the end of the season. Refreshment stands are set up around the field, with reclining chairs for spectators who want to watch the sport in comfort while the golden light fades over the peerless backdrop of glittering palace spires.

POPULAR THEATER

Touring theater companies are an essential feature of the fairs that periodically enliven rural Thai life. Perhaps the most popular are *likay*,

PRECEDING PAGE:
A GLIMPSE OF RURAL
THAI LIFE, FROM A
TRADITIONAL
PAINTING IN ONE OF
THE GUEST ROOMS.
FACING PAGE:
A DETAIL FROM THE
SAME PAINTING,
SHOWING WORK
ELEPHANTS BEING
BATHED.

which combine certain elements of the classical dance-drama with generous helpings of social satire and low comedy, and performances by well-known bands and singers. Shadow-play theater, the earliest form of Thai drama, is somewhat rarer today, though it can still be seen at many festive occasions in the far South.

The oldest version of the shadow play is known as *Nang Yai* (literally "play with big figures"), which was probably introduced to the south from the Indonesian empire of Srivijaya; it was regularly performed in Ayutthaya, the Thai capital for four centuries, when, according to a 17th century poem, "At night the sky is alight/ With blazes that make the shadows glow..."

The large cowhide figures, some as much as two meters tall, depict figures from the Ramakien, the Thai version of the Indian epic *Ramayana*, and are energetically manipulated in front of a brightly backlit white screen to the accompaniment of music and narrations in verse. Partly because of its reliance on classical storylines more familiar to educated members of the royal court than to outsiders, the *Nang Yai* declined in early Bangkok and is seldom seen nowadays, except at special performances.

Still popular, however, especially in the South, is Nang Talung, in which the figures are relatively small, manipulated behind rather than in front of the screen, and usually have at least one moving part, such as a leg, arm or jaw. There are numerous characters in a Nang Talung performance – as many as a hundred in an all-night marathon – and the plots are full of bawdy jokes and puns that often arise from topics of purely local interest.

MERIT-MAKING

Of all the ways in which Buddhism makes its presence felt in daily Thai life, none is more evident than the activities grouped under the heading of *tam boon*, or making merit. Ideologically, merit-making is aimed at instilling a sense of sacrifice, while directing the individual toward acts of generosity and loving kindness, two of Buddhism's highest virtues.

The most popular of the moralistic Jataka tales, which describe the Buddha's previous lives before attaining enlightenment, tells of noble Prince Vessantara who gives away not only his material possessions – money, jewels, palaces, and royal elephants – but also his beloved wife and children. More practically, it is a way of storing up heavenly credit and thus improving one's chances in the next life – being born a rich man, for instance, instead of a poor peasant.

Merit can be earned in a wide variety of ways, small and large. It is achieved by releasing caged birds and other animals, by giving alms to the poor, or by offering food to monks, either at a temple site or along the street in the early morning. (The often-heard Western term "begging bowl" is a misnomer; the monks are not begging but offering laymen a treasured chance to gain merit by accepting their food.) The greatest merit is earned by erecting a Buddhist temple or by contributing to the maintenance, or even restoration, of an older one.

A particularly popular form of merit-making comes at the end of the annual Rains Retreat, during which monks are supposed to remain in their monasteries, and various groups would organize ceremonies called *thot kathins* to bring a variety of useful goods as well as financial donations to the temples. These often involve festive outings by bus or train to remote parts of the country in a typical and irresistible Thai blend of piety and *sanuk*, or fun.

VILLAGE LIFE

"In the water there are fish; in the fields there is rice." This famous phrase, found in an inscription from the first Thai capital of Sukhothai, attests to the abundance of the kingdom and also to two of its favorite traditional occupations: fishing and preparing food.

In rural regions, these activities are usually closely related, since fish from neighboring streams and rice paddies form a major part of the Thai diet. An extraordinarily varied collection of traps and containers has evolved over the centuries for catching and transporting fish, sometimes differing from region to region and ingeniously adapted to the specific purposes of the community.

The *Lop Non*, for instance, found in the Central Plains, is a tubular affair made of split bamboo bound with rattan or vines and placed in a stream so that the fish swim directly into it, while the *Nang*, with a square opening and rounded bottom, is used like a scoop in shallow ponds and canals in the southern region.

Northern fishermen, on the other hand, use a bottle-shaped device known as a *Toom*, made of tightly woven bamboo with an opening in the lower part through which fish are lured by the scent of bait. There are also special baskets for storing the fish after they are caught and bringing them safely back to the village. Apart from their practicality, such traditional devices are often strikingly beautiful in both form and workmanship and thus prized by collectors of folk art.

At home the cooks are ready to transform the catch into a variety of simple but nourishing dishes on charcoal braziers, flavored with such spices as garlic, chilli peppers, ginger, coriander and basil leaves, along with fresh vegetables from the local gardens. Such activities traditionally take place on the verandah of a village home, or in the open areas below, which also serve as the site for other family industries like rearing silkworms and weaving textiles.

FACING PAGE:

VILLAGE LIFE

AROUND A TYPICAL

THAI HOME, AS

DEPICTED IN A

DETAIL FROM A

PAINTING IN

A GUEST ROOM.

ASPECTS OF DAILY
THAI LIFE, SUCH AS
KITE-FIGHTING
(TOP) AND POPULAR
THEATER (BELOW),
AS SHOWN IN
GUEST ROOM
PAINTINGS.

MERIT-MAKING BY
VILLAGERS (TOP)
AND TRAPPING FISH
IN A LOCAL STREAM
(BELOW), TWO
OTHER FAMILIAR
FEATURES OF
TRADITIONAL LIFE.

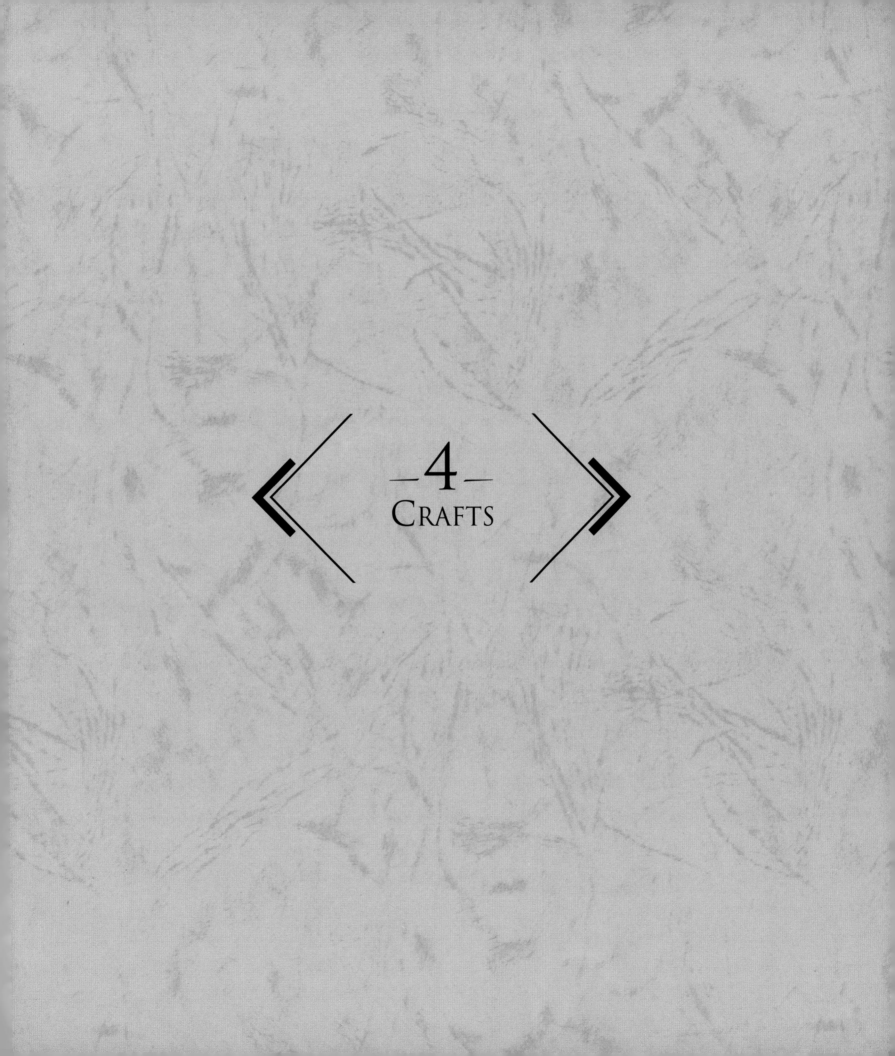

⟨ —4—
CRAFTS ⟩

I n the days of King Mongkut [Rama IV]," wrote Dr. Malcolm Smith, a long-time resident of Thailand, "it was the custom of many of the wealthy families to maintain craftsmen in their own houses. Some were employed as gold and silver smiths, some as jewellers; others were painters and wood-carvers, or workers in lacquer or in mother-of-pearl...The artists belonged to the household, they took pride in their work, they vied with each other in performance, and their children when they grew up entered the occupation and learnt it from their parents. The master of the house was, in his own way, a patron of the arts."

At the time Dr. Smith was writing his memoirs of service to the court of King Rama V, such crafts seemed in danger of extinction. Western fashions and ways of life were all the rage, and Bangkok markets were flooded with mass-produced European commodities instead of the hand-made ones that had served for centuries. This was particularly true in royal circles, where "to Europeanize his country became with [the King] one of the dominating passions of his life, and the fact that some of his reforms were quite unsuited to the climate and the habits of the people, never deterred him from introducing them".

Had the observant doctor travelled more widely in the provinces, he might have been reassured. There, relatively isolated from Bangkok's influence, the old crafts remained an integral part of daily life, the skills involved still handed down from generation to generation.

In the far north, Chiang Mai's producers of superbly textured gold and silver brocaded silk no doubt suffered when royal preference started to lean towards Western dress forms; but the court continued to support large communities of other artisans, grouped by specialty in several villages which were located outside the city walls.

In recent years, there has been a notable resurgence of interest in the country's traditional crafts, not only among visitors from abroad but also among Thais themselves. Her Majesty Queen Sirikit's SUPPORT Foundation has helped revive the popularity of a dozen or so such products, ranging from intricate basketry to handwoven silk, primarily as a way of helping rural families earn a supplementary income when their crops fail or some other natural disaster strikes.

Her Majesty also makes prominent use of SUPPORT-made items in her own wardrobe and has travelled frequently abroad to find outside markets. Moreover, many leading hotels, The Regent among them, have

PRECEDING PAGE: KNEELING FIGURE OF A PRIEST IN LACQUERED WOOD DISPLAYED IN THE LOBBY. FACING PAGE: ALSO IN THE LOBBY, A BRONZE KHMER-STYLE FIGURE OF A DANCING HINDU DEITY.

further stimulated appreciation by incorporating fine crafts in their decorative schemes, thus becoming contemporary patrons of the ancient arts as influential as any in the past.

Wood-carving is one of the most evident crafts found at The Regent, both in construction features like elevator walls and lintels, and in individual works of art. Vast forests of teak and other hard woods that once grew extensively in the north provided the material for countless royal and religious decorations: magnificently detailed gables, doors, windows and finials, images of the Buddha and his numerous disciples, thrones and palanquins, pulpits and barges used in state ceremonies. The art can also be found adorning numerous more humble items of every-day life, such as spinning wheels, furniture, cooking utensils, toys, elephant howdahs and bullock carts.

Chiang Mai is still the main center of Thai wood-carving, its artisans so celebrated that they are often brought to other parts of the country to apply their skills directly to a new project. Contemporary carvers also now produce a wide variety of creations aimed at overseas markets, from whimsical animal figures to gilded Christmas ornaments.

Another classic northern craft is lacquerware, seen in the form of bowls, trays, boxes and assorted other receptacles. The gummy resin essential to lacquerware, called *rak*, comes from a tree that grows widely in the region, and this, mixed with vegetable ash or finely-ground black clay, is applied to a base of thinly split bamboo or some-times wood. Up to fifteen coats may be given to the surface, each of which must be dried and polished before the next is applied; in damp weather, the production of a single bowl can take several months.

Many Thai lacquer objects – not only bowls and boxes but also temple doors and scripture cabinets – are further embellished by a process called *lai rod nam*, literally "ornaments washed with gold", a technique probably introduced from China during the Ayutthaya period. After the last coat of pure lacquer, a design is transferred to the surface with a perforated stencil, over which ashes or rice flour are sprinkled; when the paper is re-moved the pattern is thus visible as tiny dots against the black.

A fine brush dipped in a gummy substance is then used to fill all the parts that are to remain ungilded and the entire surface is covered with thin gold leaf. After about 20 hours the object is washed with clean water (*rod nam* in Thai), dissolving the sticky areas and leaving the fine gold designs sharply etched against a glossy black background. Lacquerware is also sometimes inlaid with complex and intricate designs of mother-of-pearl, using tiny pieces of a luminous shell found in the Gulf of Thailand. Masterpieces of this art were achieved in the late Ayutthaya and early Bangkok periods, and it continues to be one of the most impressive skills displayed by Thai craftsmen.

Among the oldest Thai crafts is fine celadon, with glazes varying in hue from jade green to pale blue. Thai legend says the art was introduced to the capital of Sukhothai in the early 14th century by potters from China, although some modern scholars do not accept this theory.

In any event, large quantities of this beautiful ware were certainly produced in Sukhothai and exported to countries like Indonesia and the Philippines, where it was believed to possess talismanic properties. After centuries of decline, the industry was revived several decades ago in Chiang Mai, using the same techniques, and handsome specimens are now widely used in decoration.

Another distinctive ceramic ware currently being made in Thailand is *Bencharong*. China was the original source of these delicate, five-colored porcelains, beginning in the 17th century toward the end of the Ming Dynasty. The designs were Thai – praying divinities, mythological animals and swirling floral patterns – and the ceramic ware was made exclusively for export to Thailand, first to the royal court of Ayutthaya and later to Bangkok. With some interruptions, imports continued throughout the 19th century, only ending with the disruption in China attending the fall of the Ch'ing Dynasty in 1911.

As we have seen from the memoirs of Dr. Smith, this coincided with the growing Thai preference for Western goods, including tablewares. Once again, however, what appeared to be a vanished craft has in recent years enjoyed a renaissance, except that this time Thai artisans have taken over the work of production, creating items that match the originals in workmanship and beauty of design.

Possibly as old as celadon – though far better known to the Western world – is lustrous handwoven Thai silk. Chou Ta-Kuan, a Chinese traveller who visited Cambodia toward the end of the 13th century, noted that while the people of that country were "not given to raising silkworms or to cultivating the mulberry tree," settlers from Siam were doing both; moreover, he says, "the Siamese use silk to weave the dark damask-like textiles with which they clothe themselves." This was shortly before the founding of the ancient capital of Sukhothai, suggesting that weaving technology had been brought by the Thais when they migrated from southern China centuries ago.

Considerable skill in the art was also evident during the Ayutthaya period, when a Thai delegation to France in 1686 wore sumptuous garments made of silk *mat mii*, a kind of weft ikat in subtle patterns that was then, as now, a specialty of northeastern weavers. These caused such a sensation that they were soon being copied by French silk manufacturers and by 1873 a French dictionary could define "Siamoise" as "a material of silk and cotton mixture in imitation of the silks worn by the Siamese Ambassador sent to the court of Louis XIV."

Weaving declined with the advent of cheaper, machine-made textiles toward the end of the 19th century, though it continued in many rural areas, especially the northeast, where silkworm cultivation was practised by many households. A dramatic new surge of interest came just after World War II, when an American named Jim Thompson settled in Thailand and, almost single-handedly, created an international export trade. Today, silk is probably Thailand's best-known handicraft, sold in thousands of shops and used extensively by fashion designers and interior decorators all over the world.

Bamboo, which grows almost everywhere in the country, has served as a basic craft material since the earliest days. Split into long, thin slivers, it is woven into countless different shapes for a wide range of practical uses, from trapping fish and measuring agricultural produce to storing valuable family possessions and steaming glutinous rice. Such common plants as reeds, rattan and a tough variety of climbing fern are also employed in fashioning similar types of household goods.

Other traditional skills also contribute to The Regent's distinctive atmosphere. Bronze-casting, for instance, is now being used for decorative figures and striking tableware, while the equally ancient art of terra cotta appears in bas reliefs depicting complex scenes from mythology. Whether spot-lighted or subtly integrated into the overall decor, such crafts form an integral part of the hotel and reflect the rich variety of Thailand's cultural heritage.

FACING PAGE: PAINTED WOODEN FIGURE IN TRADITIONAL ATTIRE LOCATED IN THE LOBBY.

FACING PAGE:
ANTIQUE DOORS
CARVED WITH
GUARDIAN FIGURES
MOUNTED ON A
DISPLAY LEADING
TO THE BALLROOM.
LEFT: TERRA COTTA
RELIEFS LOCATED
ALONG THE CABANA
WALKWAY.

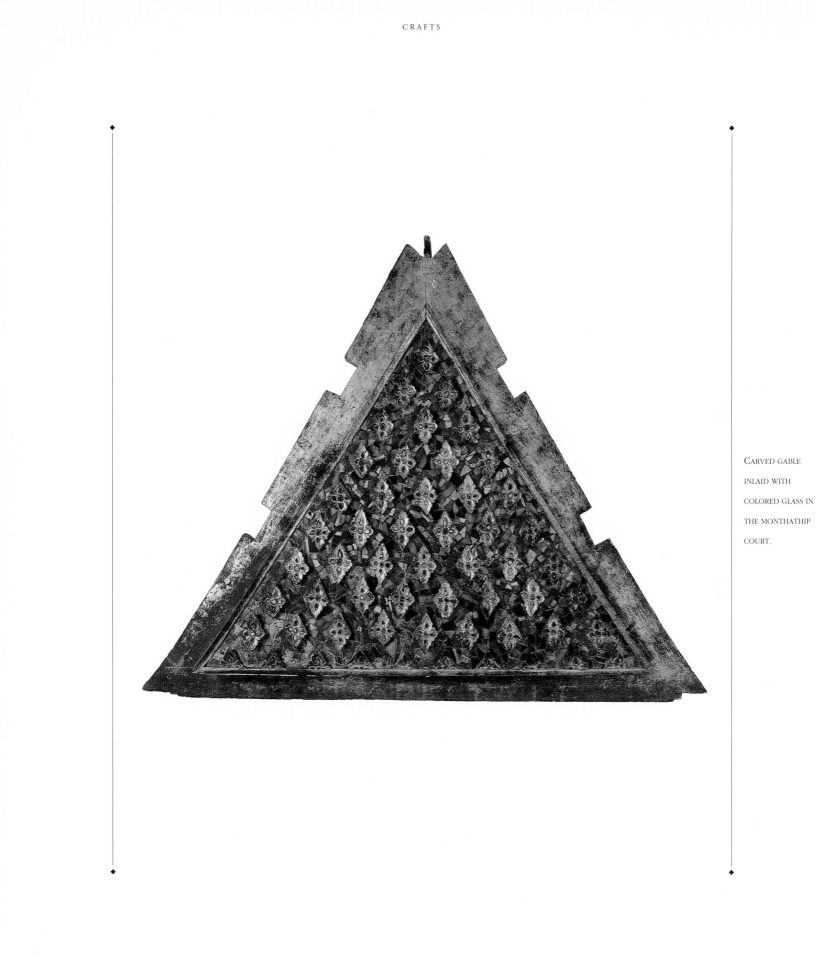

CARVED GABLE
INLAID WITH
COLORED GLASS IN
THE MONTHATHIP
COURT.

DETAIL FROM A
CARVED LINTEL ON
DISPLAY IN A
BANQUET ROOM.
FOLLOWING PAGES:
SPECIMENS OF
BENCHARONG
FOUND IN THE
HOTEL'S SUITES.

⟨ —5—
CUISINE ⟩

A Siamese makes a very good meal with a pound of rice a day, which amounts to not more than a farthing; and with a little dry or salt fish, which costs no more... Their sauces are plain, a little water with some spices, garlic, and some sweet herb. They do very much esteem a liquid sauce, like mustard, which is only crayfish corrupted because they are ill-salted; they call it *Kepi*." So wrote a French visitor to the ancient Thai capital of Ayutthaya in the 17th century. He was describing a simple form of cooking already in the process of evolving into a genuinely original cuisine, selecting elements and methods from other cultures but transforming them into something uniquely Thai: the subtle blend of flavors available at The Regent's celebrated Spice Market and currently being praised by discriminating food lovers at other Thai restaurants throughout the world.

The evolution probably began even before the Thais established their first independent capital at Sukhothai in the 13th century. A 1298 stone inscription extolling the kingdom's virtues observes that "in the water there are fish; in the fields there is rice", thus mentioning what were undoubtedly the two major ingredients of the Sukhothai diet. Black pepper was the principal seasoning, along with fermented fish sauce and assorted native roots and herbs.

Greater variety came during the 400-year rule of Ayutthaya, one of the largest and most cosmopolitan cities in Asia. The chilli pepper was introduced then from its home in South America and probably the tomato and coriander as well. No one knows who first brought these now essential ingredients, but it may have been the Portuguese, who opened relations with Ayutthaya in 1511. Spices aside, the Portuguese also left a lasting culinary impression in the form of popular sweets based on a mixture of sugar and egg yolks. Important influences came, too, from countries like China, Burma, India, Cambodia and Indonesia, in almost every case being altered slightly or drastically to suit Thai tastes.

By the mid-18th century, when Ayutthaya was destroyed by the Burmese, a distinctive Thai cuisine was firmly established, though other ingredients would be added as the kingdom increasingly came into contact with other cultures. Potatoes, for instance, were introduced by American missionaries, and a vast variety of rice-noodle dishes were

PRECEDING PAGE: SPICES USED IN THAI COOKING, AMONG THEM LEMON GRASS, PEPPER, CHILLIES, GARLIC AND GINGER. FACING PAGE: DELICATELY CARVED THAI FRUITS AND VEGETABLES, AN ART THAT ORIGINATED IN THE ROYAL COURT.

popularized by Chinese immigrants who dominated the trade of early Bangkok. Some idea of the sophisticated level Thai food had achieved is suggested by this recipe for the basic sauce called *nam phrik*, offered by Sir John Bowring in an account of his diplomatic visit in 1856:

"It is prepared by bruising a quantity of red pepper in a mortar, to which are added *kepi* (a paste made of shrimps or prawns), black pepper, garlic and onions. These being thoroughly mixed, a small quantity of brine and citron-juice is added. Ginger, tamarinds, and gourd seeds are also employed. The *nam phrik* is one of the most appetite-exciting condiments."

Regional variations also developed, both in such delicate matters as different ways of preparing *nam phrik* and also in fundamental culinary tastes. People in the north and northeast regions, for example, preferred sticky glutinous rice to the fragrant, loose-grain rice variety that accompanies meals in the central plains.

Burmese influences, too, were evident in certain northern dishes like *khao soi*, a curry broth with egg noodles and chicken, pork, or beef, and *gaeng hang lay*, a pork curry flavored with ginger, tamarind and tumeric, while northeasterners adapted a number of dishes and herbs from neighboring Laos and Cambodia.

The cooking of the far south reflected centuries of contact with Asian countries like Malaysia, India and Indonesia, and also made greater use of the coconuts and seafood (especially prawns) so abundant in the region. All these specialties eventually found their way to Bangkok, the cultural heart of the country, forming yet more threads in the rich fabric of a subtle and fascinating culinary tradition.

Wherever it is eaten, a proper Thai meal – as opposed to a quick snack at a sidewalk cafe – is almost always a social affair involving a number of people. A large bowl of rice, often replenished, is the centerpiece, around which is placed an assortment of other dishes and  condiments. A century or so ago, ladles comprised the only cutlery; the rice, glutinous or otherwise, was pressed into small balls with the right hand and then used to scoop up the contents of other dishes. Today, however, a dessert-sized spoon is used for eating and a fork to move food around on the plate; sometimes, a Chinese-style ceramic spoon is provided for soups and chopsticks when noodle dishes are included on the menu.

Thais like a combination of flavors – sweet, hot, sour, salty and bitter – sometimes one predominating, more often blended so that two or three are present together. Generally, there will be a soup of some kind, a delectable curry (very different from the dishes that go by that name in Indian cooking), a steamed fish, something fried, a spicy salad, and several condiments such as *nam phrik* and *nam pla* (fish sauce) which can be used to season dishes to suit individual tastes.

Visual appeal is important, too, especially when guests are present, and dishes are often garnished with spring onions, radishes, cherry tomatoes, turnips and other vegetables intricately carved into realistic flowers and other creations.

All these dishes are placed on the table at one time and eaten in no particular order, with each diner spooning a few mouthfuls at a time onto his serving of rice and mixing dishes at will. Dessert usually consists of one or more of Thailand's abundant fresh fruits – mango, rambutan, mangosteen, pineapple, pomelo and custard apple, to name but a few – and often, at grander meals, exquisite traditional sweets artfully displayed on a platter, like an array of precious gems.

FOLLOWING PAGES: POPULAR THAI DISHES (FROM LEFT), FISHCAKES, CHICKEN CURRY AND SPICY LEMON GRASS SHRIMP SOUP.

–6–
GARDENS

Both inside and out, gardens contribute significantly to the atmosphere of The Regent. These green and tranquil spots in all three of the hotel's connected buildings not only provide a welcome contrast to the drab uniformity of most Bangkok streets, but also remind guests that they are in a tropical country noted for its luxuriant plant life.

Traditional Thai gardens could be divided into three general categories. Those that surrounded ordinary homes of the past were primarily utilitarian rather than ornamental; a few shrubs and creepers might be included simply because they had fragrant flowers or colorful foliage, but the majority had some practical use for the inhabitants.

Thus, even in comparatively small gardens, there were always a number of fruit trees – mango, tamarind, jackfruit, rose apple, guava and papaya, as well as coconuts and bananas. One area was reserved for plants used in Thai cooking, such as lemon grass, basil, kaffir lime, coriander and ginger. And there were usually specimens that had medicinal value: a variety of crinum lily, for example, whose stem could be used in treating sprains and bruises and a small shrub whose crushed leaves were an effective antidote to snake bite.

Superstition played a role in the siting of some horticultural varieties and the omission of others. If the garden had a star-gooseberry (*ma-yom* in Thai), it was planted near the entrance, since *yom* means "admiration" and the small tree would thus attract people to the owners, while a jackfruit tree (*kha-nun*) would be planted behind the house, since *nun* suggests the idea of support.

For reasons not always clear, certain shrubs had acquired a reputation for bringing good fortune and a number of these, known collectively as *wahn*, were often prominently displayed in pots. Plumeria, or frangipani, on the other hand, was avoided because its Thai name resembles the word for "sorrow", and Bodhi trees because of their association with the sacred places of Buddhism.

"The emphasis was on the plants," one Thai authority on such arrangements has written, "with little thought of how a garden should look or of making a garden." This was not the case in the compounds of Buddhist temples and royal palaces, where aesthetic considerations played a more important role in the landscape. Temple gardens were (and, in many cases, still are) composed of cool, shimmering ponds and shady pathways, promoting a sense of tranquility. Many of the

PRECEDING PAGE:

A LUXURIANT

DISPLAY OF

TROPICAL PLANTS IN

THE MONTHATHIP

COURT.

FACING PAGE:

A WATERFALL AND

STREAM IN THE

PARICHART COURT.

plants have religious significance. The Bodhi tree, *Ficus religiosa*, under which the Buddha is supposed to have attained enlightenment, is generally given a special enclosure of its own; and other members of the Ficus family can be seen as well, with their twisting aerial roots that form mysterious grottoes, the abode of spirits according to ancient belief. Here, Plumeria trees fill the air with their delicate, heady fragrance and their perfect, five-petaled flowers adorn many offerings, while in ponds and jars grow pink and white lotus, symbols both of perfection and of the transitory nature of existence.

Classic royal gardens – few of which remain today – tended to be more formal, often a series of courtyards with pools and plants trained and clipped like the specimens grown in earthern pots along the front of The Regent hotel. Though the general arrangement was probably derived from Chinese influences, the Thais developed their own unique styles of training and clipping, each of which had an auspicious-sounding name. The best examples of this kind of garden to be seen today are those in the spacious compound of Bangkok's Grand Palace, although even here a number of modern landscape ideas, as well as new ornamental plants, have been introduced.

The sort of gardens found at The Regent hotel – that is, artful arrangements that aim at looking natural as well as pleasing to the eye – are a relatively new development in Thai landscape design but one that has become increasingly common in the past several decades. Indeed, Bangkok has become a major regional center for ornamental horticulture, with literally hundreds of new plant specimens being introduced from abroad or hybridized locally to satisfy the demands of a growing number of local plant fanciers.

Sitthiporn Dhonavanik, who was responsible for the Parichart courtyard garden at the hotel, was a pioneer in this process, not only through innovative designs but also through bringing back countless plants from his travels to exotic places like Hawaii and South America, and acclimatizing them at his nursery near the seaside resort of Pattaya.

For the Parichart Court, surrounded by shops and restaurants on the northern side, he created a small, natural-looking waterfall which cascades over boulders brought from the River Kwai and flows into a serene pool populated by colorful carp and a family of quaint Mandarin ducks. Around is a lush collection of tropical plants, among them Ficus trees, philodendrons, white-flowering spathiphyllum, variegated pandanus, fish-tail palms, red ginger and stands of lacy bamboo, while waves of mysterious greenery spill down from each floor above to enhance the cool ambience of a mini-jungle.

The smaller Monthathip Court, designed by Pusadee Muntabhorn, is more formal, with Ficus trees, a few selected shrubs, smooth river stones and a fish pool creating a serene atmosphere in a limited space.

Pusadee Muntabhorn, one of Thailand's younger landscape designers, received her training in the United States. She was also given the job of planting the 180-square-meter garden outside The Regent's ballroom. Here, plentiful sunlight encourages the luxuriant growth of colorful hibiscus, heliconias and such scented shrubs as gardenia and jasmine, spilling over the banks of a large carp-filled pool where other water plants bloom. As in the Parichart Court, the overall effect is informal and memorably tropical, a living showcase for Thailand's natural beauty in the heart of Bangkok.

FOLLOWING PAGES: GOLDEN CARP IN A SERENE POOL OUTSIDE THE BALLROOM. FICUS TREES, PALMS AND OTHER TROPICAL PLANTS IN THE PARICHART COURT GARDEN.

—7—
POPULAR
BELIEFS

Flanking the entrance to The Regent are two impressive elephants carved from white sandstone, representations of the noble animal that has played such a major role in Thailand's economic and military history and, in particular, of the rare albino variety that figures prominently in popular belief throughout most of Southeast Asia.

For countless years, the white elephant has been regarded as a sacred creature, closely associated with both religion and royalty. The Buddha, in one of his many reincarnations prior to Enlightenment, is supposed to have entered the body of such an elephant, one with a "head the color of cochineal, tusks gleaming like silver, all aglitter with precious stones, clad in the finest of golden tulle..."; and, when found among wild herds, specimens were ceremoniously presented to the king, kept in a special enclosure, and fed only the choicest foods from platters made of precious metals.

Sir John Bowring, who came on a mission in 1855, describes the exquisite care given a white elephant during the reign of King Rama IV: "A superabundance of delicacies is provided for his repast; if his tusks are grown, they are enriched with rings; a sort of diadem is placed on his head; and his attendants prostrate themselves, as in the presence of the great nobles."

Such attention no doubt gave rise to the Western myth that a ruler who wanted to ruin an enemy would give him a white elephant, whose costly maintenance would soon deplete his fortune. Actually, of course, no king would dream of parting with one of the auspicious animals, possession of which brought immense prestige to his reign; a king of the Ayutthaya period, who discovered seven during a roundup in the 16th century, proclaimed himself Lord of the White Elephants and went to war when a Burmese ruler demanded two of them.

Until the present one was adopted in 1917, Thailand's national flag displayed a white elephant against a red background, and the Most Exalted Order of the White Elephant is still one of the highest and most prestigious decorations presented by the King for services to the country. In the late 19th century, seeking adequate words to describe his impression of Queen Victoria, the leader of a Thai delegation wrote, "One cannot but be struck with the aspect of the august Queen of England, or fail to observe that she must be of pure descent from a

PRECEDING PAGE: ONE OF THE WHITE SANDSTONE ELEPHANTS THAT FLANK THE ENTRANCE TO THE HOTEL.

FACING PAGE: A *MALAI* OR GARLAND, A POPULAR TRADITIONAL THAI OFFERING.

race of godly and warlike kings and rulers of the earth, in that her eyes, complexion, and above all her bearing, are those of a beautiful and majestic white elephant."

The precise characteristics identifying such an elephant are set down in a number of detailed treatises. According to one document, a white elephant should actually display no less than seven colors on its body: white, yellow, green, red, black, purple, and silvery grey. It should have white eyes, white nails (20 in all, two more than on ordinary elephants), white hair, a white tail, and a light grey, or silvery, skin.

Outsiders were not always appreciative of these nuances. "Were I to describe him as white, I should lay myself open to the charge of color-blindness," observed Carl Bock, a Norwegian visitor who was shown a newly caught specimen during the reign of King Chulalongkorn, or Rama V.

"But he was quite an albino, the whole body being of a pale reddish-brown color, with a few real white hairs on the back. The iris of the eye, the color of which is held to be a good test of an albino, was a pale Naples yellow. He looked peaceful enough, led, not ridden, by his [keeper], and his quiet bearing was in great contrast with the excitement all around, as if he felt the importance of his position."

By tradition, and also by the Elephant Maintenance Act of 1921, all white elephants found in the country are presented to the King. The present ruler, King Bhumibol Adulyadej, has had more than 10, the most of any Thai King; the surviving ones now reside in the compound of Chitrlada Palace, the official royal residence in Bangkok, where they are treated with all the respect due to them.

Another popular belief is reflected in the hotel's spirit house, a graceful little structure that stands near the road across from Peninsula Plaza. Contrary to the assumption of some visitors, and indeed to the outward appearance of many such abodes, this is not a part of Buddhism, the faith followed by the overwhelming majority of Thais. Instead it is evidence of much older beliefs in a complex collection of invisible beings whose whims control events ranging from natural phenomena to individual fortune.

Spiritual abodes are the most obvious physical evidence of this unseen world. Perched at eye-level atop posts, they can be seen in

A *BAI-SRI*, AN
OFFERING
COMPOSED OF
DEFTLY-FOLDED
BANANA LEAVES,
ADORNED WITH
JASMINE BUDS AND
A HARD-BOILED
EGG, A FEATURE OF
MANY OFFERINGS.

almost every residential and commercial compound: traditionally a simple wooden Thai-style house consisting of a single room raised slightly from a lower platform, but often – especially in cities – a more ornate cement creation, brightly painted and closely modeled after structures in a Buddhist temple complex.

Whether grand or simple, such abodes serve as the symbolic residence of the guardian spirit who watches over the compound, known in central Thailand as *Phra Phum* (Lord of the Land or Place) or *Phra Phum Ban* (Lord of the House), sometimes as *Chao Thi*. The noted Thai scholar Phya Anuman Rajadhon has suggested that the latter term may have been derived from the Chinese *T'o Ti*, the guardian spirit of a village; he also points out that *Phra Phum Ban* originally referred to a village guardian and only later came to mean one protecting a more limited territory as towns developed and people began to live in separate compounds.

Finding a proper site for the *Phra Phum*'s spiritual residence has nothing to do with such aesthetic considerations as garden design, but is determined by a Brahmin priest or some other expert similarly versed in the lore. The limitations imposed by modern urban life may require certain compromises, but ideally the house should be close to the border of the property (so that the *Phra Phum* can keep an eye out for any approaching enemy), in a place where the shadow of the main building does not fall on it (for the human and spirit worlds should not overlap), and facing either north or south (both of which are auspicious directions). A special religious ritual, often with a Brahmin priest presiding, accompanies the raising of the post, installation of the house, and a formal request for the guardian spirit to take up residence and protect the compound.

A figure or plaque of a standing divinity, or Thevada, representing the Phra Phum is then placed inside, his head surrounded by a halo of light, his left hand holding a double-edged sword, and his right one holding either a book or a bag of money. On the outside platform are placed small figures of women and animals to serve the spirit and others of dancing girls to entertain him.

Since the hotel is located on Crown Property, a particularly grand ceremony was held for its spirit house. The Royal Astrologer attached to the Royal Household Bureau presided over the event, and among the prescribed items offered were various foods ranging from a cooked pig's head to seven different kinds of traditional Thai sweets; small cone-shaped vessels known as *bai-sri*, made of deftly folded banana leaf and decorated with flowers, candles and incense sticks; assorted fresh flowers and garlands; and miniature figures of horses, elephants, servants and Thai classical dancers. The *Phra Phum* is honored regularly with simpler offerings of flowers, lighted incense sticks and tidbits of food, and more elaborate items on special occasions, such as the anniversary of his installation, New Year's Day, or when requests are made for his spiritual intervention in personal matters.

On the other side of the hotel stands another, more ornate shrine, this one of overt Indian inspiration. It is dedicated to Brahma, the creator in the Hindu trinity of principal gods. His gilded image, with four faces and eight arms, sits inside in the position of royal ease, one leg folded and the other hanging down; one hand is pressed against his breast, while the others hold such symbolic items as a scepter, a water jar, a string of beads, a conch shell, a staff and a hollow disk. Because Brahma's traditional mount is the three-headed elephant Erawan, carved wooden elephants are preferred offerings and a large number in various sizes stand on the shrine and its surrounding platform.

Not all spirits are male. Tucked away behind the hotel, is a third little raised abode, this one dedicated to a female guardian known as *Chao Mae Saithong*. Besides being a popular girl's name, *Saithong* refers to a variety of Ficus tree often associated with spiritual residence. A venerable specimen, along with a shrine to *Chao Mae Saithong*, once stood on the site of the present Monthathip Court; during construction, the shrine was ceremoniously moved to the back of the property where another such tree displays its dramatic, twisting aerial roots, and there it has remained, regularly honored with the fragrant flowers and nine burning incense sticks its resident is believed to prefer.

The floral decorations presented to such shrines, and also used in many ceremonies, are frequently ephemeral but exquisite works of living art. These are sometimes referred to as "arrangements" but the term could mislead a Westerner, suggesting as it does a more or less natural configuration for purely decorative purposes. The Thai achievement, on the other hand, is to transform leaves and flowers into beautiful objects that have no counterpart in nature but that proudly proclaim the artistic skills of man.

It would be more accurate, however, to say the skills of women, for the making of such decorations has traditionally been a female occupation. It originated at the royal court, where secluded ladies and their attendants had a great deal of leisure time and were expected to master various elegant arts, of which working with flowers was one. Malcolm Smith, a British physician who attended the principal Queen of King Rama V and whose duties often took him into the women's quarter of the Grand Palace, was greatly impressed by the pains taken with certain creations.

"Some of the finest effects," he wrote, "were produced by sewing flowers together in great sheets to form curtains or covers. Productions of this kind had to be done quickly and at the last moment, and on some occasions hundreds of women and girls would be employed, working all through the night to get them completed. By the morning they would be finished and for a few brief hours they served their purpose. The 'natural' arrangement of flowers as a form of decoration was never practiced by the Siamese until they learnt it from the Europeans."

Even today, this royal legacy is still very much alive. Groups of women gather daily in the shady courtyards of the old palace to make the garlands used by the royal family in its numerous ceremonial duties, as well as other special arrangements for regular outside customers like The Regent.

Thai floral creations can be roughly divided into three general categories: those made by the *roy* method, in which the colorful components are threaded together into garlands of many types; the *jad paan*, in which they are embedded in, or sewn over, a mound of damp, semi-solid material; and those involving deftly-folded and decorated banana leaves.

The first method is the most commonly seen, for it is used to make the *malai*, or garlands, that play such a major role in Thai social and religious life. The basis for most is fragrant jasmine buds, but other flowers may also be included, among them roses, orchids, and African

SHRINE DEDICATED
TO THE FEMALE
SPIRIT *CHAO MAE
SAITHONG*, LOCATED
BENEATH AN OLD
FICUS TREE BEHIND
THE HOTEL.

THE HOTEL'S SPIRIT
HOUSE LOCATED AT
THE SIDE ENTRANCE,
WHERE THE *PHRA
PHUM*, OR
GUARDIAN SPIRIT, IS
REGULARLY
HONORED WITH
OFFERINGS.

daisies. *Malai* range from reasonably simple ones like those sold outside almost every shrine to large and extremely complex wreaths requiring hours of labor and costing hundreds of *baht*.

Their uses are equally varied. Everyone who visits a temple or shrine brings one as an offering, and taxi drivers hang a garland from the dashboard to avert accidents. You are also likely to be given a *malai* if you move into a new house, receive a promotion at work, get engaged or married – in other words, on just about any auspicious occasion that calls for something a little special.

Jad paan, or bowl arrangements, are often called *poom*, in a reference to the traditional rounded pyramidal shape, which resembles a budding lotus. The core, usually six to eight inches high, is made of moistened earth or clay, sometimes sawdust, the whole of which is covered with flowers in various patterns. This is then set in a low-footed bowl and often placed on an altar for religious ceremonies.

The customary flower used in this sort of decoration is *Gomphrene globosa*, popularly called Bachelor's Button or Everlasting Flower (in Thai, *ban-mai-ru-roey*). These blooms have the advantage of fitting tightly together like a woven cloth, and also of lasting for weeks. The natural colors are white, pinky mauve and purple, but the tough little flowers are often dyed brilliant green, red, orange, and yellow. Grander *pooms*, like those made by the experts of the Grand Palace, may be fashioned of jasmine and other short-lived blossoms and resemble delicate, multi-colored pieces of porcelain.

The supple leaf of the banana tree is turned by skilled hands into a number of lovely objects. One group, known collectively as *bai-sri*, is not only beautiful, but also essential to many ancient religious ceremonies, especially those of Brahmin origin, such as the installation of a spirit house for the *Phra Phum*.

Bai-sri pak cham, for instance, consists of a central banana-leaf cone filled with cooked rice and surmounted by a boiled egg, and often adorned with a jasmine crown. Surrounding the base are other elongated cones decorated with various flowers. This concoction is placed in spirit houses to inspire good fortune, given as a token of respect by a student to his teacher, or presented as an offering when an infant is four days old. In the past – and even now in a few traditional families – it was also a prominent feature of the *koon chuk* ceremony, during which a child's topknot is shaved off to symbolize his coming of age. Other kinds of *bai-sri*, usually of simpler construction but no less graceful, are given to revered monks on their birthdays or on other auspicious occasions that call for merit-making.

Another memorable banana leaf and flower composition is the *krathong*, which legend says was originated by a court lady during the Sukhothai period to celebrate the festival of Loy Krathong. Plastic, styrofoam and other unnatural modern materials have invaded *krathong*-making in recent years, and innovators have come up with bizarre new designs; but to the average Thai the true *krathong* is still made of fresh leaves, carefully folded into the shape of an open lotus blossom. After being embellished with burning incense sticks, a lighted candle, and varied flowers, this is set adrift in rivers, streams, and pools under the full moon of the eleventh lunar month, a gift to the water spirits and one of the most spectacular examples of Thai floral art.

FACING PAGE:
SHRINE LOCATED TO
THE SOUTH OF THE
MAIN ENTRANCE,
DEDICATED TO
BRAHMA.

OUR PEOPLE ARE THE SOURCE

OF OUR STRENGTH,

OUR CUSTOMERS ARE THE FOCUS

OF ALL THAT WE DO.

I deally, a hotel is more than a collection of accommodations and related service facilities, however superior these may be. It should also reflect something of its surroundings: the culture and traditions, the spirit that defines the place and makes it unique.

The Regent, Bangkok achieves this in a variety of ways. Most immediately, of course, there is the staff, whose grace and hospitality embody the very essence of Thailand's particular charm, from the spontaneous smile to the genuine concern for a guests's well-being. But in addition, the hotel has numerous features that reveal other aspects of the Thai experience, some prominently displayed, others – perhaps the majority – briefly glimpsed and wondered at in passing, like half-open windows on an unfamiliar landscape.

Some of these are examined in the following pages for the benefit of those whose curiosity has been stirred and who want to know more about the distinctive culture of which The Regent is such a vital part.

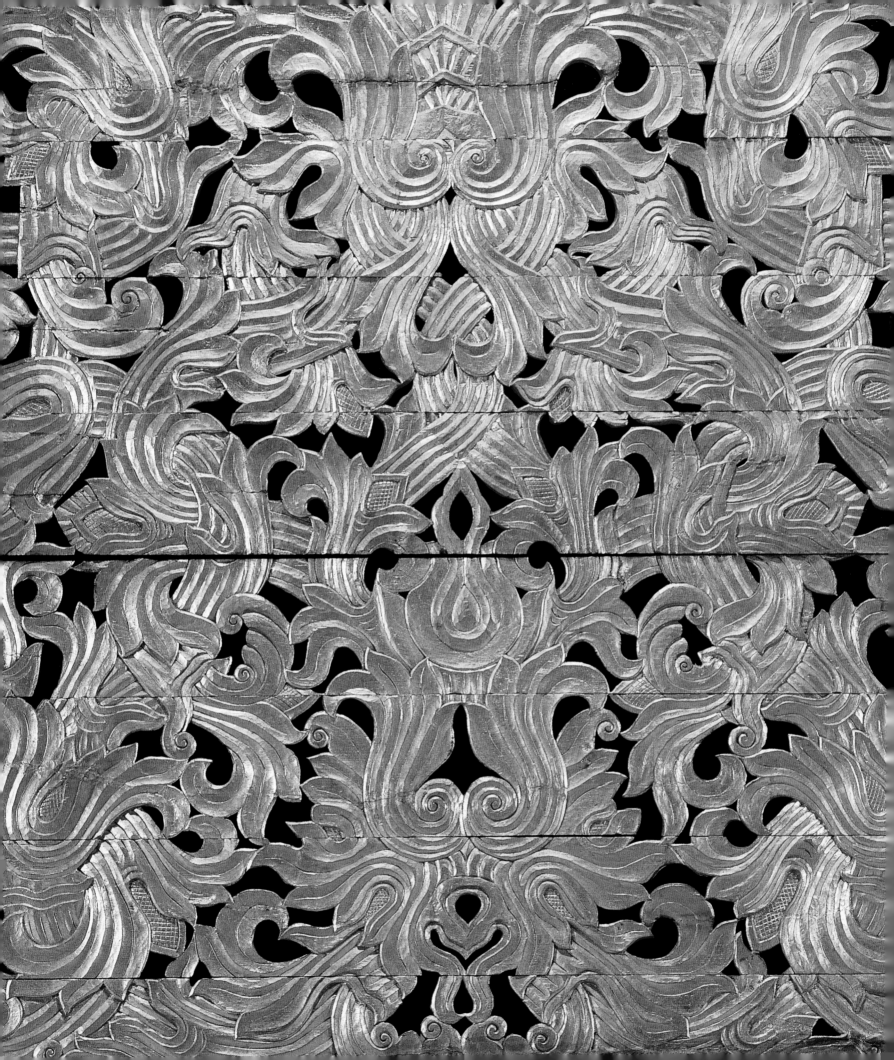

that this shift was facilitated by his laboratory research on that most hard-to-specify stimulus, the human face, and that this experience provided awareness of the crucial role of pattern and context in achieving knowledge.

This valuable background has not kept him from thoroughly immersing himself in the classic social science case studies and becoming in the process a leader of nonlaboratory social science methodology. I know of no comparable text. It meets a long-standing need. I am confident that it will become a standard text in social science research methods courses.

DONALD T. CAMPBELL
BETHLEHEM, PENNSYLVANIA

Preface

The case study has long been stereotyped as a weak sibling among social science methods. Investigators who do case studies are regarded as having deviated from their academic disciplines, their investigations as having insufficient precision (that is, quantification), objectivity, and rigor.

Despite this stereotype, case studies continue to be used extensively in social science research—including the traditional disciplines (psychology, sociology, political science, anthropology, history, and economics) as well as practice-oriented fields such as urban planning, public administration, public policy, management science, social work, and education. The method also is a frequent mode of thesis and dissertation research in all of these disciplines and fields. Moreover, case studies are increasingly commonplace even in evaluation research, supposedly the province of other methods such as surveys and quasi-experiments. All of this suggests a striking paradox: If the case study method has serious weaknesses, why do investigators continue to use it?

One explanation is that some people just do not know any better and are not trained to use alternative methods. However, a perusal of the illustrative case studies cited as examples throughout this book will reveal a distinguished group of scholars, including a few who have served as heads of their respective professions. (See the numbered BOXES throughout the text and the reference section, in which full bibliographical information is provided.) A second, minor argument given these days is that U.S. federal agencies have made surveys and questionnaires a bureaucratically hazardous affair, due to the clearance procedures required. Case studies therefore have become a preferred method. However, federally sponsored research does not dominate the social sciences—and certainly not in Europe and other countries—and the nature of federal rules cannot account for the broader pattern of methodologies used in the social sciences.

In contrast, this book makes a third argument—that the stereotype of the case study method may be wrong. According to this argument, the continuing relevance of the method raises the possibility that we have misunderstood its strengths and weaknesses and that a different perspective is needed. This book tries to develop such a perspective, by disentangling the case study, as a research tool, from (a) the case study as a teaching tool, (b) ethnographies and participant-observation, and (c) "qualitative" methods. The essence of the case study goes beyond all of these, even though there can be overlaps with the latter two. Thus the truly distinguishing features of the case study method, throughout all phases of research—problem definition, design, data collection, data analysis, and composition and reporting—are the subjects of the chapters of this book.

The object of the book is to guide investigators and students who are trying to do case studies as a rigorous method of research. The book claims to be distinctive in that case study designs and analysis are given more attention than the traditional topic of case study data collection. The former have received too little attention in existing social science texts, yet they create the greatest problems for those trying to do case studies. The book also claims to be distinctive in that references to widely known case studies in different fields are described individually, illustrating points made in the text (see the BOXES in the text). Finally, the book is also distinctive in that it is starting to pass the test of time, the first edition (1984) having gone through 8 printings and the revised edition (1989) having gone through another 16.

The ideas contained in this book are based on a mixture of my own research over the past 20 years, on case study methods courses taught at the Massachusetts Institute of Technology for 5 years and at the American University for 3, as well as on discussions with many scholars interested in case study research, including Herbert Kaufman (while at the Brookings Institution), Alexander George of Stanford University, Lawrence Susskind of MIT, Matthew Miles of the Center for Policy Research, Karen Seashore Louis (while at the University of Massachusetts), Elliot Liebow (while at the National Institute of Mental Health), and Carol Weiss of Harvard University. More recently, I have been privileged to conduct annual seminars under the auspices of the Aarhus School of Business in Denmark (and shared insights with Professors Erik Maaloe, Finn Borum, and Erik Albaek). These colleagues, as well as those at the RAND Corporation (1970 to 1978) and at COSMOS Corporation (1980 to the present time), have provided continuing stimulation, debate, and support in helping me to articulate the various aspects of case study research discussed in this book.

Two anonymous reviewers commented helpfully on the manuscript of the first edition. All three versions of this book (1984, 1989, and the present version) benefited directly from the continued and careful attention from Leonard Bickman and Debra Rog (the series editors) as well as from C. Deborah Laughton and the fine staff at Sage Publications. Their detailed attention, cheerful support, and periodic nudging all make an author want to finish a text and get on to the next challenge in life. Nonetheless, as with the earlier versions, I alone bear the responsibility for this second edition.

Of course, anyone's ideas about case studies—and about social science methods more generally—must have deeper roots, and mine go back to the two disciplines in which I was trained: history as an undergraduate and experimental psychology as a graduate. History and historiography first raised my consciousness regarding the importance of methodology in the social sciences. The unique brand of experimental psychology I learned at MIT then taught me that empirical research advances only when it is accompanied by logical thinking, and not when treated as a mechanistic endeavor. This lesson turns out to be a basic theme of the case study method. I have therefore dedicated this book to the person at MIT who taught me this best, and under whom I completed a dissertation on face recognition, though he might only barely recognize the resemblances between past and present, were he alive today.

NOTE TO THE SECOND EDITION

The first edition of this book received increasing attention by those doing social and psychological investigations, evaluation research, public policy studies, and business, management, and international studies. An intriguing development was the turn toward the case study as a research (and not just teaching) tool on the part of business schools across the country. Similarly, investigators of international programs had rediscovered the importance of the case study as a serious research tool. Overall, a significant trend may have been toward appreciating the complexity of organizational phenomena, for which the case study may be the most appropriate research method.

In response to comments about the first edition (1984), the revised edition (1989) tried to clarify further the critical role of theory, both in designing case studies and in generalizing from them. Also, further guidance was provided regarding the problem of determining the number of cases to be used in a multiple-case study. Both discussions were found in Chapter 2. Yet another response to these earlier comments was a companion book, *Applications of Case Study Research* (1993), which provides extensive examples of the case study method in practice.

This second edition updates the original and revised versions, without duplicating any of the examples in the applications book. First, the text integrates many additional publications, some that have appeared only recently.

Some of these are significant and deal directly with the case study method (e.g., Agranoff & Radin, 1991; Feagin, Orum, & Sjoberg, 1991; Hamel, 1992; Platt, 1992a; Stake, 1994; U.S. General Accounting Office, 1990). Of special note is Platt's article tracing the historic development of the case study as a research method.

Other significant publications deal with closely related topics, including qualitative methods, pattern-matching, and writing and composition (Becker, 1986; Lincoln, 1991; Marshall & Rossman, 1989; Merton, Fiske, & Kendall, 1990; Strauss & Corbin, 1990; Trochim, 1989; Van Maanen, 1988; Wolcott, 1990). These publications have helped to clarify further the areas of contrast and overlap between the case study method and other research strategies.

Second, the text gives increased emphasis to examples covering the world marketplace and international economy—topics somehow more publicly salient than before. These examples are in the text itself as well as in new illustrations (see BOXES 5b, 6, 11, and 29). Overall, although the number of BOXES appears to have diminished from the first edition, this observation is misleading because the first edition contained four BOXES that were actually figures, and not illustrative examples. (The figures are still part of the text but are now labeled figures and not BOXES.)

Third, the text tries to clarify several issues even further. These include (a) expanded discussion of the raging debate in evaluation between qualitative and quantitative research (Chapter 1), (b) even more on the development of theory (Chapter 2), (c) clarification of the five levels of questions, (d) a new distinction between data collection units and design units (Chapter 3), (e) a more refined comparison of the six data sources' strengths and weaknesses, (f) a more extensive discussion of triangulation as the rationale for multiple sources of evidence (Chapter 4), (g) the use of program logic models as an analytic strategy, (h) additional guidance on carrying out high-quality analyses (Chapter 5), and a bit more on (i) writing structures and (j) writing and rewriting (Chapter 6). In sum, the updating has affected every chapter in one way or another, although in most other respects the book remains largely unchanged.

A final and significant change has been a more detailed articulation of the original definition of case studies. Whereas the earlier versions considered case studies to have three characteristics, the present edition (Chapter 1) identifies two additional characteristics that were implicit but not clearly enumerated earlier. This more articulated definition should lead to an improved understanding of the case study method as a research tool.

I would like to close this note by expressing thanks to all the budding and experienced investigators who have practiced case study research over the past 10 years. There seem to be more of you, and collectively I hope that we are doing a better job than would have been true 10 years ago. However, the challenge of innovating and significantly advancing the craft still remains. The present update still reflects incremental changes. The desired advance would make case study research even more commonplace and at the same time raise its quality to unquestioned heights.

1

Introduction

The case study is but one of several ways of doing social science research. Other ways include experiments, surveys, histories, and the analysis of archival information (as in economic studies). Each strategy has peculiar advantages and disadvantages, depending upon three conditions: (a) the type of research question, (b) the control an investigator has over actual behavioral events, and (c) the focus on contemporary as opposed to historical phenomena.

In general, case studies are the preferred strategy when "how" or "why" questions are being posed, when the investigator has little control over events, and when the focus is on a contemporary phenomenon within some real-life context. Such "explanatory" case studies also can be complemented by two other types—"exploratory" and "descriptive" case studies. Regardless of the type of case study, investigators must exercise great care in designing and doing case studies to overcome the traditional criticisms of the method.

THE CASE STUDY
AS A RESEARCH STRATEGY

This book is about the design and conduct of case studies *for research purposes*. As a research strategy, the case study is used in many situations, including:

- Policy, political science, and public administration research
- Community psychology and sociology
- Organizational and management studies
- City and regional planning research, such as studies of plans, neighborhoods, or public agencies
- The conduct of dissertations and theses in the social sciences—the academic disciplines as well as professional fields such as business administration, management science, and social work

This book covers the distinctive characteristics of the case study strategy, compared with other types of research. Importantly, the book deals with design, analysis, and reporting issues—and not merely the more traditional focus on data collection or fieldwork.

The overall goal of this book is to help investigators deal with some of the more difficult questions commonly neglected by available research texts. So often, for instance, the author has been confronted by a student or colleague who has asked (a) how to define the case being studied, (b) how to determine the relevant data to be collected, or (c) what should be done with the data, once collected. This book, it is hoped, answers these questions.

However, this book does not cover all uses of case studies. For example, it is not intended to help those who might use case studies as teaching devices, popularized in the fields of law, business, medicine, or public policy (see Llewellyn, 1948; Stein, 1952; Towl, 1969; Windsor & Greanias, 1983) but now prevalent in virtually every academic field, including the natural sciences. For teaching purposes, a case study need not contain a complete or accurate rendition of actual events; rather, its purpose is to establish a framework for discussion and debate among students. The criteria for developing good cases for teaching—usually of the single- and not multiple-case variety—are far different than those for doing research (e.g., Caulley & Dowdy, 1987). Teaching case studies need not be concerned with the rigorous and fair presentation of empirical data; research case studies need to do exactly that.

Similarly, this book is not intended to cover those situations in which cases are used as a form of record keeping. Medical records, social work files, and other case records are used to facilitate some practice, such as medicine, law, or social work. Again, the criteria for developing good cases for practice are different than those for designing case studies for research.

In contrast, the rationale for this book is that case studies are increasingly used as a research tool (e.g., Hamel, 1992; Perry & Kraemer, 1986) and that you—who may be a seasoned or budding social scientist—would like to know how to design and conduct single- or multiple-case studies to investigate a research issue. This book concentrates heavily on the problem of designing and analyzing case studies and is not merely a guide to collecting case study evidence. In this sense, the book fills a void in social science methodology, which is dominated by texts on "field methods," offering few guides on how to start a case study, how to analyze the data, or even how to minimize the problems of composing the case study report. This book covers all of the phases of design, data collection, analysis, and reporting.

As a research endeavor, the case study contributes uniquely to our knowledge of individual, organizational, social, and political phenomena. Not surprisingly, the case study has been a common research strategy in psychology, sociology, political science, business, social work, and planning (Yin,

1983). Case studies are even found in economics, in which the structure of a given industry, or the economy of a city or a region, may be investigated by using a case study design. In all of these situations, the distinctive need for case studies arises out of the desire to understand complex social phenomena. In brief, the case study allows an investigation to retain the holistic and meaningful characteristics of real-life events—such as individual life cycles, organizational and managerial processes, neighborhood change, international relations, and the maturation of industries.

COMPARING CASE STUDIES WITH OTHER RESEARCH STRATEGIES

When and why would you want to do case studies on some topic? Should you consider doing an experiment instead? A survey? A history? A computer-based analysis of archival records such as student records?

These and other choices represent different research strategies. (The following discussion focuses only on five choices and does not attempt to catalog all of them, however.) Each is a different way of collecting and analyzing empirical evidence, following its own logic. And each strategy has its own advantages and disadvantages. To get the most out of using the case study strategy, you need to know these differences.

A common misconception is that the various research strategies should be arrayed hierarchically. We were once taught to believe that case studies were appropriate for the exploratory phase of an investigation, that surveys and histories were appropriate for the descriptive phase, and that experiments were the only way of doing explanatory or causal inquiries. The hierarchical view reinforced the idea that case studies were only an exploratory tool and could not be used to describe or test propositions (Platt, 1992a).

This hierarchical view, however, is incorrect. Experiments with an exploratory motive have certainly always existed. In addition, the development of causal explanations has long been a serious concern of historians, reflected by the subfield known as historiography. Finally, case studies are far from being only an exploratory strategy. Some of the best and most famous case studies have been both descriptive (for example, Whyte's *Street Corner Society*, 1943/1955; see BOX 1) and explanatory (see Allison's *Essence of Decision: **Explaining** the Cuban Missile Crisis*, 1971 [emphasis added to title]; see BOX 2).

The more appropriate view of these different strategies is a pluralistic one. Each strategy can be used for all three purposes—exploratory, descriptive, or

---

BOX 1
A Famous Descriptive Case Study

Street Corner Society (1943/1955), by William F. Whyte, has for decades been recommended reading in community sociology. The book is a classic example of a descriptive case study. Thus it traces the sequence of interpersonal events over time, describes a subculture that had rarely been the topic of previous study, and discovers key phenomena—such as the career advancement of lower income youths and their ability (or inability) to break neighborhood ties.

The study has been highly regarded despite its being a single-case study, covering one neighborhood ("Cornerville") and a time period now more than 50 years old. The value of the book is, paradoxically, its generalizability to issues on individual performance, group structure, and the social structure of neighborhoods. Later investigators have repeatedly found remnants of Cornerville in their work, even though they have studied different neighborhoods and different time periods.

---

explanatory. There may be exploratory case studies, descriptive case studies, or explanatory case studies (Yin, 1981a, 1981b). There also may be exploratory experiments, descriptive experiments, and explanatory experiments. What distinguishes the strategies is not this hierarchy but three other conditions, discussed below. Nevertheless, this does not imply that the boundaries between the strategies—or the occasions when each is to be used—are always clear and sharp. Even though each strategy has its distinctive characteristics, there are large areas of overlap among them (e.g., Sieber, 1973). The goal is to avoid gross misfits—that is, when you are planning to use one type of strategy but another is really more advantageous.

When to Use Each Strategy

The three conditions consist of (a) the type of research question posed, (b) the extent of control an investigator has over actual behavioral events, and (c) the degree of focus on contemporary as opposed to historical events. Figure 1.1 displays these three conditions and shows how each is related to five major research strategies in the social sciences: experiments, surveys, archival analysis, histories, and case studies. The importance of each condition, in distinguishing among the five strategies, is discussed below.

BOX 2
An Explanatory Case Study

Even a single-case study can often be used to pursue an explanatory, and not merely exploratory (or descriptive), purpose. The analyst's objective should be to pose competing explanations for the same set of events and to indicate how such explanations may apply to other situations.

This strategy was followed by Graham Allison in *Essence of Decision: Explaining the Cuban Missile Crisis* (1971). The single case is the confrontation between the United States and the Soviet Union over the placement of offensive missiles in Cuba. Allison posits three competing theories or models to explain the course of events, including answers to three key questions: why the Soviet Union placed offensive (and not merely defensive) missiles in Cuba in the first place, why the United States responded to the missile deployment with a blockade (and not an air strike or invasion), and why the Soviet Union eventually withdrew the missiles. By comparing each theory with the actual course of events, Allison develops the best explanation for this type of crisis.

Allison suggests that this explanation is applicable to other situations, thereby extending the usefulness of his single-case study. Thus Allison cites the U.S. involvement in Vietnam, nuclear confrontation more generally, and the termination of wars by nations as other situations for which the theory can offer useful explanation.

Types of research questions (Figure 1.1, column 1). The first condition covers your research question(s) (Hedrick, Bickman, & Rog, 1993). A basic categorization scheme for the types of questions is the familiar series: "who," "what," "where," "how," and "why."

If research questions focus mainly on "what" questions, either of two possibilities arises. First, some types of "what" questions are exploratory, such as this one: "What are the ways of making schools effective?" This type of question is a justifiable rationale for conducting an exploratory study, the goal being to develop pertinent hypotheses and propositions for further inquiry. However, as an exploratory study, any of the five research strategies can be used—for example, an exploratory survey, an exploratory experiment, or an exploratory case study. The second type of "what" question is actually a form of a "how many" or "how much" line of inquiry—for example, "What have been the outcomes from a particular managerial reorganization?" Identifying such outcomes is more likely to favor survey or archival strategies than others. For example, a survey can be readily designed to enumerate the

strategy	form of research question	requires control over behavioral events?	focuses on contemporary events?
experiment	how, why	yes	yes
survey	who, what, where, how many, how much	no	yes
archival analysis	who, what, where, how many, how much	no	yes/no
history	how, why	no	no
case study	how, why	no	yes

Figure 1.1. Relevant Situations for Different Research Strategies
SOURCE: COSMOS Corporation.

"whats," whereas a case study would not be an advantageous strategy in this situation.

Similarly, like this second type of "what" question, "who" and "where" questions (or their derivatives—"how many" and "how much") are likely to favor survey strategies or the analysis of archival records, as in economic research. These strategies are advantageous when the research goal is to describe the incidence or prevalence of a phenomenon or when it is to be *predictive* about certain outcomes. The investigation of prevalent political attitudes (in which a survey or a poll might be the favored strategy) or of the spread of a disease like AIDS (in which an analysis of health statistics might be the favored strategy) would be typical examples.

In contrast, "how" and "why" questions are more *explanatory* and likely to lead to the use of case studies, histories, and experiments as the preferred research strategies. This is because such questions deal with operational links needing to be traced over time, rather than mere frequencies or incidence. Thus, if you wanted to know how a community successfully thwarted a proposed highway (see Lupo et al., 1971), you would be less likely to rely on a survey or an examination of archival records and might be better off doing a history or a case study. Similarly, if you wanted to know why bystanders fail to report emergencies under certain conditions, you could design and conduct a series of experiments (see Latané & Darley, 1969).

Let us take two more examples. If you were studying "who" participated in riots, and "how much" damage had been done, you might survey residents, examine business records (an archival analysis), or conduct a "windshield survey" of the riot area. In contrast, if you wanted to know "why" riots occurred, you would have to draw upon a wider array of documentary information, in addition to conducting interviews; if you focused on the "why" question in more than one city, you would probably be doing a multiple-case study.

Similarly, if you wanted to know "what" the outcomes of a new governmental program had been, you could answer this frequency question by doing a survey or by examining economic data, depending upon the type of program involved. Thus consider such questions as these: How many clients did the program serve? What kinds of benefits were received? How often were different benefits produced? These could all be answered without doing a case study. But if you needed to know "how" or "why" the program had worked (or not), you would lean toward either a case study or a field experiment.

Some "how" and "why" questions are ambivalent and need clarification. "How" and "why" Bill Clinton got elected in 1992 can be studied by either a survey or a case study. The survey might examine voting patterns, showing that voters for Ross Perot drew largely from supporters of then President Bush, and this could satisfactorily address the how and why questions. In contrast, the case study might examine how Clinton conducted his campaign to achieve the necessary nomination and to manipulate public opinion in his favor. The study would cover the potentially helpful role of the weak U.S. economy in denying support for the Bush-Quayle ticket as incumbents. This approach also would be an acceptable way of addressing the "how" and "why" questions but would be different than the survey study.

To summarize, the first and most important condition for differentiating among the various research strategies is to identify the type of research question being asked. In general, "what" questions may either be exploratory (in which case any of the strategies could be used) or about prevalence (in which surveys or the analysis of archival records would be favored). "How" and "why" questions are likely to favor the use of case studies, experiments, or histories.

Defining the research questions is probably the most important step to be taken in a research study, so patience and sufficient time should be allowed for this task. The key is to understand that research questions have both *substance*—for example, What is my study about?—and *form*—for example, Am I asking a "who," "what," "where," "why," or "how" question? Others have focused on some of the substantively important issues (see Campbell,

Daft, & Hulin, 1982); the point of the preceding discussion is that the form of the question provides an important clue regarding the appropriate research strategy to be used. Remember, too, the large areas of overlap among the strategies, so that, for some questions, a choice among strategies might actually exist. Remember, finally, that you may be predisposed to pursue a particular strategy regardless of the study question. If so, be sure to create the form of the study question best matching the strategy you were inclined to pursue in the first place.

Extent of control over behavioral events (Figure 1.1, column 2) and degree of focus on contemporary as opposed to historical events (Figure 1.1, column 3). Assuming that "how" and "why" questions are to be the focus of study, a further distinction among history, case study, and experiment is the extent of the investigator's control over and access to actual behavioral events. Histories are the preferred strategy when there is virtually no access or control. Thus the distinctive contribution of the historical method is in dealing with the "dead" past—that is, when no relevant persons are alive to report, even retrospectively, what occurred, and when an investigator must rely on primary documents, secondary documents, and cultural and physical artifacts as the main sources of evidence. Histories can, of course, be done about contemporary events; in this situation, the strategy begins to overlap with that of the case study.

The case study is preferred in examining contemporary events, but when the relevant behaviors cannot be manipulated. The case study relies on many of the same techniques as a history, but it adds two sources of evidence not usually included in the historian's repertoire: direct observation and systematic interviewing. Again, although case studies and histories can overlap, the case study's unique strength is its ability to deal with a full variety of evidence—documents, artifacts, interviews, and observations—beyond what might be available in the conventional historical study. Moreover, in some situations, such as participant-observation, informal manipulation can occur.

Finally, experiments are done when an investigator can manipulate behavior directly, precisely, and systematically. This can occur in a laboratory setting, in which an experiment may focus on one or two isolated variables (and presumes that the laboratory environment can "control" for all the remaining variables beyond the scope of interest), or it can be done in a field setting, where the term *social experiment* has emerged to cover research in which investigators "treat" whole groups of people in different ways, such as providing them with different kinds of vouchers (Boruch, forthcoming). Again, the methods overlap. The full range of experimental science also includes those situations in which the experimenter cannot manipulate behavior (see Blalock, 1961; Campbell & Stanley, 1966; Cook & Campbell, 1979) but in which the logic of experimental design may still be applied. These situations have been commonly regarded as "quasi-experimental" situations. The quasi-experimental approach can even be used in a historical setting, in which, for instance, an investigator may be interested in studying race riots or lynchings (see Spilerman, 1971) and may use a quasi-experimental design because no control over the behavioral event was possible.

Summary. We can identify some situations in which all research strategies might be relevant (such as exploratory research), and other situations in which two strategies might be considered equally attractive (such as how and why Clinton got elected). We also can use more than one strategy in any given study (for example, a survey within a case study or a case study within a survey). To this extent, the various strategies are not mutually exclusive. But we can also identify some situations in which a specific strategy has a distinct advantage. For the *case study*, this is when

- a "how" or "why" question is being asked about a contemporary set of events over which the investigator has little or no control.

To determine the questions that are most significant for a topic, and to gain some precision in formulating these questions, requires much preparation. One way is to review the literature on the topic (Cooper, 1984). Note that such a literature review is therefore a means to an end, and not—as most students think—an end in itself. Budding investigators think that the purpose of a literature review is to determine the *answers* about what is known on a topic; in contrast, experienced investigators review previous research to develop sharper and more insightful *questions* about the topic.

Traditional Prejudices Against the Case Study Strategy

Although the case study is a distinctive form of empirical inquiry, many research investigators nevertheless have disdain for the strategy. In other words, as a research endeavor, case studies have been viewed as a less desirable form of inquiry than either experiments or surveys. Why is this?

Perhaps the greatest concern has been over the lack of rigor of case study research. Too many times, the case study investigator has been sloppy and has allowed equivocal evidence or biased views to influence the direction of the findings and conclusions.

The possibility also exists that people have confused case study teaching with case study research. In teaching, case study materials may be deliberately altered to demonstrate a particular point more effectively. In research, any such step would be strictly forbidden. Every case study investigator must work hard to report all evidence fairly, and this book will help him or her to do so. What is often forgotten is that bias also can enter into the conduct of experiments (see Rosenthal, 1966) and the use of other research strategies, such as designing questionnaires for surveys (Sudman & Bradburn, 1982) or conducting historical research (Gottschalk, 1968). The problems are not different, but in case study research, they may have been more frequently encountered and less frequently overcome.

A second common concern about case studies is that they provide little basis for scientific generalization. "How can you generalize from a single case?" is a frequently heard question. The answer is not a simple one (Kennedy, 1976). However, consider for the moment that the same question had been asked about an experiment: "How can you generalize from a single experiment?" In fact, scientific facts are rarely based on single experiments; they are usually based on a multiple set of experiments, which have replicated the same phenomenon under different conditions. The same approach can be used with multiple-case studies but requires a different concept of the appropriate research designs; this is discussed in detail in Chapter 2. The short answer is that case studies, like experiments, are generalizable to theoretical propositions and not to populations or universes. In this sense, the case study, like the experiment, does not represent a "sample," and the investigator's goal is to expand and generalize theories (analytic generalization) and not to enumerate frequencies (statistical generalization). Or, as three notable social scientists describe in their *single* case study, the goal is to do a "generalizing" and not a "particularizing" analysis (Lipset, Trow, & Coleman, 1956, pp. 419-420).

A third frequent complaint about case studies is that they take too long, and they result in massive, unreadable documents. This complaint may be appropriate, given the way case studies have been done in the past (e.g., Feagin, Orum, & Sjoberg, 1991), but this is not necessarily the way case studies must be done in the future. Chapter 6 discusses alternative ways of writing the case study—including ones in which the traditional, lengthy narrative can be avoided altogether. Nor need case studies take a long time. This incorrectly confuses the case study strategy with a specific method of data collection, such as ethnography or participant-observation. Ethnographies usually require long periods of time in the "field" and emphasize detailed, observational evidence. Participant-observation may not require the same length of time but still assumes a hefty investment of field efforts. In contrast, case studies are a form of inquiry that does *not* depend solely on ethnographic or participant-observer data. One could even do a valid and high-quality case study without leaving the library and the telephone, depending upon the topic being studied.

Despite the fact that these common concerns can be allayed, as above, one major lesson is still that good case studies are very difficult to do. The problem is that we have little way of screening or testing for an investigator's ability to do good case studies. People know when they cannot play music; they also know when they cannot do mathematics; and they can be tested for other skills, such as by the bar examination in law. Somehow, the skills for doing good case studies have not yet been defined, and as a result,

> most people feel that they can prepare a case study, and nearly all of us believe we can understand one. Since neither view is well founded, the case study receives a good deal of approbation it does not deserve. (Hoaglin, Light, McPeek, Mosteller, & Stoto, 1982, p. 134)

This quotation is from a book by five prominent *statisticians*. Surprisingly, even from another field, they recognize the challenge of doing good case studies.

DIFFERENT TYPES OF CASE STUDIES, BUT A COMMON DEFINITION

The discussion has progressed without a formal definition of case studies. Moreover, commonly asked questions about case studies have still been unanswered. For example, is it still a case study when more than one case is included in the same study? Do case studies preclude the use of quantitative evidence? Can case studies be used to do evaluations? Can case studies include journalistic accounts? Let us now attempt to define the case study strategy and answer these questions.

Definition of the Case Study as a Research Strategy

The most frequently encountered definitions of case studies have merely repeated the types of topics to which case studies have been applied. For example, in the words of one observer, the essence of a case study, the central tendency among all types of case study, is that it tries to illuminate a *decision* or set of decisions: why they were taken, how they were implemented, and with what result. (Schramm, 1971, emphasis added)

This definition thus cites the topic of "decisions" as the major focus of case studies. Similarly, other topics have been listed, including "individuals," "organizations," "processes," "programs," "neighborhoods," "institutions," and even "events." However, citing the topic is surely insufficient for establishing the needed definition.

Alternatively, most social science textbooks have failed to consider the case study a formal research strategy at all (the major exception is the book by five statisticians from Harvard University—Hoaglin et al., 1982). As discussed earlier, one common flaw was to consider the case study as the exploratory stage of some other type of research strategy, and the case study itself was only mentioned in a line or two of text.

Another common flaw has been to confuse case studies with ethnographies (Fetterman, 1989) or with participant-observation (Jorgensen, 1989), so that a textbook's presumed discussion of case studies was in reality a description either of the ethnographic method or of participant-observation as a data collection technique. The most popular contemporary texts (e.g., Kidder & Judd, 1986; Nachmias & Nachmias, 1992), in fact, still cover "fieldwork" only as a data collection technique and omit any further discussion of case studies.

In a historical overview of the case study in American methodological thought, Jennifer Platt (1992a) explains the reasons for these treatments. She traces the practice of doing case studies back to the conduct of life histories, the work of the Chicago school of sociology, and casework in social work. She then shows how "participant-observation" emerged as a data collection technique, leaving the further definition of any distinctive case study strategy in suspension. Finally, she explains how the first edition of this book (1984) definitively dissociated the case study strategy from the limited perspective of doing participant-observation (or any type of fieldwork). The case study strategy, in her words, begins with "a logic of design . . . a strategy to be preferred when circumstances and research problems are appropriate rather than an ideological commitment to be followed whatever the circumstances" (Platt, 1992a, p. 46).

And just what is this logic of design? The technically critical features had been worked out prior to the first edition of this book (Yin, 1981a, 1981b) but now may be restated in two ways. First, the technical definition begins with the scope of a case study:

1. A case study is an empirical inquiry that

- investigates a contemporary phenomenon within its real-life context, especially when
- the boundaries between phenomenon and context are not clearly evident.

In other words, you would use the case study method because you deliberately wanted to cover contextual conditions—believing that they might be highly pertinent to your phenomenon of study. This first part of our logic of design therefore helps us to understand case studies by continuing to distinguish them from the other research strategies that have been discussed.

An experiment, for instance, deliberately divorces a phenomenon from its context, so that attention can be focused on only a few variables (typically, the context is "controlled" by the laboratory environment). A history, by comparison, does deal with the entangled situation between phenomenon and context, but usually with *non*contemporary events. Finally, surveys can try to deal with phenomenon and context, but their ability to investigate the context is extremely limited. The survey designer, for instance, constantly struggles to limit the number of variables to be analyzed (and hence the number of questions that can be asked) to fall safely within the number of respondents that can be surveyed.

Second, because phenomenon and context are not always distinguishable in real-life situations, a whole set of other technical characteristics, including data collection and data analysis strategies, now become the second part of our technical definition:

2. The case study inquiry

- copes with the technically distinctive situation in which there will be many more variables of interest than data points, and as one result
- relies on multiple sources of evidence, with data needing to converge in a triangulating fashion, and as another result
- benefits from the prior development of theoretical propositions to guide data collection and analysis.

In other words, the case study as a research strategy comprises an all-encompassing method—with the logic of design incorporating specific approaches to data collection and to data analysis. In this sense, the case study is not either a data collection tactic or merely a design feature alone (Stoecker, 1991) but a comprehensive research strategy.[1] How the strategy is defined and implemented is the topic of this entire book.

Certain other features of the case study strategy are not critical for defining the strategy but may be considered variations within case study research and also provide answers to common questions.

Variations Within Case Studies as a Research Strategy

Yes, case study research can include both single- and multiple-case studies. Though some fields, such as political science and public administration, have tried to delineate sharply between these two approaches (and have used such terms as the *comparative case method* as a distinctive form of multiple-case studies; see Agranoff & Radin, 1991; George, 1979; Lijphart, 1975), single- and multiple-case studies are in reality but two variants of case study designs (see Chapter 2 for more).

And, yes, case studies can include, and even be limited to, quantitative evidence. In fact, the contrast between quantitative and qualitative evidence does not distinguish the various research strategies. Note that, as analogous examples, some experiments (such as studies of psychophysical perceptions) and some survey questions (such as those seeking categorical rather than numerical responses) rely on qualitative, and not quantitative, evidence. Likewise, historical research can include enormous amounts of quantitative evidence.

As a related but important note, the case study strategy should not be confused with "qualitative research" (see Schwartz & Jacobs, 1979; Strauss & Corbin, 1990; Van Maanen, 1988; Van Maanen, Dabbs, & Faulkner, 1982). Some qualitative research follows ethnographic methods and seeks to satisfy two conditions: (a) the use of close-up, detailed observation of the natural world by the investigator and (b) the attempt to avoid prior commitment to any theoretical model (Jacob, 1987, 1989; Lincoln & Guba, 1986; Stake, 1983; Van Maanen et al., 1982, p. 16). However, ethnographic research does not always produce case studies (for example, see the brief ethnographies in G. Jacobs, 1970), nor are case studies limited to these two conditions. Instead, case studies can be based on any mix of quantitative and qualitative evidence. In addition, case studies need not always include direct, detailed observations as a source of evidence.

As a further note, some investigators distinguish between quantitative research and qualitative research—not on the basis of the type of evidence but on the basis of wholly different philosophical beliefs (e.g., Guba & Lincoln, 1989; Lincoln, 1991; Sechrest, 1991; Smith & Heshusius, 1986). These distinctions have produced a sharp debate within the field of evaluation research. Although some believe that these philosophical beliefs are irreconcilable, the counterargument can still be posed—that regardless of whether one favors qualitative or quantitative research, there is a strong and essential common ground between the two (Yin, 1994).

And, yes, case studies have a distinctive place in evaluation research (see Cronbach et al., 1980; Guba & Lincoln, 1981; Patton, 1980; U.S. General Accounting Office, 1990; Yin, 1993, chap. 4). There are at least five different applications. The most important is to *explain* the causal links in real-life interventions that are too complex for the survey or experimental strategies. In evaluation language, the explanations would link program implementation with program effects (U.S. General Accounting Office, 1990). A second application is to *describe* an intervention and the real-life context in which it occurred. Third, case studies can *illustrate* certain topics within an evaluation, again in a descriptive mode—even from a journalistic perspective. Fourth, the case study strategy may be used to *explore* those situations in which the intervention being evaluated has no clear, single set of outcomes. Fifth, the case study may be a "*meta-evaluation*"—a study of an evaluation study (N. Smith, 1990; Stake, 1986). Whatever the application, one constant theme is that program sponsors—rather than research investigators alone—may have the prominent role in defining the evaluation questions and relevant data categories (U.S. General Accounting Office, 1990).

And, finally, yes, certain journalistic efforts can qualify as case studies. Actually, one of the best written and most interesting case studies is about the Watergate scandal, by two reporters from *The Washington Post* (see BOX 3).

SUMMARY

This chapter has introduced the importance of the case study as a research strategy. The case study, like other research strategies, is a way of investigating an empirical topic by following a set of prespecified procedures. These procedures will largely dominate the remainder of this book.

The chapter also has attempted to distinguish the case study from alternative research strategies in social science, indicating the situations in which doing a single- or multiple-case study may be preferred, for instance, to doing a survey. Some situations may have no clearly preferred strategy, as the strengths and weaknesses of the various strategies may overlap. The basic approach, however, is to consider all the strategies in a pluralistic fashion—as part of a repertoire for doing social science research from which the investigator may draw according to a given situation.

BOX 3
A Journalistic Case Study

Although public memory of President Richard M. Nixon's resignation has receded, Bernstein and Woodward's *All the President's Men* (1974) remains a fascinating account of the Watergate scandal. The book is dramatic and suspenseful, relies on solid journalistic methods, and serendipitously represents a common design for case studies.

The "case," in this book, is not the Watergate burglary itself, or even the Nixon administration more generally. Rather, the case is the "coverup," a complex set of events that occurred in the aftermath of the burglary. Bernstein and Woodward continually confront the reader with two "how" and "why" questions: How did the coverup occur, and why did it occur? Neither is answered easily, and the book's appeal lies in its piecing together of fact after fact, each piece adding up curiously and then potently to an explanation for the coverup.

Establishing the how and why of a complex human situation is a classic example of the use of case studies, whether done by journalists or social scientists. If the case involves a significant public event and an appealing explanation, the ingredients may add up, as in *All the President's Men,* to a best-seller.

Finally, the chapter has discussed some of the major criticisms of case study research and has suggested that these criticisms are misdirected. However, we must all work hard to overcome the problems of doing case study research, including the recognition that some of us were not meant, by skill or disposition, to do such research in the first place. Case study research is remarkably hard, even though case studies have traditionally been considered to be "soft" research. Paradoxically, the "softer" a research strategy, the harder it is to do.

EXERCISES

1. *Defining a case study question.* Develop a question that would be the rationale for a case study you might conduct. Instead of doing a case study, now imagine that you could only do a history, a survey, or an experiment (but not a case study) in order to answer this question. What aspects of the question, if any, could not be answered through these other research strategies? What would be the distinctive advantage of doing a case study to answer this question?

2. *Defining "significant" case study questions.* Name a topic you think is worthy of making the subject of a case study. Identify the three major questions your case

study would try to answer. Now assume that you were actually able to answer these questions with sufficient evidence (i.e., that you had successfully conducted your case study). How would you justify, to a colleague, the significance of your findings? Would you have advanced some major theory? Would you have discovered something rare? (If you are unimpressed by your answers, perhaps you should consider redefining the major questions of your case.)

3. *Identifying "significant" questions in other research strategies.* Locate a research study based solely on the use of survey, historical, or experimental (but not case study) methods. Describe the ways in which the findings of this study are significant. Does it advance some major theory? Has it discovered something rare?

4. *Examining case studies used for teaching purposes.* Obtain a copy of a case study designed for teaching purposes (e.g., a case in a textbook used in a business school course). Identify the specific ways in which this type of "teaching" case is different than research case studies. Does the teaching case cite primary documents, contain evidence, or display data? Does the teaching case have a conclusion? What appears to be the main objective of the teaching case?

5. *Defining different types of case studies used for research purposes.* Define the three types of case studies used for research (but not teaching) purposes: (a) explanatory or causal case studies, (b) descriptive case studies, and (c) exploratory case studies. Compare the situations in which these different types of case studies would be most applicable, and then name a case study you would like to conduct. Would it be explanatory, descriptive, or exploratory? Why?

NOTE

1. Robert Stake (1994) has yet another approach for defining case studies. He considers them not to be "a methodological choice but a choice of object to be studied." Further, the object must be a "functioning specific" (such as a person or classroom) but not a generality (such as a policy). This definition is too broad. Every study of entities qualifying as objects (e.g., people, organizations, and countries) would then be a case study, regardless of the methodology used (e.g., psychological experiment, management survey, economic analysis).

2

Designing Case Studies

A research design is the logic that links the data to be collected (and the conclusions to be drawn) to the initial questions of a study. Every empirical study has an implicit, if not explicit, research design.

For case studies, four major types of designs are relevant, following a 2×2 matrix. The first pair of categories consists of single-case and multiple-case designs. The second pair, which can occur in combination with either of the first pair, is based on the unit or units of analysis to be covered—and distinguishes between holistic and embedded designs.

The case study investigator also must maximize four aspects of the quality of any design: (a) construct validity, (b) internal validity (for explanatory or causal case studies only), (c) external validity, and (d) reliability. How the investigator should deal with these four aspects of quality control is summarized in Chapter 2 but also is a major theme throughout the remainder of the book.

GENERAL APPROACH TO
DESIGNING CASE STUDIES

In identifying the research strategy for your research project, Chapter 1 has shown when you should select the case study strategy, as opposed to other strategies. The next task is to design your case study. For this purpose, as in designing any other type of research investigation, a plan, or *research design*, is needed.

The development of this research design is a difficult part of doing case studies. Unlike other research strategies, a comprehensive "catalog" of research designs for case studies has yet to be developed. There are no textbooks like those in the biological and psychological sciences, covering such design considerations as the assignment of subjects to different "groups," the selection of different stimuli or experimental conditions, or the identification of various response measures (see Cochran & Cox, 1957; Fisher, 1935, cited in Cochran & Cox, 1957; Sidowski, 1966). In a laboratory experiment, each of these choices reflects an important logical connection to the issues being studied. Similarly, there are not even textbooks like the well-known volumes by Campbell and Stanley (1966) or by Cook and Campbell (1979), which summarize the various research designs for quasi-experimental situations. Nor have there emerged any common designs—for example, "panel" studies—such as those now recognized in doing survey research (see Kidder & Judd, 1986, chap. 6).

One pitfall to be avoided, however, is to consider case study designs to be a subset or variant of the research designs used for other strategies, such as experiments. For the longest time, scholars incorrectly thought that the case study was but one type of quasi-experimental design (the one-shot posttest-only design). This misperception has finally been corrected, with the following statement appearing in a revision on quasi-experimental designs: "Certainly the case study as normally practiced should not be demeaned by identification with the one-group post-test-only design" (Cook & Campbell, 1979, p. 96).

In other words, the one-shot, posttest-only design as a quasi-experimental design still may be considered flawed, but the case study has now been recognized as something different. In fact, the case study is a separate research strategy that has its own research designs.

Unfortunately, case study research designs have not been codified. The following chapter therefore expands on the new methodological ground broken by the first edition of this book and describes a basic set of research designs for doing single- and multiple-case studies. Although these designs will need to be continually modified and improved in the future, in their present form they will nevertheless help you to design more rigorous and methodologically sound case studies.

Definition of Research Designs

Every type of empirical research has an implicit, if not explicit, research design. In the most elementary sense, the design is the logical sequence that connects the empirical data to a study's initial research questions and, ultimately, to its conclusions. Colloquially, a research design is *an action plan for getting from here to there*, where *here* may be defined as the initial set of questions to be answered, and *there* is some set of conclusions (answers) about these questions. Between "here" and "there" may be found a number of major steps, including the collection and analysis of relevant data. As a summary definition, another textbook has described a research design as a plan that

guides the investigator in the process of collecting, analyzing, and interpreting observations. It is a *logical model of proof* that allows the researcher to draw inferences concerning causal relations among the variables under investigation. The research design also defines the domain of generalizability, that is, whether the obtained interpretations can be generalized to a larger population or to different situations. (Nachmias & Nachmias, 1992, pp. 77-78, emphasis added)

Another way of thinking about a research design is as a "blueprint" of research, dealing with at least four problems: what questions to study, what data are relevant, what data to collect, and how to analyze the results (see F. Borum, personal communication, Copenhagen Business School, Copenhagen, Denmark, 1991; Philliber, Schwab, & Samsloss, 1980).

Note that a research design is much more than a work plan. The main purpose of the design is to help to avoid the situation in which the evidence does not address the initial research questions. In this sense, a research design deals with a *logical* problem and not a *logistical* problem. As a simple example, suppose you want to study a single organization. Your research questions, however, have to do with the organization's relationships with other organizations—their competitive or collaborative nature, for example. Such questions can be answered only if you collect information directly from the other organizations and not merely from the one you started with. If you complete your study by examining only one organization, you cannot draw accurate conclusions about interorganizational partnerships. This is a flaw in your research design, not in your work plan. The outcome could have been avoided if you had developed an appropriate research design in the first place.

Components of Research Designs

For case studies, five components of a research design are especially important:

1. a study's questions,
2. its propositions, if any,
3. its unit(s) of analysis,
4. the logic linking the data to the propositions, and
5. the criteria for interpreting the findings.

Study questions. This first component has already been described in Chapter 1. Although the substance of your questions will vary, Chapter 1 suggested that the *form* of the question—in terms of "who," "what," "where," "how," and "why"—provides an important clue regarding the most relevant research strategy to be used. The case study strategy is most likely to be appropriate for "how" and "why" questions, so your initial task is to clarify precisely the nature of your study questions in this regard.

Study propositions. As for the second component, each proposition directs attention to something that should be examined within the scope of the study. For instance, assume that your research, on the topic of interorganizational partnerships, began with the question: How and why do organizations collaborate with one another to provide joint services (for example, a manufacturer and a retail store collaborating to sell certain computer products)? These "how" and "why" questions, capturing what you are really interested in answering, led you to the case study as the appropriate strategy in the first place. Nevertheless, these "how" and "why" questions do not point to what you should study. Only if you are forced to state some propositions will you move in the right direction. For instance, you might think that organizations collaborate because they derive mutual benefits. This proposition, in addition to reflecting an important theoretical issue (that other incentives for collaboration do not exist or are unimportant), also begins to tell you where to look for relevant evidence (to define and ascertain the extent of specific benefits to each organization).

At the same time, some studies may have a legitimate reason for not having any propositions. This is the condition—which exists in experiments, surveys, and the other research strategies alike—in which a topic is the subject of "exploration." Every exploration, however, should still have some purpose. Instead of stating propositions, the design for an exploratory study should state a purpose, as well as the criteria by which an exploration will be judged successful. Consider the analogy in BOX 4 for exploratory case studies. Can you imagine how you would ask for support from Queen Isabella to do your exploratory study?

Unit of analysis. This third component is related to the fundamental problem of defining what the "case" is—a problem that has plagued many investigators at the outset of case studies. For instance, in the classic case study, a "case" may be an individual. Jennifer Platt (1992a, 1992b) has noted how the early case studies in the Chicago school of sociology were life histories of such roles as juvenile delinquents or derelict men. You also can imagine case studies of clinical patients, of exemplary students, or of certain types of leaders. In each situation, an individual person is the case being studied, and the individual is the primary unit of analysis. Information about each relevant individual would be collected, and several such individuals or "cases" might be included in a multiple-case study. Propositions would still be needed to help identify the relevant information about this individual or

---

BOX 4
"Exploration" as an Analogy for an
Exploratory Case Study

When Christopher Columbus went to Queen Isabella to ask for support for his "exploration" of the New World, he had to have some reasons for asking for three ships (Why not one? Why not five?), and he had some rationale for going westward (Why not south? Why not south and then east?). He also had some (mistaken) criteria for recognizing the Indies when he actually encountered them. In short, his exploration began with some rationale and direction, even if his initial assumptions might later have been proved wrong (Wilford, 1992). This same degree of rationale and direction should underlie even an exploratory case study.

---

individuals. Without such propositions, an investigator might be tempted to collect "everything," which is impossible to do. For example, the propositions in studying these individuals might involve the influence of early childhood or the role of peer relationships. Such topics already represent a vast narrowing of the relevant data. The more a study contains specific propositions, the more it will stay within feasible limits.

Of course, the "case" also can be some event or entity that is less well defined than a single individual. Case studies have been done about decisions, about programs, about the implementation process, and about organizational change. Feagin, Orum, & Sjoberg (1991) contains some classic examples of these single cases in sociology and political science. Beware of these types of topics—none is easily defined in terms of the beginning or end points of the "case." For example, a case study of a specific program may reveal (a) variations in program definition, depending upon the perspective of different actors, and (b) program components that existed prior to the formal designation of the program. Any case study of such a program would therefore have to confront these conditions in delineating the unit of analysis.

As a general guide, the definition of the unit of analysis (and therefore of the case) is related to the way the initial research questions have been defined. Suppose, for example, you want to study the role of the United States in the world economy. Peter Drucker (1986) has written a provocative essay about fundamental changes in the world economy, including the importance of "capital movements" independent of the flow of goods and services. The unit of analysis for your case study might be a country's economy, an industry in

---

BOX 5a
What Is the Unit of Analysis?

The Soul of a New Machine (1981) was a Pulitzer prize-winning book by Tracy Kidder. The book, also a best-seller, is about the development of a new minicomputer produced by Data General Corporation, intended to compete directly with one produced by Digital Equipment Corporation.

This easy-to-read book describes how Data General's engineering team invented and developed the new computer. The book begins with the initial conceptualization of the computer and ends when the engineering team relinquishes control of the machine to Data General's marketing staff.

The book is an excellent example of a case study. However, the book also illustrates a fundamental problem in doing case studies—that of defining the *unit of analysis*. Is the case study about the minicomputer, or is it about the dynamics of a small group—the engineering team? The answer is critical if we want to understand how the case study relates to a broader body of knowledge—that is, whether to generalize to a technology topic or to a group dynamics topic. Because the book is not an academic study, it does not need to, nor does it, provide an answer.

---

the world marketplace, an economic policy, or the trade or capital flow between two countries. Each unit of analysis would call for a slightly different research design and data collection strategy. Selection of the appropriate unit of analysis results from your accurately specifying the primary research questions. If your questions do not lead to the favoring of one unit of analysis over another, your questions are probably either too vague or too numerous—and you may have trouble conducting your case study.

Sometimes, the unit of analysis may have been defined one way, even though the phenomenon being studied calls for a different definition. Most frequently, investigators have confused case studies of neighborhoods with case studies of small groups (for another example, confusing an innovation with a small group in organizational studies, see BOX 5a). How a general *area* such as a neighborhood copes with racial transition, upgrading, and other phenomena can be quite different than how a small *group* copes with these same phenomena. *Street Corner Society* (Whyte, 1943/1955—also see BOX 1 in Chapter 1 of this book) and *Tally's Corner* (Liebow, 1967—also see BOX 9, this chapter), for instance, have often been mistaken for being case studies of neighborhoods when in fact they are case studies of small groups (note that in neither book is the neighborhood geography described, even though

---

BOX 5b
A Clearer Choice Among Units of Analysis

Ira Magaziner and Mark Patinkin's book *The Silent War: Inside the Global Business Battles Shaping America's Future* (1989) presents nine case studies. Each case study helps the reader to understand a real-life situation of international economic competition.

Two of the cases appear similar but in fact have different main units of analysis. One case, about the Korean firm Samsung, is a case study of the critical policies that make the firm competitive. Understanding Korean economic development is part of the context, and the case study also contains an embedded unit—Samsung's development of the microwave oven as an illustrative product. The other case, about the development of an Apple computer factory in Singapore, is in fact a case study of Singapore's critical policies that make the country competitive. The Apple computer factory experience—an embedded unit of analysis—is actually an illustrative example of how national policies affect foreign investments.

These two cases show how the definition of the main and embedded units of analyses, as well as the definition of the contextual events surrounding these units, depends on the level of inquiry. The main unit of analysis is likely to be at the level being addressed by the main study questions.

---

the small groups lived in a small area with clear neighborhood implications). BOX 5b, however, presents a good example of how units of analyses can be defined in a more discriminating manner—in the field of world trade.

Most investigators will encounter this type of confusion in defining the unit of analysis. To reduce the confusion, one good practice is to discuss the potential case with a colleague. Try to explain to that person what questions you are trying to answer and why you have chosen a specific case or group of cases as a way of answering those questions. This may help you to avoid incorrectly identifying the unit of analysis.

Once the general definition of the case has been established, other clarifications in the unit of analysis become important. If the unit of analysis is a small group, for instance, the persons to be included within the group (the immediate topic of the case study) must be distinguished from those who are outside it (the context for the case study). Similarly, if the case is about services in a specific geographic area, decisions need to be made about public services whose district boundaries do not coincide with the area. Finally, for almost any topic that might be chosen, specific time boundaries are needed to define the beginning and end of the case. All of these types of questions need to be considered and answered to define the unit of analysis and thereby to determine the limits of the data collection and analysis.

One final point needs to be made about defining the case and the unit of analysis, pertaining to the role of the available research literature. Most researchers will want to compare their findings with previous research; for this reason, the key definitions should not be idiosyncratic. Rather, each case study and unit of analysis either should be similar to those previously studied by others or should deviate in clear, operationally defined ways. In this manner, the previous literature therefore also can become a guide for defining the case and unit of analysis.

Linking data to propositions, and criteria for interpreting the findings. The fourth and fifth components have been the least well developed in case studies. These components represent the data analysis steps in case study research, and a research design should lay the foundations for this analysis.

Linking data to propositions can be done any number of ways, but none has become as precisely defined as the assignment of subjects and treatment conditions in psychological experiments (which is the way that hypotheses and data are connected in psychology). One promising approach for case studies is the idea of "pattern-matching" described by Donald Campbell (1975), whereby several pieces of information from the same case may be related to some theoretical proposition. In a related article on one type of pattern—a time-series pattern—Campbell (1969) illustrated this approach but without labeling it as such.

In his article, Campbell first showed how the annual number of traffic fatalities in Connecticut had seemed to decline after the passage of a new state law limiting the speed to 55 miles per hour. However, further examination of the fatality rate, over a number of years before and after the legal change, showed unsystematic fluctuation rather than any marked reduction. A simple eyeball test was all that was needed to show that the actual pattern *looked* unsystematic rather than following a downtrend (see Figure 2.1), and thus Campbell concluded that the speed limit had had no effect on the number of traffic fatalities.

What Campbell did was describe two potential patterns and then show that the data matched one better than the other. If the two potential patterns are considered rival propositions (an "effects" proposition and a "no effects" proposition, regarding the impact of the new speed limit law), the pattern-matching technique is a way of relating the data to the propositions, even though the entire study consists of only a single case (the state of Connecticut).

This article also illustrates the problems in dealing with the fifth component, *the criteria for interpreting a study's findings*. Campbell's data matched

a priori propositions:

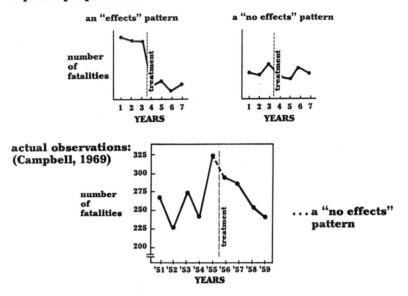

Figure 2.1. An Example of Pattern-Matching
SOURCE: COSMOS Corporation.

one pattern much better than they matched the other. But how close does a match have to be so as to be considered a match? Note that Campbell did not do any statistical test to make the comparison. Nor would a statistical test have been possible, because each data point in the pattern was a single number—the number of fatalities for that year—for which one could not calculate a variance and could not conduct any statistical test. Currently, there is no precise way of setting the criteria for interpreting these types of findings. One hopes that the different patterns are sufficiently contrasting that (as in Campbell's case) the findings can be interpreted in terms of comparing at least two rival propositions.

Summary. A research design should include five components. Although the current state of the art does not provide detailed guidance on the last two, the complete research design should not only indicate what data are to be collected—as indicated by (a) a study's questions, (b) its propositions, and (c) its units of analysis. The design also should tell you what is to be done after the data have been collected—as indicated by (d) the logic linking the data to the propositions and (e) the criteria for interpreting the findings.

The Role of Theory in Design Work

Covering these preceding five components of research designs will effectively force you to begin constructing a preliminary theory related to your topic of study. This role of theory development, prior to the conduct of any data collection, is one point of difference between case studies and related methods such as ethnography (Lincoln & Guba, 1985, 1986; Van Maanen, 1988; Van Maanen et al., 1982) and "grounded theory" (Strauss & Corbin, 1990). Typically, these related methods deliberately avoid specifying any theoretical propositions at the outset of an inquiry. As a result, students wrongly think that by using the case study method, they can proceed quickly into the data collection phase of their work, and they have been encouraged to make their "field contacts" as quickly as possible. No guidance could be more misleading. Among other considerations, the relevant field contacts depend upon an understanding—or theory—of what is being studied.

Theory development. For case studies, theory development as part of the design phase is essential, whether the ensuing case study's purpose is to develop or to test theory. Using a case study on the implementation of a new management information system (MIS) as an example (Markus, 1983), the simplest ingredient of a theory is a statement such as the following:

> The case study will show why implementation only succeeded when the organization was able to re-structure itself, and not just overlay the new MIS on the old organizational structure. (Markus, 1983)

The statement presents the nutshell of a theory of MIS implementation—that is, that organizational restructuring is needed to make MIS implementation work.

Using the same case, an additional ingredient might be the following statement:

> The case study will also show why the simple replacement of key persons was not sufficient for successful implementation. (Markus, 1983)

This second statement presents the nutshell of a *rival* theory—that is, that MIS implementation fails because of the resistance to change on the part of

individual people, and that the replacement of such people is the only requirement for implementation to succeed.

You can see that, as these two initial ingredients are elaborated, the stated
ideas will increasingly cover the questions, propositions, units of analysis,
logic connecting data to propositions, and criteria for interpreting the findings—that is, the five components of the needed research design. In this sense,
the complete research design embodies a "theory" of what is being studied.
This theory should by no means be considered with the formality of grand
theory in social science, nor are you being asked to be a masterful theoretician.
Rather, the simple goal is to have a sufficient blueprint for your study, and
this requires theoretical propositions. Then, the complete research design will
provide surprisingly strong guidance in determining what data to collect and
the strategies for analyzing the data. For this reason, theory development prior
to the collection of any case study data is an essential step in doing case
studies.

However, theory development takes time and can be difficult (Eisenhardt,
1989). For some topics, existing works may provide a rich theoretical framework for designing a specific case study. If you are interested in international
economic development, for instance, Peter Drucker's "The Changed World
Economy" (1986) is an exceptional source of theories and hypotheses.
Drucker claims that the world economy has changed significantly from the
past. He points to the "uncoupling" between the primary products (raw
materials) economy and the industrial economy, a similar uncoupling between
low labor costs and manufacturing production, and the uncoupling between
financial markets and the real economy of goods and services. To test these
propositions might require different studies, some focusing on the different
uncouplings, others focusing on specific industries, and yet others explaining
the plight of specific countries. Each different study would likely call for a
different unit of analysis. Drucker's theoretical framework would provide
guidance for designing these studies and even for collecting relevant data.

In other situations, the appropriate theory may be a descriptive theory (see
BOX 6, and also BOX 1 for another example), and your concern should focus
on such issues as (a) the purpose of the descriptive effort, (b) the full but
realistic range of topics that might be considered a "complete" description of
what is to be studied, and (c) the likely topic(s) that will be the essence of the
description. Good answers to these questions, including the rationales underlying the answers, will help you go a long way toward developing the needed
theoretical base—and research design—for your study.

For yet other topics, the existing knowledge base may be poor, and the
available literature will provide no conceptual framework or hypotheses of
note. Such a knowledge base does not lend itself to the development of good

---

BOX 6
Using a Metaphor to
Develop Descriptive Theory

Whether four countries—the American colonies, Russia, England, and France—all underwent similar courses of events during their major political revolutions is the topic of Crane Brinton's famous historical study—*The Anatomy of a Revolution* (1938). Tracing and analyzing these events is done in a descriptive manner, as the author's purpose is not so much to explain the revolutions as to determine whether they followed similar courses.

The "cross-case" analysis reveals major similarities: All societies were on the upgrade, economically; there were bitter class antagonisms; the intellectuals deserted from positions of leadership; government machinery was inefficient; and the ruling class exhibited immoral, dissolute, or inept behavior (or all three). However, rather than relying solely on this "factors" approach to description, the author also develops the metaphor of a human body suffering from a fever as a way of describing the pattern of events over time. The author adeptly uses the cyclic pattern of fever and chills, rising to a critical point and followed by a false tranquility, to describe the ebb and flow of events in the four revolutions.

---

theoretical statements, and any new empirical study is likely to assume the characteristic of being an "exploratory" study. Nevertheless, as noted earlier with the illustrative case in BOX 4, even an exploratory case study should be preceded by statements about (a) what is to be explored, (b) the purpose of the exploration, and (c) the criteria by which the exploration will be judged successful.

Illustrative types of theories. In general, to overcome the barriers to theory development, you should try to prepare for your case study by doing such things as reviewing the literature related to what you would like to study (also see Cooper, 1984); discussing your topic and ideas with colleagues or teachers; and asking yourself challenging questions about what you are studying, why you are proposing to do the study, and what you hope to learn as a result of the study.

As a further reminder, you should be aware of the full range of theories that might be relevant to your study. For instance, note that the MIS example illustrates MIS "implementation" theory, and that this is but one type of theory that can be the subject of study. Other types of theories for you to c
include the following:

- Individual theories—for example, theories of individual development, cognitive behavior, personality, learning and disability, individual perception, and interpersonal interactions
- Group theories—for example, theories of family functioning, informal groups, work teams, supervisory-employee coordination, and interpersonal networks
- Organizational theories—for example, theories of bureaucracies, organizational structure and functions, excellence in organizational performance (e.g., Harrison, 1987), and interorganizational partnerships
- Societal theories—for example, theories of urban development, international behavior, cultural institutions, technological development, and marketplace functions

Other examples cut across some of these illustrative types. Decision-making theory (Carroll & Johnson, 1992), for instance, can involve individuals, organizations, or social groups. As another example, a common topic of case studies is the evaluation of publicly supported programs, such as federal, state, or local programs. In this situation, the development of a theory of how a program is supposed to work is essential to the design of the evaluation but has been commonly underemphasized in the past (Bickman, 1987). According to Bickman, analysts have frequently confused the theory of the program (e.g., how to make education more effective) with the theory of program implementation (e.g., how to install an effective program). Where policymakers want to know the desired substantive steps (e.g., describe a newly effective curriculum), the analysts unfortunately recommend managerial steps (e.g., hire a good project director). This mismatch can be avoided by giving closer attention to the substantive theory.

Generalizing from case study to theory. Theory development does not only facilitate the data collection phase of the ensuing case study. The appropriately developed theory also is the level at which the generalization of the case study results will occur. This role of theory has been characterized throughout this book as "analytic generalization" and has been contrasted with another way of generalizing results, known as "statistical generalization." Understanding the distinction between these two types of generalization may be your most important challenge in doing case studies.

Let us take the more commonly recognized way of generalizing—"statistical generalization"—first, although it is the less relevant one for doing case studies. In statistical generalization, an inference is made about a population (or universe) on the basis of empirical data collected about a sample. This is shown as a *Level One Inference* in Figure 2.2.[1] This method of generalizing

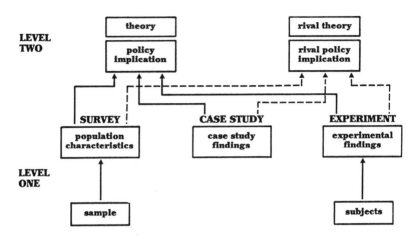

Figure 2.2. Making Inferences: Two Levels
SOURCE: COSMOS Corporation.

is commonly recognized because research investigators have ready access to formulas for determining the confidence with which generalizations can be made, depending mostly upon the size and internal variation within the universe and sample. Moreover, this is the most common way of generalizing when doing surveys (e.g., Fowler, 1988; Lavrakas, 1987), and it is an integral (though not the only) part of generalizing from experiments.

A fatal flaw in doing case studies is to conceive of statistical generalization as the method of generalizing the results of the case. This is because cases are not "sampling units" and should not be chosen for this reason. Rather, individual case studies are to be selected as a laboratory investigator selects the topic of a new experiment. Multiple cases, in this sense, should be considered like multiple experiments (or multiple surveys). Under these circumstances, the method of generalization is "analytic generalization," in which a previously developed theory is used as a template with which to compare the empirical results of the case study. If two or more cases are shown to support the same theory, replication may be claimed. The empirical results may be considered yet more potent if two or more cases support the same theory but do not support an equally plausible, *rival* theory. Graphically, this type of generalization is shown as a *Level Two Inference* in Figure 2.2.

Analytic generalization can be used whether your case study involves one or several cases, which shall be later referenced as single-case or multiple-case studies. Further, the logic of replication and the distinction between statistical and analytic generalization will be covered in greater detail in the discussion of multiple-case study designs. The main point at this juncture is that you should try to aim toward analytic generalization in doing case studies, and you should avoid thinking in such confusing terms as "the sample of cases" or the "small sample size of cases," as if a single case study were like a single respondent in a survey or a single subject in an experiment. In other words, in terms of Figure 2.2, you should aim for *Level Two Inferences* when doing case studies.

Because of the importance of this distinction between the two ways of generalizing, you will find repeated examples and discussion throughout the remainder of this chapter as well as in Chapter 5.

Summary. This subsection has suggested that a complete research design, covering the five components described earlier, in fact requires the development of a theoretical framework for the case study that is to be conducted. Rather than resisting such a requirement, a good case study investigator should make the effort to develop this theoretical framework, no matter whether the study is to be explanatory, descriptive, or exploratory. The use of theory, in doing case studies, not only is an immense aid in defining the appropriate research design and data collection but also becomes the main vehicle for generalizing the results of the case study.

CRITERIA FOR JUDGING
THE QUALITY OF RESEARCH DESIGNS

Because a research design is supposed to represent a logical set of statements, you also can judge the quality of any given design according to certain logical tests. Concepts that have been offered for these tests include trustworthiness, credibility, confirmability, and data dependability (U.S. General Accounting Office, 1990).

Four tests, however, have been commonly used to establish the quality of any empirical social research. Because case studies are one form of such empirical research, the four tests also are relevant to case study research. Therefore, an important innovation of this book is the identification of several tactics for dealing with these four tests when doing case studies. Figure 2.3 lists the four widely used tests and the recommended case study tactics as well as a cross-reference to the phase of research when the tactic is to be used. (Each tactic is later described in detail in the relevant chapter of this book.)

tests	case study tactic	phase of research in which tactic occurs
construct validity	– use multiple sources of evidence – establish chain of evidence – have key informants review draft case study report	data collection data collection composition
internal validity	– do pattern-matching – do explanation-building – do time-series analysis	data analysis data analysis data analysis
external validity	– use replication logic in multiple-case studies	research design
reliability	– use case study protocol – develop case study data base	data collection data collection

Figure 2.3. Case Study Tactics for Four Design Tests
SOURCE: COSMOS Corporation.

Because the four tests are common to all social science methods, the tests have been summarized in numerous textbooks (see Kidder & Judd, 1986, pp. 26-29):

- *Construct validity*: establishing correct operational measures for the concepts being studied
- *Internal validity* (for explanatory or causal studies only, and not for descriptive or exploratory studies): establishing a causal relationship, whereby certain conditions are shown to lead to other conditions, as distinguished from spurious relationships
- *External validity*: establishing the domain to which a study's findings can be generalized
- *Reliability*: demonstrating that the operations of a study—such as the data collection procedures can be repeated, with the same results

This list is much more complex than the standard "validity" and "reliability" notions to which most students have been exposed, and each item deserves explicit attention. For case studies, an important revelation is that the several tactics to be used in dealing with these tests should be applied throughout the subsequent conduct of the case study, and not just at the beginning. In this sense, "design work" actually continues beyond the initial design plans.

Construct Validity

This first test is especially problematic in case study research. People who have been critical of case studies often point to the fact that a case study investigator fails to develop a sufficiently operational set of measures and that "subjective" judgments are used to collect the data. Take an example such as studying "neighborhood change"—a common case study topic.

Over the years, concerns have arisen over how certain urban neighborhoods have changed their character. Any number of case studies have examined the types of changes and their consequences. However, without any prior specification of the significant, operational events that constitute "change," a reader cannot tell whether the recorded changes in a case study genuinely reflect critical events in a neighborhood or whether they happen to be based on an investigator's impressions only.

Neighborhood change can indeed cover a wide variety of phenomena: racial turnover, housing deterioration and abandonment, changes in the pattern of urban services, shifts in a neighborhood's economic institutions, or the turnover from low- to middle-income residents in "gentrifying" neighborhoods. To meet the test of construct validity, an investigator must be sure to cover two steps:

1. Select the specific types of changes that are to be studied (in relation to the original objectives of the study) and
2. Demonstrate that the selected measures of these changes do indeed reflect the specific types of change that have been selected.

For example, suppose you satisfy the first step by stating that you plan to study the rise in neighborhood crime. The second step now demands that you also justify why you might be using police-reported crime (which happens to be the standard measure used in the FBI Uniform Crime Reports) as your measure of crime. Perhaps this is not a valid measure, given that large proportions of crimes are not reported to the police.

As Figure 2.3 shows for doing case studies, three tactics are available to increase construct validity. The first is the use of *multiple sources of evidence*, in a manner encouraging convergent lines of inquiry, and this tactic is relevant during data collection (see Chapter 4). A second tactic is to establish a *chain of evidence*, also relevant during data collection (Chapter 4). The third tactic is to have the draft case study report reviewed by key informants (a procedure described further in Chapter 6).

Internal Validity

This second test has been given the greatest attention in experimental and quasi-experimental research (see Campbell & Stanley, 1966; Cook & Campbell, 1979). Numerous "threats" to validity have been identified, mainly dealing with spurious effects. However, because so many textbooks already cover this topic, only two points need to be made here.

First, internal validity is a concern only for causal (or explanatory) case studies, in which an investigator is trying to determine whether event x led to event y. If the investigator incorrectly concludes that there is a causal relationship between x and y without knowing that some third factor—z—may actually have caused y, the research design has failed to deal with some threat to internal validity. Note that this logic is inapplicable to descriptive or exploratory studies (whether the studies are case studies, surveys, or experiments), which are not concerned with making causal statements.

Second, the concern over internal validity, for case study research, may be extended to the broader problem of making inferences. Basically, a case study involves an inference every time an event cannot be directly observed. Thus an investigator will "infer" that a particular event resulted from some earlier occurrence, based on interview and documentary evidence collected as part of the case study. Is the inference correct? Have all the rival explanations and possibilities been considered? Is the evidence convergent? Does it appear to be airtight? A research design that has anticipated these questions has begun to deal with the overall problem of making inferences and therefore the specific problem of internal validity.

However, the specific tactics for achieving this result are difficult to identify. This is especially true in doing case studies. As one set of suggestions, Figure 2.3 shows that the analytic tactic of *pattern-matching*, already touched upon but to be described further in Chapter 5, is one way of addressing internal validity. Two related analytic tactics, *explanation-building* and *time-series analysis*, also are described in Chapter 5.

External Validity

The third test deals with the problem of knowing whether a study's findings are generalizable beyond the immediate case study. In the simplest example, if a study of neighborhood change focused on one neighborhood, are the results applicable to another neighborhood? The external validity problem has been a major barrier in doing case studies. Critics typically state that single cases offer a poor basis for generalizing. However, such critics are implicitly contrasting the situation to survey research, in which a "sample" (if selected correctly) readily generalizes to a larger universe. *This analogy to samples and universes is incorrect when dealing with case studies.* This is because survey research relies on *statistical* generalization, whereas case studies (as with experiments) rely on *analytical* generalization. In analytical generalization, the investigator is striving to generalize a particular set of results to some broader theory (see BOX 7).

For example, the theory of neighborhood change that led to a case study in the first place is the same theory that will help to identify the other cases to which the results are generalizable. If a study had focused on "gentrification" (see Auger, 1979), the procedure for selecting a neighborhood for study also will have identified those types of neighborhoods within which gentrification was occurring. In principle, theories about changes in all of these neighborhoods would be the target to which the results could later be generalized.

The generalization is not automatic, however. A theory must be tested through replications of the findings in a second or even a third neighborhood, where the theory has specified that the same results should occur. Once such replication has been made, the results might be accepted for a much larger number of similar neighborhoods, even though further replications have not been performed. This *replication logic* is the same that underlies the use of experiments (and allows scientists to generalize from one experiment to another) and, as shown in Figure 2.3, will be discussed further in this chapter in the section on multiple-case designs.

Reliability

Most people are probably already familiar with this final test. The objective is to be sure that, if a later investigator followed exactly the same procedures as described by an earlier investigator and conducted the same case study all over again, the later investigator should arrive at the same findings and conclusions. (Note that the emphasis is on doing the *same* case over again, not on "replicating" the results of one case by doing *another* case study.) The goal of reliability is to minimize the errors and biases in a study.

One prerequisite for allowing this other investigator to repeat an earlier case study is the need to document the procedures followed in the earlier case. Without such documentation, you could not even repeat your own work

---

BOX 7
How Case Studies
Can Be Generalized to Theory

A common complaint about case studies is that it is difficult to generalize from one case to another. Thus analysts fall into the trap of trying to select a "representative" case or set of cases. Yet no set of cases, no matter how large, is likely to deal satisfactorily with the complaint.

The problem lies in the very notion of generalizing to other case studies. Instead, an analyst should try to generalize findings to "theory," analogous to the way a scientist generalizes from experimental results to theory. (Note that the scientist does not attempt to select "representative" experiments.)

This approach is well illustrated by Jane Jacobs in her famous book, *The Death and Life of Great American Cities* (1961). The book is based mostly on experiences from New York City. However, the chapter topics, rather than reflecting the single experiences of New York, cover broader theoretical issues in urban planning, such as the role of sidewalks, the role of neighborhood parks, the need for primary mixed uses, the need for small blocks, and the processes of slumming and unslumming. In the aggregate, these issues in fact represent the building of a theory of urban planning.

Jacob's book created heated controversy in the planning profession. As a partial result, new empirical inquiries were made in other locales to examine one or another facet of her rich and provocative ideas. Her *theory*, in essence, became the vehicle for examining other cases, and the theory still stands as a significant contribution to the field of urban planning.

(which is another way of dealing with reliability). In the past, case study research procedures have been poorly documented, making external reviewers suspicious of the reliability of the case study. As remedies, Chapter 3 will discuss the use of a *case study protocol* to deal with the documentation problem in detail, and Chapter 4 will describe another tactic, the development of a *case study database*.

The general way of approaching the reliability problem is to make as many steps as operational as possible and to conduct research as if someone were always looking over your shoulder. In accounting and bookkeeping, one is always aware that any calculations must be capable of being audited. In this sense, an auditor is also performing a reliability check and must be able to produce the same results if the same procedures are followed. A good guideline for doing case studies is therefore to conduct the research so that an auditor could repeat the procedures and arrive at the same results.

Summary. Four tests may be considered relevant in judging the quality of a research design. In designing and doing case studies, various tactics are available to deal with these tests, though not all of the tactics occur at the formal stage of designing a case study. Some of the tactics occur during the data collection, data analysis, or compositional phases of the research and are therefore described in greater detail in subsequent chapters of this book.

CASE STUDY DESIGNS

These general characteristics of research designs serve as a background for considering the specific designs for case studies. Four types of designs will be discussed, based on a 2 × 2 matrix (see Figure 2.4). The matrix assumes that single- and multiple-case studies reflect different design situations and that, within these two types, there also can be a unitary or multiple units of analysis. Thus, for the case study strategy, the four types of designs are (a) single-case (holistic) designs, (b) single-case (embedded) designs, (c) multiple-case (holistic) designs, and (d) multiple-case (embedded) designs. The rationale for these four types of designs is as follows.

What Are the Potential Single-Case Designs?

Rationale for single-case designs. A primary distinction in designing case studies is between *single-* and *multiple-*case designs. This means the need for a decision, prior to any data collection, on whether a single-case study or multiple cases are going to be used to address the research questions.

The single-case study is an appropriate design under several circumstances. First, recall that a single-case study is analogous to a single experiment, and many of the same conditions that justify a single experiment also justify a single-case study. One rationale for a single case is when it represents the *critical case* in testing a well-formulated theory (again, note the analogy to the critical experiment). The theory has specified a clear set of propositions as well as the circumstances within which the propositions are believed to be true. To confirm, challenge, or extend the theory, there may exist a single case, meeting all of the conditions for testing the theory. The single case can then be used to determine whether a theory's propositions are correct or whether some alternative set of explanations might be more relevant. In this manner, like Graham Allison's comparison of three theories of bureaucratic functioning and the Cuban missile crisis (described in Chapter 1, BOX 2), the single case can represent a significant contribution to knowledge and

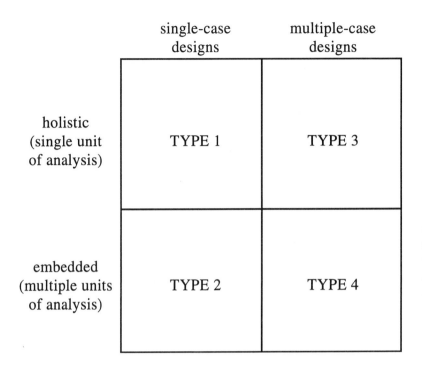

Figure 2.4. Basic Types of Designs for Case Studies
SOURCE: COSMOS Corporation.

theory-building. Such a study can even help to refocus future investigations in an entire field. (See BOX 8 for another example, in the field of organizational innovation.)

A second rationale for a single case is one in which the case represents an *extreme or unique case*. This has commonly been the situation in clinical psychology, in which a specific injury or disorder may be so rare that any single case is worth documenting and analyzing. For instance, one rare clinical syndrome is the inability of certain clinical patients to recognize familiar faces. Given visual cues alone, such patients are unable to recognize loved ones, friends, pictures of famous people, or (in some cases) their own image in a mirror. This syndrome appears to be due to some physical injury to the brain. Yet the syndrome occurs so rarely that scientists have been unable to establish any common patterns (Yin, 1970, 1978). In such circumstances, the single-case study is an appropriate research design whenever a new person with this syndrome—known as prosopagnosia—is encountered. The case

---

BOX 8
The Single Case Study as the Critical Case

One rationale for selecting a single-case rather than a multiple-case design is that the single case represents the *critical test of a significant theory*. Neal Gross et al. used such a design by focusing on a single school in their book, *Implementing Organizational Innovations* (1971).

The school was selected because it had a prior history of innovation and could not be claimed to suffer from "barriers to innovation." In the prevailing theories, such barriers had been prominently cited as the major reason that innovations failed. Gross et al. showed that, in this school, an innovation also failed but that the failure could not be attributed to any barriers. Implementation processes, rather than barriers, appeared to account for the outcomes.

In this manner, the book, though limited to a single case, represents a watershed in innovation theory. Prior to the study, analysts had focused on the identification of barriers; since the study, the literature has been much more dominated by studies of the implementation process.

---

study would document the person's abilities and disabilities to determine the precise nature of the face recognition deficit but also to ascertain whether related disorders exist.

A third rationale for a single case study is the *revelatory case*. This situation exists when an investigator has an opportunity to observe and analyze a phenomenon previously inaccessible to scientific investigation, such as Whyte's *Street Corner Society*, previously described in Chapter 1, BOX 1. A latter-day example is Elliot Liebow's famous case study of unemployed blacks, *Tally's Corner* (see BOX 9). Liebow had the opportunity to meet the men in one neighborhood in Washington, DC, and to learn about their every-day lives. His observations of and insights into the problems of unemployment formed a significant case study, because few social scientists had previously had the opportunity to investigate these problems, even though the problems were common across the country (as distinguished from the rare or unique case). When other investigators have similar types of opportunities and can uncover some prevalent phenomenon previously inaccessible to scientists, such conditions justify the use of a single-case study on the grounds of its revelatory nature.

These three rationales serve as the major reasons for conducting a single-case study. There are other situations in which the single-case study may be conducted as a prelude to further study, such as the use of case studies as

---

BOX 9
The Revelatory Case as a Single Case

Another rationale for selecting a single-case rather than a multiple-case design is that the investigator has access to a situation previously inaccessible to scientific observation. The case study is therefore worth conducting because the descriptive information alone will be revelatory.

Such was the situation in Elliot Liebow's sociological classic, *Tally's Corner* (1967). The book is about a single group of black men, living in a poor, inner-city neighborhood. By befriending these men, the author was able to learn about their lifestyles, their coping behavior, and in particular their sensitivity to unemployment and failure. The book provides insights into a subculture that has prevailed in many U.S. cities for a long period of time, but one that had been only obscurely understood. The single case showed how investigations of such topics could be done, stimulating much further research and eventually the development of policy actions.

---

exploratory devices or such as the conduct of a pilot case that is the first of a multiple-case study. However, in these latter instances, the single-case study cannot be regarded as a complete study on its own.

Whatever the rationale for doing single cases (and there may be more than the three mentioned here), a potential vulnerability of the single-case design is that a case may later turn out not to be the case it was thought to be at the outset. Single-case designs therefore require careful investigation of the potential case to minimize the chances of misrepresentation and to maximize the access needed to collect the case study evidence. A fair warning is not to commit oneself to the single case until these major concerns have been covered.

Holistic versus embedded case studies. The same case study may involve *more than one unit of analysis*. This occurs when, within a single case, attention also is given to a subunit or subunits (see BOX 10). For instance, even though a case study might be about a single public program, the analysis might include outcomes from individual projects within the program (and possibly even some quantitative analyses of large numbers of projects). In an organizational study, the embedded units also might be "process" units—such as meetings, roles, or locations. In either situation, these embedded units can be selected through sampling or cluster techniques (McClintock, 1985). However the units are selected, the resulting design

---

BOX 10
An Embedded, Single-Case Design

Union Democracy (1956) is a highly regarded case study by three eminent academicians—Seymour Martin Lipset, Martin Trow, and James Coleman. The case study is about the inside politics of the International Typographical Union and involves *several* units of analysis (see the following table). The main unit was the organization as a whole, the smallest unit was the individual member, and several intermediary units also were important. At each level of analysis, different data collection techniques were used, ranging from historical to survey analysis.

---

would be called an *embedded case study design* (see Figure 2.4, Type 2). In contrast, if the case study examined only the global nature of a program or of an organization, a *holistic design* would have been used (see Figure 2.4, Type 1).

Both variations of single-case studies have different strengths and weaknesses. The holistic design is advantageous when no logical subunits can be identified and when the relevant theory underlying the case study is itself of a holistic nature. Potential problems arise, however, when a global approach allows an investigator to avoid examining any specific phenomenon in operational detail. Another typical problem with the holistic design is that the entire case study may be conducted at an abstract level, lacking any clear measures or data.

A further problem with the holistic design is that the entire nature of the case study may shift, unbeknownst to the researcher, during the course of study. The initial study questions may have reflected one orientation, but as the case study proceeds, a different orientation may emerge, and the evidence begins to address different questions. Although some people have claimed such flexibility to be a strength of the case study approach, in fact, the largest criticism of case studies is based on this type of shift—in which the original research design is no longer appropriate for the research questions being asked (see Yin, Bateman, & Moore, 1983). Because of this problem, such unsuspected slippage needs to be avoided; if the relevant research questions really do change, you should simply start over again, with a new research design. One way to increase the sensitivity to such slippage is to have a set of subunits. With such subunits, an embedded design can serve as an important device for focusing a case study inquiry.

Kinds of Data (BOX 10 Continued)

Unit Being Characterized	Total System	Intermediate Units		Individuals	
	Issues, Data on Occupation; Union Laws; Policies; Historical Data; Convention Reports	Locals' Histories and Voting Records; Issues on Local Level; Size of Locals	Shops' Voting Records; Shop Size	Interviews with Leaders	Interviews of the Sample of Man
ITU as a whole	Structural, environmental, behavioral properties	By inference, communication network (structural)			
Locals	Behavioral properties (militancy, etc.)	Behavioral properties, size	By inference, communication network (structural)	Structural, environmental, behavioral properties	
Shops			Behavioral properties, size		Distributions of individual properties
Other immediate social environment of men	The social climate, by inference from dominant issues and election outcome	The social climate, by inference from dominant issues and election outcome			Chapel chairman's attributes; friends' attributes
Men	By inference, dominant values and interests	By inference: values, interests, and loyalties (e.g., local over international)	By inference: values, interests, loyalties (e.g., to shop over local)	By inference: values	Behavior, background, values, attitudes

SOURCE: Lipset, Trow, & Coleman (1956, p. 422). Reprinted by permission.

An embedded design, however, also has some pitfalls. A major one occurs when the case study focuses only on the subunit level and fails to return to the larger unit of analysis. A program evaluation that includes project characteristics as a subunit of analysis, for instance, becomes a project study if no investigating is done at the larger unit—that is, the "program." Similarly, a study of organizational climate may involve individual employees as a subunit of study. However, if the data focus only on individual employees, the study will in fact become an employment and not an organizational study. What has happened is that the original phenomenon of interest (organizational climate) has become the context and not the target of study.

Summary. Single cases are a common design for doing case studies, and two types have been described: those using holistic designs and those using embedded units of analysis. Overall, the single-case design is eminently justifiable under certain conditions—where the case represents a critical test of existing theory, where the case is a rare or unique event, or where the case serves a revelatory purpose.

A major step in designing and conducting a single case is defining the unit of analysis (or the case itself). An operational definition is needed and some precaution must be taken—before a total commitment to the whole case study is made—to ensure that the case in fact is relevant to the issues and questions of interest.

Within the single case may still be incorporated subunits of analyses, so that a more complex—or embedded—design is developed. The subunits can often add significant opportunities for extensive analysis, enhancing the insights into the single case. However, if too much attention is given to these subunits, and if the larger, holistic aspects of the case begin to be ignored, the case study itself will have shifted its orientation and changed its nature. This shift might in fact be justifiable, but it should not come as a surprise to the investigator.

What Are the Potential Multiple-Case Designs?

The same study may contain more than a single case. When this occurs, the study has to use a multiple-case design, and such designs have increased in frequency in recent years. A common example is a study of school innovations (such as open classrooms, teacher aides, or new technology) in which independent innovations occur at different sites. Thus each site might be the subject of an individual case study, and the study as a whole would have used a multiple-case design.

Multiple- versus single-case designs. In some fields, multiple-case studies have been considered a different "methodology" than single-case studies. For example, both anthropology and political science have developed one set of rationales for doing single-case studies and a second set for doing what have been considered "comparative" (or multiple-case) studies (see Eckstein, 1975; George, 1979). From the perspective of this book, however, the choice between single- and multiple-case designs remains within the same methodological framework—and no broad distinction is made between the so-called classic (that is, single-) case study and multiple-case studies. The choice is considered one of research design, with both being included under the case study strategy.

Multiple-case designs have distinct advantages and disadvantages in comparison with single-case designs. The evidence from multiple cases is often considered more compelling, and the overall study is therefore regarded as being more robust (Herriott & Firestone, 1983). At the same time, the rationale for single-case designs usually cannot be satisfied by multiple cases. The unusual or rare case, the critical case, and the revelatory case are all likely to involve only single cases, by definition. Moreover, the conduct of a multiple-case study can require extensive resources and time beyond the means of a single student or independent research investigator.

Therefore, the decision to undertake multiple-case studies cannot be taken lightly. Every case should serve a specific purpose within the overall scope of inquiry. Here, *a major insight is to consider multiple cases as one would consider multiple experiments*—that is, to follow a "replication" logic. This is far different from a mistaken analogy in the past, which incorrectly considered multiple cases to be similar to the multiple respondents in a survey (or to the multiple subjects *within* an experiment)—that is, to follow a "sampling" logic. The methodological differences between these two views are revealed by the different rationales underlying the replication as opposed to sampling logics.

Replication, not sampling logic, for multiple-case studies. The replication logic is analogous to that used in multiple experiments (see Hersen & Barlow, 1976). Thus, if one has access only to three cases of a rare, clinical syndrome in psychology or medical science, the appropriate research design is one in which the same results are predicted for each of the three cases, thereby producing evidence that the three cases did indeed involve the same syndrome. If similar results are obtained from all three cases, replication is said to have taken place. This replication logic is the same whether one is repeating certain critical experiments, is limited to a few cases due to the expense or difficulty in performing a surgical preparation in animals, or is limited by the rarity of occurrence of a clinical syndrome. In each of these situations, an individual case or subject is considered akin to a single experiment, and the analysis must follow cross-experiment rather than *within*-experiment design and logic.

The logic underlying the use of multiple-case studies is the same. Each case must be carefully selected so that it either (a) predicts similar results (a *literal replication*) or (b) produces contrasting results but for predictable reasons (a *theoretical replication*). The ability to conduct six or ten case studies, arranged effectively within a multiple-case design, is analogous to the ability to conduct six to ten experiments on related topics; a few cases (two or three) would be literal replications, whereas a few other cases (four to six) might be designed to pursue two different patterns of theoretical replications. If all the cases turn out as predicted, these six to ten cases, in the aggregate, would have provided compelling support for the initial set of propositions. If the cases are in some way contradictory, the initial propositions must be revised and retested with another set of cases. Again, this logic is similar to the way scientists deal with contradictory experimental findings.

An important step in all of these replication procedures is the development of a rich, theoretical framework. The framework needs to state the conditions under which a particular phenomenon is likely to be found (a literal replication) as well as the conditions when it is not likely to be found (a theoretical replication). The theoretical framework later becomes the vehicle for generalizing to new cases, again similar to the role played in cross-experiment designs. Furthermore, just as with experimental science, if some of the empirical cases do not work as predicted, modification must be made to the theory. Remember, too, that theories can be practical, and not just academic. The study in BOX 11 contains an excellent example of a multiple-case study (two cases) whose cases and conclusions are tied together by a practical, policy-oriented theory.

To take another example, one might consider the initial proposition that an increase in microcomputer use in school districts will occur when such technologies are used for both administrative and instructional applications, but not either alone. To pursue this proposition in a multiple-case study design, three or four cases might be selected in which both types of applications are present, to determine whether, in fact, microcomputer use did increase over a period of time (the investigation would be predicting a literal replication in these three or four cases). Three or four additional cases might be selected in which only administrative applications are present, with the prediction being little increase in use (predicting a theoretical replication). Finally, three or four other cases would be selected in which only instructional applications

---

BOX 11
Multiple-Case Studies
and a Policy-Oriented Theory

The international marketplace of the 1970s and 1980s was marked by Japan's prominence. Much of its strength was attributable to the role of centralized planning and support by government agencies. In contrast, the United States was considered to have no counterpart support structures. Gregory Hooks's excellent case study (1990) points to a counterexample, frequently ignored by advocates: the role of the U.S. defense department in implementing an industrial planning policy within defense-related industries.

Hooks provides quantitative data on two cases—the aeronautics industry and the microelectronics industry. One industry was much more dependent upon government than the other. However, in both cases, Hooks's evidence shows how the defense department supported the development of these industries through financial support, ensuring demand, and support of R&D.

---

are present, with the same prediction of little increase in use, but for different reasons than the administrative-only cases (another theoretical replication). If this entire pattern of results across these multiple cases is indeed found, the nine to twelve cases, in the aggregate, would provide substantial support for the initial proposition. (See BOX 12 for another example of a multiple-case replication design, but from the field of urban studies.)

This replication logic, whether applied to experiments or to case studies, must be distinguished from the sampling logic commonly used in surveys. According to the sampling logic, a number of respondents (or subjects) are assumed to "represent" a larger pool of respondents (or subjects), so that data from a smaller number of persons are assumed to represent the data that might have been collected from the entire pool.

The sampling logic demands an operational enumeration of the entire universe or pool of potential respondents and then a statistical procedure for selecting the specific subset of respondents to be surveyed. This logic is applicable whenever an investigator is interested in determining the prevalence or frequency of a particular phenomenon and when it is too expensive or impractical to survey the entire universe or pool. The resulting data from the sample that is actually surveyed are assumed to reflect the entire universe or pool, with inferential statistics used to establish the confidence intervals for which this representation is actually accurate.

BOX 12
A Multiple-Case, Replication Design

A common problem of the 1960s and 1970s was how to get good advice to city governments. Peter Szanton's book, *Not Well Advised* (1981), reviewed the experiences of numerous attempts by university and research groups to collaborate with city officials.

The book is an excellent example of a multiple-case, replication design. Szanton starts with eight case studies, showing how different university groups all failed to help cities. The eight cases are sufficient "replications" to convince the reader of a general phenomenon. Szanton then provides five more case studies, in which nonuniversity groups also failed, concluding that failure was therefore not necessarily inherent in the academic enterprise. Yet a third group of cases shows how university groups have successfully helped business, engineering firms, and sectors other than city government. A final set of three cases shows that those few groups able to help city government were concerned with implementation and not just with the production of new ideas, leading to the major conclusion that city governments may have peculiar needs in receiving advice.

Within each of the four groups of case studies, Szanton has illustrated the principle of *literal* replication. Across the four groups, he has illustrated *theoretical* replication. This potent case study design can and should be applied to many other topics.

Any application of this sampling logic to case studies would be misplaced. First, case studies should not generally be used to assess the incidence of phenomena. Second, a case study would have to cover both the phenomenon of interest and its context, yielding a large number of potentially relevant variables. In turn, this would require an impossibly large number of cases—too large to allow any statistical consideration of the relevant variables.

Third, if a sampling logic had to be applied to all types of research, many important topics could not be empirically investigated, such as in the following problem: Your investigation deals with the role of the presidency of the United States, and you are interested in studying the behavior of the incumbent from some leadership perspective. The leadership perspective, to be at all faithful to the complexity of reality, must incorporate dozens if not hundreds of relevant variables. Any sampling logic simply would be misplaced under such circumstances, as there have been only 42 presidents since the beginning of the Republic. Moreover, you would probably not have the resources to

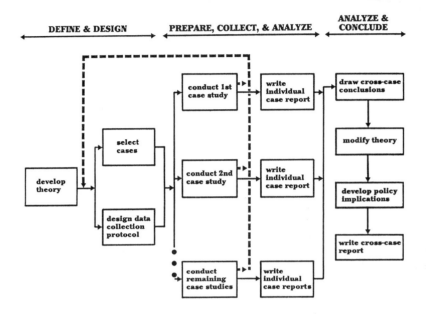

Figure 2.5. Case Study Method
SOURCE: COSMOS Corporation.

conduct a full study of all 42 incumbents (and even if you did, you would still have too many variables in relation to the 42 data points available). This type of study just could not be done, following the sampling logic; if the replication logic is followed, however, the study is eminently feasible.

The replication approach to multiple-case studies is illustrated in Figure 2.5. (This figure is derived from research on the case study method; see Yin, Bateman, & Moore, 1983.) The figure indicates that the initial step in designing the study must consist of theory development and then shows that case selection and the definition of specific measures are important steps in the design and data collection process. Each individual case study consists of a "whole" study, in which convergent evidence is sought regarding the facts and conclusions for the case; each case's conclusions are then considered to be the information needing replication by other individual cases. Both the individual cases and the multiple-case results can and should be the focus of a summary report. For each individual case, the report should indicate how and why a particular proposition was demonstrated (or not demonstrated). Across cases, the report should indicate the extent of the replication logic and why certain cases were predicted to have certain results, whereas other cases—if any—were predicted to have contrasting results.

Again, Figure 2.5 depicts a very different logic than that of sampling design. This is a difficult step to perceive and is worth extensive discussion with colleagues before proceeding with any case study design.

When using a multiple-case design, a further question you will encounter has to do with the *number* of cases deemed necessary or sufficient for your study. However, because a sampling logic should not be used, the typical criteria regarding sample size also are irrelevant. Instead, you should think of this decision as a reflection of the number of case replications—both literal and theoretical—that you would like to have in your study.

For the number of literal replications, an appropriate analogy from statistical studies is the selection of the criterion for establishing levels of significance. Much as the choice of "p < .05" or "p < .01" is not derived from any formula but is a matter of discretionary, judgmental choice, the selection of the number of replications depends upon the certainty you want to have about your multiple-case results (as with the higher criterion for establishing statistical significance, the greater certainty lies with the larger number of cases). For example, you may want to settle for two or three literal replications when the rival theories are grossly different and the issue at hand does not demand an excessive degree of certainty. However, if your rivals have subtle differences or if you want a high degree of certainty, you may press for five, six, or more replications.

For the number of theoretical replications, the important consideration is related to your sense of the complexity of the realm of external validity. When you are uncertain whether external conditions will produce different case study results, you may want to articulate these relevant conditions more explicitly at the outset of your study and identify a larger number of cases to be included. For example, in the neighborhood example used previously in discussing external validity (see the section titled "External Validity"), a common concern from the standpoint of policy research (e.g., Majchrzak, 1984) is that ethnically and racially different neighborhoods do not usually follow similar courses of change. A study of gentrification would therefore want to include at least some number of cases that varied along ethnic or racial lines (and *within* each type of case, one would still want a minimum of two or three literal replications). In contrast, when external conditions are not thought to produce much variation in the phenomenon being studied, a smaller number of theoretical replications is needed.

Multiple-case studies: Holistic or embedded. The fact that a design calls for multiple-case studies does not eliminate the variation identified earlier with single cases: Each individual case may still be holistic or embedded. In other words, a multiple-case study may consist of multiple holistic cases (see Figure 2.4, Type 3) or of multiple embedded cases (see Figure 2.4, Type 4).

The difference between these two designs depends upon the type of phenomenon being studied. In an embedded design, a study may even call for the conduct of a survey at each case study site. For instance, supposing a study is concerned with the delivery of services by different community mental health centers (facilities) (see Larsen, 1982). Each center may rightfully be the topic of a case study; the theoretical framework may dictate that nine such centers be included as case studies, three to replicate a direct result (literal replication) and six others to deal with contrasting conditions (theoretical replications).

In all nine centers, an embedded design is used because surveys of the centers' clients will be conducted. However, the results of each survey will *not* be pooled across centers. Rather, the survey data will be part of the findings for each individual center, or case. These data may be highly quantitative, focusing on the attitudes and behavior of individual clients, and the data will be used along with archival information to interpret the success and operations at the given center. If, in contrast, the survey data are pooled across centers, a multiple-case study design is no longer being used, and the investigation is likely to be using a survey rather than case study design.

Summary. This section has dealt with situations in which the same investigation may call for multiple-case studies. These types of designs are becoming more prevalent, but they are more expensive and time-consuming to conduct.

Any use of multiple-case designs should follow a replication, not a sampling, logic, and an investigator must choose each case carefully. The cases should serve in a manner similar to multiple experiments, with similar results (a literal replication) or contrasting results (a theoretical replication) predicted explicitly at the outset of the investigation.

The replication design does not necessarily mean that each case study needs to be either holistic or embedded. The individual cases, within a multiple-case study design, may be either. When an embedded design is used, each individual case study may in fact include the collection and analysis of highly quantitative data, including the use of surveys within each case.

How Case Study Designs Can Be Kept Flexible

A final reminder is that a case study design is not something completed only at the outset of a study. The design can be altered and revised after the initial stages of a study, but only under stringent circumstances.

As an example, *pilot* case studies may reveal inadequacies in the initial design or may help to articulate it. In the event of a single-case design, what was thought to be a revelatory or unique case may not turn out to be so after all. In the event of a multiple-case design, the selection of cases may have to be modified because of new information about the cases. In other words, after some early data collection and analysis, an investigator has every right to conclude that the initial design was faulty and to modify the design. This is an appropriate and desirable use of pilot studies. (Also see Chapter 3 for more on pilot case studies.)

At the same time, an investigator must be careful not to shift, unknowingly, the theoretical concerns or objectives. If these, rather than the cases themselves, are changed, the investigator can correctly be accused of exercising a bias in conducting the research and interpreting the findings. The point is that the flexibility of case study designs is *in selecting cases different from those initially identified* (with appropriate documentation of this shift) but not in changing the purpose or objectives of the study to suit the case(s) that were found. The former situation is much like changing experiments when it is obvious that an experimental procedure is infeasible; the latter is a more subtle but still illegitimate change.

EXERCISES

1. *Defining the boundaries of a case study.* Select a topic for a case study you would like to do. Identify some basic questions to be answered by your case study. Does the naming of these questions clarify the boundaries of your case, with regard to the relevant length of time for which evidence is to be collected? The relevant organization or geographic area? The type of evidence that should be collected? The priorities for doing analysis?

2. *Defining the unit of analysis for a case study.* Examine or read the case study *The Soul of a New Machine.* What is the main unit of analysis in this book? What alternatives did you consider, and why did you select the unit that you did? Carry out the same exercise for some other case study of your choosing.

3. *Defining a case study research design.* Select one of the case studies described in the BOXES of this book. Describe the research design of this case study. How did it justify the relevant evidence to be sought, given the basic research

questions to be answered? What methods were used to draw conclusions, based on the evidence? Is the design a single- or multiple-case design? Is it holistic or does it have embedded units of analysis?

4. *Establishing the rationale for single- and multiple-case studies.* Name the rationales for using a single-case study design, then name those for using a multiple-case design. Give examples of each type of design, either from the case studies described in the BOXES of this book or from other case studies with which you are acquainted. What are the advantages of each type of design?

5. *Defining the criteria for judging the quality of research designs.* Define the four criteria for judging the quality of research designs: (a) construct validity, (b) internal validity, (c) external validity, and (d) reliability. Give an example of each type of criterion in a case study you might want to do.

NOTE

1. Figure 2.2 focuses only on the formal research design process, not on data collection activities. For all three types of research, data collection techniques might be depicted as a third level and also can involve inferences—for example, for case studies this might include searching for patterns among converging types of evidence, as described further in Chapter 5; similar data collection techniques can be described for surveys or experiments—for example, questionnaire design for surveys or stimulus presentation strategies for experiments.

3

Conducting Case Studies: Preparing for Data Collection

The preparation for doing a case study includes the prior skills of the investigator, the training and preparation for the specific case study, the development of a case study protocol, and the conduct of a pilot case study. With regard to prior skills, many people incorrectly believe they are sufficiently skilled to do case studies because they think the method is easy to use. In fact, case study research is among the hardest types of research to do.

To help prepare an investigator to do a high-quality case study, intensive training sessions should be planned, a case study protocol should be developed and refined, and a pilot study conducted. These procedures are especially desirable if the research is based on a multiple-case design or involves multiple investigators (or both).

Chapters 1 and 2 have shown that doing a case study begins with the definition of the problems or issues to be studied and the development of a case study design. However, most people associate the "doing" of a case study with the collection of the case study data, and this chapter and the following one focus on this activity. This chapter deals with preparing for data collection; the next chapter covers the data collection techniques themselves.

Preparing for data collection can be complex and difficult. If not done well, the entire case study investigation can be jeopardized, and all of the earlier work—in defining the problem and designing the case study—will have been for naught.

Good preparation begins with *desired skills* on the part of the case study investigator. These skills have seldom been the subject of separate attention in the past. Yet some are critical and can be learned or practiced. Three additional topics also should be a formal part of any case study preparation: the *training* for a specific case study, the development of a *protocol* for the investigation, and the conduct of a *pilot case study*. The protocol is an especially effective way of dealing with the overall problems of increasing the reliability of case studies. However, success with all four topics is needed to ensure that case studies are conducted with high quality and managed smoothly. All demand a certain amount of patience, which has too frequently been overlooked in the past. Each of these topics is therefore discussed in the remainder of this chapter.

THE CASE STUDY INVESTIGATOR:
DESIRED SKILLS

Too many people are drawn to the case study strategy because they believe it is "easy." As noted in Chapter 1, many social scientists—especially budding ones—think the case study strategy can be mastered without much difficulty. Their perception is that they will have to learn only a minimal set of technical procedures, that any deficiencies in formal, analytic skills will be irrelevant, and that a case study will allow them simply to "tell it like it is." No perception could be farther from the truth.

In actuality, the demands of a case study on a person's intellect, ego, and emotions are far greater than those of any other research strategy. This is because the data collection procedures are *not* routinized. In laboratory experiments or in surveys, for instance, the data collection phase of a research project can be largely, if not wholly, conducted by a research assistant. The assistant is to carry out the data collection activities with a minimum of discretionary behavior, and in this sense the activity is routinized—and boring. There is no such parallel in conducting case studies.

In fact, a point to be emphasized throughout this chapter is that the skills required for collecting case study data are much more demanding than those for experiments and surveys. In case studies, there is little room for the traditional research assistant. Rather, a well-trained and experienced investigator is needed to conduct a high-quality case study because of the continuous interaction between the theoretical issues being studied and the data being collected. During data collection, only a more experienced investigator will be able to take advantage of unexpected opportunities rather than being trapped by them—and also to exercise sufficient care against potentially biased procedures.

Unfortunately, there are no tests for determining which persons are likely to become good case study investigators and which persons are not. Compare this situation, briefly mentioned in Chapter 1, to that in mathematics or even a profession such as law. In math, people are able to score themselves for their abilities and to screen themselves from further advancement because they simply cannot carry out certain levels of math problems. Similarly, to practice law, a person must first gain entrance into a law school and later pass the bar examination in a particular state. Again, many people screen themselves out of the field by failing to pass either of these tests.

No such devices exist for assessing case study skills. However, a basic list of commonly required skills is as follows:

- A person should be able to *ask good questions*—and to interpret the answers.
- A person should *be a good "listener"* and not be trapped by his or her own ideologies or preconceptions.
- A person should *be adaptive and flexible*, so that newly encountered situations can be seen as opportunities, not threats.
- A person must *have a firm grasp of the issues being studied*, whether this is a theoretical or policy orientation, even if in an exploratory mode. Such a grasp focuses the relevant events and information to be sought to manageable proportions.
- A person should *be unbiased by preconceived notions*, including those derived from theory. Thus a person should be sensitive and responsive to contradictory evidence.

Each of these attributes is described below. Many of the attributes are remediable, and anyone missing one or more of these skills can work on developing them. But everyone must be honest in assessing his or her capabilities in the first place.

Question-Asking

An inquiring mind is a major prerequisite *during* data collection, not just before or after the activity. Data collection follows a formal plan, but the specific information that may become relevant to a case study is not readily predictable. As you do your fieldwork, you must constantly ask yourself why events appear to have happened or to be happening. If you are able to ask good questions, you also will be mentally and emotionally exhausted at the end of a day in the field. This is far different than the experience in collecting experimental or survey data, in which a person may become physically exhausted but has been mentally untested after a day of data collection.

One insight into asking good questions is to understand that research is about questions and not necessarily about answers. If you are the type of person for whom one tentative answer immediately leads to a whole host of new questions, and if these questions eventually aggregate to some significant inquiry about how or why the world works as it does, you are likely to be a good asker of questions.

"Listening"

Listening includes observing and sensing more generally and is not limited to the aural modality. Being a good listener means being able to assimilate large amounts of new information without bias. As an interviewee recounts an incident, a good listener hears the exact words used by the interviewee (sometimes, the terminology reflects an important orientation), captures the mood and affective components, and understands the context from which the interviewee is perceiving the world.

This type of skill also needs to be applied to the inspection of documentary evidence as well as to making direct observations of real-life situations. In reviewing documents, a good question to ask is whether there is any important message *between* the lines; any inferences, of course, would need to be corroborated with other sources of information, but important insights may be gained in this way. Poor "listeners" may not even realize that there can be information between the lines. Others who are deficient are those whose minds are closed or who indeed have poor memories.

Adaptiveness and Flexibility

Very few case studies will end up exactly as planned. Inevitably, you will have to make minor if not major changes, ranging from the need to pursue an unexpected lead (potentially minor) to the need to identify a new "case" for study (potentially major). The skilled investigator must remember the original purpose of the investigation but then must be willing to change procedures or plans if unanticipated events occur (see BOX 13).

When a shift is made, you must maintain an unbiased perspective and acknowledge those situations in which, in fact, a totally new investigation may be under way. When this occurs, many completed steps—including the initial design of the case study—must be repeated and redocumented. One of the worst complaints about the conduct of case study research is that investigators change directions without knowing that their original research design was inadequate for the revised investigation, thereby leaving unknown gaps and biases. Thus the need to balance adaptiveness with *rigor*—but not rigidity—cannot be overemphasized.

BOX 13
Maintaining Flexibility in Designing a Case Study

Peter Blau's study of behavior in large government agencies (*The Dynamics of Bureaucracy*, 1955) is still valued for its insights into the relationship between the formal and informal organization of work groups.

Although his study focused on two government agencies, that was not Blau's initial design. As the author notes, he first intended to study a single organization and later switched to a plan to compare two organizations—a public one and a private one (pp. 272-273). However, his initial attempts to gain access to a private firm were unsuccessful, and in the meanwhile he had developed a stronger rationale for comparing two government agencies but of different types.

These shifts in the initial plans are examples of the types of changes that can occur in the design of a case study, and Blau's experience shows how a skilled investigator can take advantage of changing opportunities, as well as shifts in theoretical concerns, to produce a classic case study.

Grasp of the Issues Being Studied

The main way of staying on target, of course, is to understand the purpose of the case study investigation in the first place. Each case study investigator must understand the theoretical or policy issues, because judgments have to be made (and intelligence exercised) during the data collection phase. Without a firm grasp of the issues, you could miss important clues and would not know when a deviation was acceptable or even desirable. The point is that case study data collection is not merely a matter of *recording* data in a mechanical fashion, as it is in some other types of research. You must be able to interpret the information as it is being collected and to know immediately, for instance, if several sources of information contradict one another and lead to the need for additional evidence—much like a good detective.

In fact, the detective role offers some rich insights into case study fieldwork. Note that the detective arrives on a scene *after* a crime has occurred and is basically being called upon to make *inferences* about what actually transpired. The inferences, in turn, must be based on convergent evidence from witnesses and physical artifacts as well as some unspecifiable element of common sense. Finally, the detective may have to make inferences about multiple crimes, to determine whether the same perpetrator committed them. This last step is similar to the replication logic underlying multiple-case studies.

Lack of Bias

All of the preceding conditions will be negated if an investigator seeks to use a case study only to substantiate a preconceived position. Case study investigators are especially prone to this problem because they must understand the issues and exercise discretion (see Becker, 1958, 1967). In contrast, the traditional research assistant, though mechanistic and possibly even sloppy, is not likely to introduce bias into the research.

One test of this possible bias is the degree to which you are open to contrary findings. For example, researchers studying "nonprofit" organizations may be surprised to find that many of these organizations have entrepreneurial and capitalistic motives. If such findings are based on compelling evidence, the conclusions of the case study would have to reflect these contrary findings. To test your own tolerance for contrary findings, report your preliminary findings—possibly while still in the data collection phase—to two or three critical colleagues. The colleagues should offer alternative explanations and suggestions for data collection. If the quest for contrary findings can produce documentable rebuttals, the likelihood of bias will have been reduced.

TRAINING AND PREPARATION FOR A SPECIFIC CASE STUDY

The key to understanding the training needed for collecting case study data is to understand that every case study investigator must be able to operate as a "senior" investigator. Once in the field, each case study fieldworker is an independent investigator and cannot rely on a rigid formula to guide his or her behavior. One must be able to make intelligent decisions about the data being collected.

In this sense, training for a case study investigation actually begins with the definition of the problem being studied and the development of the case study design. If these steps have been satisfactorily conducted, as described in Chapters 1 and 2, only minimal further effort may be needed, especially if there is only a single case study investigator.

However, it often happens that a case study investigation must rely on *multiple investigators*, because of any of three conditions:

1. a single case calls for intensive data collection at the same site, requiring a "team" of investigators (see BOX 14);
2. a case study involves multiple cases, with different persons needed to cover each site or to rotate among the sites; or
3. a combination of the first two conditions exists.

BOX 14
The Logistics of Field Research,
Circa 1924-1925

Arranging schedules and gaining access to relevant sources of evidence are important to the *management* of a case study. The modern researcher may feel that these activities have emerged only with the growth of "big" social science during the 1960s and 1970s.

In a famous field study done 70 years ago, however, many of the same management techniques had already been practiced. The two principal investigators and their staff secretary opened a local office in the city they were studying, and this office was used by other project staff for extended periods of time. From this vantage point, the research team participated in local life, examined documentary materials, compiled local statistics, conducted interviews, and distributed and collected questionnaires. This extensive fieldwork resulted 5 years later in the publication of the now classic study of small-town America, *Middletown* (1929), by Robert and Helen Lynd.

Furthermore, some members of the research team may not have participated in the initial problem-definition or research-design phases of a study. Under these conditions, formal training and preparation are essential preludes to actual data collection.

Case Study Training as a Seminar Experience

When multiple investigators are to be trained, they can work on becoming "senior" investigators if the training takes the form of a seminar rather than rote instruction. As in a seminar, much time has to be allowed for reading, preparing for the training sessions, and the sessions themselves. In most instances, the seminar requires at least a week's worth of preparation and discussions. (See Figure 3.1 for an illustrative agenda.)

Typically, the seminar will cover all phases of the planned case study investigation, including readings on the subject matter, the theoretical issues that led to the case study design, and case study methods and tactics. The goal of the training is to have all participants understand the basic concepts, terminology, and issues relevant to the study. Each investigator needs to know:

- Why the study is being done
- What evidence is being sought

I. Purpose of case studies

II. Field assignments

III. Tasks for case studies

    A. Orientation and preparation

    B. Field appointments and travel arrangements

    C. Site visit

    D. Writing case study

    E. Review and approval of draft

    F. Field appointments and travel arrangements for next case study

IV. Training reminders

    A. Read overview, interview guide, and procedural reminders

    B. Read about doing fieldwork: watching and listening

       —ask questions nondirectively

       —organize note-taking around major sections of interview guide

    C. Read model case study

    D. Keep clearly written (and *correctly spelled*) lists of all contacts: name, title, organization, telephone number

    E. Collect documents and records in field and submit with case study; list documents in form of *annotated bibliography*

Figure 3.1. Training Session Agenda

- What variations can be anticipated (and what should be done if such variations occur)
- What would constitute supportive or contrary evidence for any given proposition

Discussions, rather than lectures, are the key part of the training effort, to ensure that the desired level of understanding has been achieved.

This seminar approach to case study training again can be contrasted to the training for survey interviewers. The survey training does involve discussions, but it mainly emphasizes the questionnaire items or terminology to be used and takes place over an intensive but short period of time. Moreover, the training avoids the global or conceptual concerns of the study, as the interviewer is discouraged from having any broader understanding than the mechanics of the survey instrument. Survey training rarely involves any outside reading about the substantive issues, and the survey interviewer generally has no knowledge of how the survey data are to be analyzed and what issues are to be investigated. Such an outcome would be insufficient for case study training.

Protocol Development and Review

The next subsection will say more about the *contents* of the case study protocol. However, a legitimate and desirable training task is the coauthorship of the protocol by all of the case study investigators.

A major task of the training seminar may therefore be to develop a draft protocol. In this situation, each coinvestigator may be assigned one portion of the substantive topics to be covered by the case study. The investigator is then responsible for reviewing the appropriate reading materials on this topic, adding any other information that may be relevant, and drafting the initial set of protocol questions on this topic. In the seminar, the entire group of case study investigators can discuss and review the individual drafts. Such a discussion not only will lead to the completion of the protocol but also will ensure that each investigator has mastered the contents of the protocol by participating in its development.

If the case study team is not sharing the task of developing the protocol, the training sessions should include a thorough review of the protocol. All aspects of the protocol, whether procedural or substantive, need to be discussed, and modifications in the protocol may be made.

Problems to Be Addressed

The training also has the purpose of uncovering problems within the case study plan or the research team's capabilities. If such problems do emerge, one consolation is that they will be more troublesome if they are not recognized until later, after the data collection begins. Good case study investigators should therefore press to be certain, during the training period, that potential problems are brought into the open.

The most obvious problem is that the training may reveal flaws in the case study design or even the initial definition of the study problem. If this occurs, you must be willing to make the necessary revisions, even if more time and effort are necessary. Sometimes the revisions will challenge the basic purpose of the investigation, as in a situation in which the original objective may have been to investigate a technological phenomenon, such as the use of microcomputers, but in which the case study really turns out to be about an organizational phenomenon. Any revisions, of course, also may lead to the need to review of a slightly different literature and a recasting of the entire study and its audience. Nevertheless, such changes are warranted if the training has demonstrated the unrealistic (or uninteresting) nature of the original plan.

A second problem is that the training sessions may reveal some incompatibilities among the investigating team—and in particular the fact that some of the investigators may not share the ideology of the project or its sponsors. In one multiple-case study of community organizations, for instance, fieldworkers varied in their beliefs regarding the efficacy of such organizations (U.S. National Commission on Neighborhoods, 1979). When such biases are discovered, one way of dealing with the contrary ideologies is to suggest to the fieldworker that contrary evidence will be respected if it is collected and verifiable. The fieldworker still has the choice, of course, of continuing to participate in the study or deciding to drop out.

A third problem is that the training may uncover some unreal time deadlines or expectations regarding available resources. For instance, a case study may have assumed that 20 persons were to be interviewed, in an open-ended manner, as part of the data collection. The training may have revealed, however, that the time needed for interviewing these persons is much longer than anticipated. Under such circumstances, any expectation that 20 persons could be interviewed would have to be considered unrealistic.

Finally, the training may uncover some positive traits, such as the fact that two or more field investigators are able to work productively together. Such rapport and productivity during the training session may readily extend to the actual data collection period and may therefore suggest certain pairings for the case study teams. In general, the training should have the effect of creating group norms for the ensuing data collection activity. This norm-building process is more than an amenity; it will help ensure supportive reactions should unexpected problems arise during the data collection.

THE CASE STUDY PROTOCOL

A case study protocol is more than an instrument. The protocol contains the instrument but also contains the procedures and general rules that should be followed in using the instrument. Having a case study protocol is desirable under all circumstances, but it is essential if you are using a multiple-case design.

The protocol is a major tactic in increasing the *reliability* of case study research and is intended to guide the investigator in carrying out the case study. (Figure 3.2 gives a table of contents from an illustrative protocol, which was used for a study of microcomputer implementation and its organizational effects in 12 school districts.) The protocol should have the following sections:

CONTENTS

Figure 3.2. Protocol for Conducting Case Studies of Microcomputer Use in Special Education

- An overview of the case study project (project objectives and auspices, case study issues, and relevant readings about the topic being investigated)
- Field procedures (credentials and access to the case study "sites," general sources of information, and procedural reminders)
- Case study questions (the specific questions that the case study investigator must keep in mind in collecting data, "table shells" for specific arrays of data, and the potential sources of information for answering each question)

Figure 3.2. Continued

- A guide for the case study report (outline, format for the narrative, and specification of any bibliographical information and other documentation)

A quick glance at these topics will indicate why the protocol is so important. First, it reminds the investigator what the case study is about. Second, the preparation of the protocol forces an investigator to anticipate several problems, including that of how the case study reports might be completed. This means, for instance, that the *audience* for such reports will have to be identified, even before the case study has been conducted. Such forethought will help to avoid disastrous outcomes in the long run. Each section of the protocol is discussed next.

Overview of the Case Study Project

The overview should cover the background information about the project, the substantive issues being investigated, and the relevant readings about the issues.

As for background information, every project has its own context and perspective. Some projects, for instance, are funded by government agencies having a general mission and clientele that need to be remembered in conducting the research. Other projects have broader theoretical concerns or related research—such as a survey—that in fact led to the design of the case study investigation. Whatever the situation, this type of background information, in summary form, belongs in the overview section.

A procedural element of this background section is a statement about the project that you can present to anyone who may want to know about the project, its purpose, and the people involved in conducting and sponsoring the project. This statement can even be accompanied by a letter of introduction, to be sent to all major interviewees and organizations that may be the subject of study. (See Figure 3.3 for an illustrative letter.) The bulk of the overview, however, should be devoted to the substantive issues being investigated. This may include the rationale for selecting the sites, the propositions or hypotheses being examined, and the broader theoretical or policy relevance of the inquiry. For all of these topics, relevant readings should be cited, and the essential reading materials should be made available to each member of the case study team.

A good overview will communicate to the intelligent reader (that is, someone familiar with the general topic of inquiry) the purpose of and setting for the case study. Some of the materials (such as the summary statement of the project) will be needed for other purposes anyway, so that writing the overview should be seen as a worthwhile activity.

Field Procedures

Chapter 1 has previously defined case studies as studies of events within their real-life contexts. This has important implications for problem definition and design, which have been discussed in Chapters 1 and 2.

For data collection, however, this characteristic of case studies also raises an important issue, for which properly designed field procedures are essential. The data are to be collected from existing people and institutions, not within

NATIONAL COMMISSION ON NEIGHBORHOODS
2000 K Street, N.W., Suite 350
Washington, D.C. 20006
202-632-5200

May 30, 1978

To Whom It May Concern:

     This is to introduce
a highly qualified individual with wide experience
in the field of neighborhood revitalization and community organization.   has been engaged
by the National Commission on Neighborhoods to join
a team of experts now undertaking a series of 40-50
case studies commissioned by our Task Force on Gover-
nance.

     Ultimately, by means of this case study
approach, the Commission hopes to identify and document answers to such questions as: What enables some
neighborhoods to survive, given the forces, attitudes
and investment policies (both public and private)
working against them? What preconditions are necessary in order to expand the number of neighborhoods
where successful revitalization, benefiting existing
residents, is possible? What can be done to promote
these preconditions?

     This letter is directed to community leaders,
administrative staff and city officials. We must ask
you to give your time, experience and patience to our
interviewers. Your cooperation is most essential if
the case studies are to successfully guide and support
the final policy recommendations which the Commission
must forward to the President and to Congress.

     On behalf of all twenty members of the Commission,
I wish to express our gratitude for your assistance.
Should you wish to be entered on our mailing list for
the Commission newsletter and final report, our interviewer will be glad to make the proper arrangements.

     Again, thank you very much.

                         Sincerely,

                         /signed/
                         Senator Joseph F. Timilty
                         Chairman

Figure 3.3. Illustrative Letter of Introduction

the controlled confines of a laboratory, the sanctity of a library, or the structured limitations of a rigid questionnaire. Thus, in a case study, the investigator must learn to integrate real-world events with the needs of the data collection plan; in this sense, the investigator does not control the data collection environment as one might using other research strategies.

Note that in a laboratory experiment, human "subjects" are solicited to enter into the laboratory—that is, an environment controlled nearly entirely by the research investigator. The subject, within ethical and physical constraints, must follow the instructions of the investigator, which carefully prescribe the desired behavior. Similarly, the human "respondent" to a survey questionnaire cannot deviate from the agenda set by the questions. The respondent's behavior is constrained by the ground rules of the investigator. Of course, the subject or respondent who does not wish to follow the prescribed behaviors may freely drop out of the experiment or survey. Finally, in the historical archive, pertinent documents may not always be available, but the investigator can generally inspect what exists at his or her own pace and at a time convenient to his or her schedule. In all three situations, the formal data collection activity is closely controlled by the research investigator.

Doing case studies involves an entirely different situation. When interviewing key persons, you must cater to the interviewee's schedule and availability, not your own. The nature of the interview is much more open-ended, and an interviewee may not necessarily cooperate fully in answering the questions. Similarly, in making observations of real-life activities, you are intruding into the world of the subject being studied rather than the reverse; under these conditions, you may have to make special arrangements to be able to act as an observer (or even as a participant-observer), and your behavior—and not that of the subject or respondent—is the one likely to be constrained.

This contrasting process of doing data collection leads to the need to have explicit and well-planned field procedures regarding "coping" behaviors and guidelines. Imagine, for instance, sending someone to camp; because you do not know what to expect, the best preparation is to have the resources to be prepared. Case study field procedures should be the same.

With this orientation in mind, the field procedures of the protocol need to emphasize the major tasks in collecting data, including:

- Gaining access to key organizations or interviewees
- Having sufficient resources while in the field—including a personal computer, writing instruments, paper, paper clips, and a preestablished, quiet place to write notes privately

- Developing a procedure for calling for assistance and guidance, if needed, from other case study investigators or colleagues
- Making a clear schedule of the data collection activities that are expected to be completed within specified periods of time
- Providing for unanticipated events, including changes in the availability of interviewees as well as changes in the mood and motivation of the case study investigator

These are the types of topics that can be included in the field procedures section of the protocol. Depending upon the type of study being done, the specific procedures will vary.

The more operational these procedures are, the better. To take but one minor issue as an example, case study data collection frequently results in the accumulation of numerous documents at the field site. The burden of carrying such bulky documents can be reduced by two procedures. First, the case study team may have had the foresight to bring large envelopes (jiffy bags), allowing them to mail the documents back to the office rather than carry them. Second, field time may have been set aside for perusing the documents and then going to a local copier facility and copying only the few relevant pages of each document. These are the kinds of operational details that can enhance the overall quality and efficiency of case study data collection.

Case Study Questions

The heart of the protocol is a set of substantive questions reflecting the actual inquiry. Two characteristics distinguish these questions from those in a survey interview. (See Figure 3.4 for an illustrative question from a study of a school program; the complete protocol included dozens of such questions.)

First, the questions are posed *to you, the investigator*, not to a respondent. The questions, in essence, are your reminders regarding the information that needs to be collected, and why. In some instances, the specific questions also may serve as prompts in asking questions during a case study interview; however, the main purpose of these questions is to keep the investigator on track as data collection proceeds.

Second, each question should be accompanied by a list of probable sources of evidence. Such sources may include the names of individual interviewees, documents, or observations. This pathway between the questions of interest and the likely sources of evidence is extremely helpful in collecting the data. Before starting a particular interview, for instance, a case study investigator

Q. How is the program organized, who is employed by it, when are decisions made, and who makes them?

Sources of Data:

— Program director

— Director's immediate supervisor

— Organizational chart

— Job descriptions

Sample Strategies:

— Obtain or draw an organizational chart that shows the location of the program office.

— List the type and number of instructional and noninstructional personnel (including specialists, coordinators, managers).

— To whom does the program director report?

— Who reports to the program director?

— Whom does the program director supervise?

— What kinds of decisions does the director have to formally sign off and with whom?

— Create an organizational chart of the program (if one doesn't exist) that shows the directors and any intermediaries (either in schools or in the program office) and their relations to principals, regular teachers, and special teachers.

— Fill in the following table by ranking the order in which the following decisions and events occur.

(continued)

Figure 3.4. Illustrative Protocol Question

can quickly review the major questions that the interview should cover. (Again, these questions form the structure of the inquiry and are not intended as the literal questions to be asked of the interviewee.)

The questions in the case study protocol should reflect the full set of concerns from the initial design—but only those to be addressed at the single-case level, not those at other levels. In fact, distinguishing among levels of questions is crucial when a single case is part of a multiple-case study, because there may be five levels of questions—only the first two of which can be covered by the single case:

	Order	Month Completed in Calendar 1994	Month Completed in Calendar 1993	Title of People Involved in Decisions
Determining budget				
Hiring or firing of staff				
Assigning staff to schools				
Purchasing of materials and equipment				
Deciding subjects and grades				
Testing students				
Selecting students				
Selecting schools				
Evaluating school programs				
Preparation and submission of application				

Figure 3.4. Continued

Level 1: questions asked of specific interviewees

Level 2: questions asked of the individual case (these are the questions in the case study protocol)

Level 3: questions asked of the findings across multiple cases

Level 4: questions asked of an entire study—for example, calling on information beyond the multiple cases and including other literature that may have been reviewed

Level 5: normative questions about policy recommendations and conclusions, going beyond the narrow scope of the study

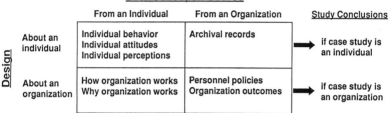

Figure 3.5. Design Versus Data Collection: Different Units of Analysis
SOURCE: COSMOS Corporation.

Among these levels, considerable confusion may occur, so your understanding of these levels is critical.

The first two levels deal with the single case (even if such a case is part of a multiple-case study). The common confusion between these two levels is that a data collection source may be at Level 1, whereas the unit of analysis of your case study may be at Level 2—a design frequently used when the case is about an organization (Level 2). Even though your data collection may rely heavily on information from Level 1, your conclusions cannot be based entirely on interviews as a source of information (you would then have collected information about how individuals *perceived* the organization, but not about the organization itself).

However, the reverse situation also can be true. Your case study may be about an individual, but the sources of information about the individual can include archival records (e.g., personnel files or student records) from the organizational level. In this situation, you would also want to avoid basing your conclusions about the individual on the organizational sources of information only. Figure 3.5 illustrates these two situations, where the unit of analysis for the case study is different from the unit of analysis for the data collection source.

The other levels also should be understood clearly. A cross-case question, for instance (Level 3), may be whether larger school districts are more responsive than smaller school districts, or whether complex bureaucratic structures make the larger districts more cumbersome and less responsive. However, the protocol for the single case can address only the responsiveness of a specific school district. What cannot be asked is whether such an arrangement appears to be more responsive than that found in other districts. Only the cross-case analysis can cover this topic. Similarly, the questions at Levels 4 and 5 also are unanswerable when doing each individual case study, and you should note this limitation when including such questions in the case study protocol. Remember: *The protocol is for the data collection from a single case and is not intended to serve the entire project.*

The protocol questions also can include empty "table shells" (for more detail, see Miles & Huberman, 1984). These are the outlines of a table, arraying a specific set of data. The outlines give the exact columnar and row headings, indicating the data categories to be covered. The case study investigator's job is to collect the data called forth by the table. The provision of such table shells helps in several ways. First, it forces you to identify exactly what data are being sought. Second, it ensures that parallel information will be collected at different sites where a multiple-case design is being used. Finally, it aids in understanding what will be done with the data once they have been collected.

Guide for the Case Study Report

This element is generally missing in most case study plans. Investigators neglect to think about the outline, format, or audience for the case study report until after the data have been collected. Yet some planning at this preparatory stage—admittedly out of sequence in the typical planning of most research— means that a tentative outline can appear in the case study protocol. (A detailed discussion of the possible topics in the case study report is found in Chapter 6 of this book.)

Again, one reason for the traditional, linear sequence is related to practices with other research strategies. One does not worry about the report from an experiment until after the experiment has been completed, because the format of the report and its likely audience are going to be dictated by an academic journal. Thus most experiments follow a similar outline: the posing of the research questions and hypotheses; a description of the research design, apparatus, and data collection procedures; the presentation of the data collected; and a discussion of findings and conclusions.

Unfortunately, case study reports do not have such a uniformly acceptable outline. Nor, in many instances, do case study reports end up in journals (Feagin, Orum, & Sjoberg, 1991, pp. 269-273). For this reason, each investigator must be concerned, throughout the conduct of a case study, with the design of the final case study report. The problem is not easy to deal with.

In addition, the protocol also can indicate the extent of documentation for the case study report. The fieldwork is likely to lead to large amounts of documentary evidence, in the form of published reports, publications, memoranda, and other documents collected from the site. What is to be done with this documentation for later presentation? In most studies, the documents are filed away and seldom retrieved. Yet this documentation is an important part of the "database" for a case study (see Chapter 6) and should not be ignored until after the case study has been completed. One possibility is to have the case study report include an annotated bibliography in which each of the available documents is itemized. The annotations would help a reader (or the investigator, at some later date) to know which documents might be relevant for further inquiry.

In summary, to the extent possible, the basic outline of the case study report should be part of the protocol. This will facilitate the collection of relevant data, in the appropriate format, and will reduce the possibility that a return visit to the case study site will be necessary. At the same time, the existence of such an outline should not imply rigid adherence to a predesigned protocol. In fact, case study plans can change as a result of the initial data collection, and you are encouraged to consider these flexibilities—if used properly and without bias—to be an advantage of the case study strategy.

THE PILOT CASE STUDY

A final preparation for data collection is the conduct of a pilot study. The pilot case may be chosen for several reasons unrelated to the criteria for selecting the final cases in the case study design. For example, the informants at the pilot site may be unusually congenial and accessible, or the site may be geographically convenient, or it may have an unusual amount of documentation and data. One other possibility is that the pilot site represents the most complicated of the real cases, so that nearly all relevant data collection issues will be encountered at this site.

The pilot case study helps investigators to refine their data collection plans with respect to both the content of the data and the procedures to be followed. In this regard, it is important to note that a *pilot test* is not a *pretest*. The pilot case is used more formatively, assisting an investigator to develop relevant lines of questions—possibly even providing some conceptual clarification for the research design as well. In contrast, the pretest is the occasion for a formal "dress rehearsal," in which the intended data collection plan is used as faithfully as possible as a final test run.

The pilot case study can be so important that more resources may be devoted to this phase of the research than to the collection of data from any of the actual cases. For this reason, several subtopics are worth further discussion: the selection of pilot cases, the nature of the inquiry for the pilot cases, and the nature of the reports from the pilot cases.

Selection of Pilot Cases

In general, convenience, access, and geographic proximity can be the main criteria for selecting the pilot case or cases. This will allow for a less structured and more prolonged relationship to develop between the interviewees and the case study investigator than might occur in the "real" case study sites. The pilot site could then assume the role of a "laboratory" for the investigators, allowing them to observe different phenomena from many different angles or to try different approaches on a trial basis.

One study of technological innovations in local services (Yin, 1979, 1981c, 1982c) actually had seven pilot cases, each focusing on a different type of technology. Four of the cases were located in the same metropolitan area as the research team's and were visited first. Three of the cases, however, were located in a different city and were the basis for a second set of visits. The cases were not chosen because of their distinctive technologies or for any other substantive reason. The main criterion, in addition to proximity, was the fact that access to the sites was made easy by some prior personal contact on the part of the research team. Finally, the interviewees at the sites also were congenial to the notion that the investigators were at an early stage of their research and would not have a fixed agenda.

Nature of the Pilot Inquiry

The inquiry for the pilot case can be much broader and less focused than the ultimate data collection plan. Moreover, the inquiry can cover both substantive and methodological issues.

In the above-mentioned example, the research team used the seven pilot cases to improve its conceptualization of different types of technologies and their related organizational effects. The pilot studies were done prior to the selection of specific technologies for the final data collection—and prior to the final articulation of the study's theoretical propositions. Thus the pilot data provided considerable insight into the basic issues being studied. This information was used in parallel with an ongoing review of relevant literature, so that the final research design was informed both by prevailing theories and by a fresh set of empirical observations. The dual sources of information help to ensure that the study to be done reflected significant theoretical or policy issues as well as questions relevant to contemporary cases.

Methodologically, the work at the pilot sites can provide information about relevant field questions and about the logistics of the field inquiry. In the technology pilot sites, one important logistical question was whether to observe the technology in action first or to collect information about the prevalent organizational issues first. This choice interacted with a further question about the deployment of the field team: If the team consisted of two or more persons, what assignments required the team to work together and what assignments could be completed separately? Variations in these procedures were tried during the pilot case studies, the trade-offs were acknowledged, and eventually a satisfactory procedure was developed for the formal data collection plan.

Reports From the Pilot Cases

The pilot case reports are mainly of value to the investigators and need to be written clearly, even if in the form of memoranda. One difference between the pilot reports and the actual case study reports is that the pilot reports should be explicit about the lessons learned for both research-design and field procedures. The pilot reports might even contain subsections on these topics.

If more than a single pilot case is planned, the report from one pilot case also can indicate the modifications to be attempted in the next pilot case. In other words, the report can contain the agenda for the ensuing pilot case. If enough pilot cases are done in this manner, the final agenda may actually become a good prototype for the final case study protocol.

SUMMARY

This chapter has reviewed the preparations for data collection. Depending upon the scope of a case study—whether single or multiple sites will be involved or whether single or multiple investigators will be involved—the preparatory tasks will be correspondingly straightforward or complex.

The major topics have been the desired skills of the case study investigator, the preparation and training of the case study investigators for a specific case study, the nature of the case study protocol, and the role and purpose of a pilot case. Every case study should follow these different steps to varying degrees, depending upon the specific inquiry.

As with the management of other affairs, the expertise with which these activities is conducted will improve with practice. One desirable sequence is for you to complete a relatively straightforward case study before attempting to do a more complex one, such as one from a managerial standpoint. With the successful completion of each case study, these preparatory tasks may even become second nature. Furthermore, if the same case study team has conducted several different studies together, the team will work with increasing efficiency and professional satisfaction with each ensuing case study.

EXERCISES

1. *Identifying skills for doing case studies.* Name the various skills that are important for a case study investigator to have. Do you know any people that have been successful in doing case study research? What strengths and weaknesses do they have as research investigators? Are these similar to the ones you have just named?

2. *Retrospectively developing an "old" protocol.* Select one of the case studies cited in the BOXES of this book. For just one of the chapters in this case study, design the protocol that would have yielded the findings now found in the chapter. What questions would have been posed by the protocol? What procedures followed in answering these questions and collecting the relevant data?

3. *Developing a "new" protocol.* Select some phenomenon in need of explanation from your university's everyday life. Illustrative topics might be, for example, why the university recently changed some policy, or how your department makes decisions about its curriculum requirements.

   For this phenomenon, design a case study protocol to collect the information needed to make an adequate explanation. Whom would you interview? What documents would you seek? What observations, if any, would you make? How would all of these relate to the key questions of your case study?

4. *Conducting training for case study research.* Describe the major ways in which the preparation and training to do a case study project are *different* than those for doing projects using other types of research strategies (e.g., surveys, experiments, histories, and archival analysis). Develop a training agenda to prepare for a case study you might be considering, in which two or three persons are to collaborate.

5. *Selecting a case for doing a pilot study.* Define the desired features for a pilot case as a prelude to a new case study research project. How would you go about contacting and using such a case? Describe why you might want only one pilot site, as opposed to two or more pilot sites.

4

Conducting Case Studies: Collecting the Evidence

Evidence for case studies may come from six sources: documents, archival records, interviews, direct observation, participant-observation, and physical artifacts. The use of these six sources calls for slightly different skills and methodological procedures.

In addition to the attention given to these individual sources, some overriding principles are important to any data collection effort in doing case studies. These include the use of (a) multiple sources of evidence, that is, evidence from two or more sources, but converging on the same set of facts or findings; (b) a case study database, that is, a formal assembly of evidence distinct from the final case study report; and (c) a chain of evidence, that is, explicit links between the questions asked, the data collected, and the conclusions drawn. The incorporation of these principles into a case study investigation will increase its quality substantially.

Data collection for case studies can rely on many sources of evidence. Six important ones are discussed in this chapter: documentation, archival records, interviews, direct observation, participant-observation, and physical artifacts. One purpose of this chapter is to review, briefly, the ways of collecting data from these sources. A second purpose is to convey three essential data collection principles, regardless of the source or sources of evidence used.

As for the first purpose, the review of the six sources is necessarily brief because numerous textbooks and research articles—such as the comprehensive works on "field methods" by Schatzman and Strauss (1973), Murphy (1980), and Webb, Campbell, Schwartz, Sechrest, and Grove (1981)—already contain similar information. Such books are easy to use and discuss specific data collection techniques relevant to case studies, including the logistics of planning and conducting the fieldwork (see Fiedler, 1978). Similarly, there also are many works on more specialized but related topics, including the following:

- *Organizational and management studies*: Bouchard (1976) and Webb and Weick (1979)
- *Participant-observation*: McCall and Simmons (1969), Lofland (1971), and Jorgenson (1989)
- *Anthropological methods*: Pelto and Pelto (1978), Naroll and Cohen (1973), and Wax (1971)
- *Observational techniques*: Douglas (1976), Johnson (1976), and Webb et al. (1981)
- *Clinical psychology*: Bolgar (1965) and Rothney (1968)
- *Program evaluation*: King, Morris, and Fitz-Gibbon (1987)
- *Historical techniques and the use of documents*: Barzun and Graff (1985)

Anyone needing further detail about data collection should consult one or more of these works.

However, most of these works fail to deal with the case study as a separate research strategy, and they also tend to treat data collection in isolation from the other aspects of the research process. Little is said, for instance, about how these techniques can help to deal with the design problems enumerated in Chapter 2: construct validity, internal validity, external validity, and reliability. For this reason, this chapter gives much emphasis to its second purpose, the discussion of three principles of data collection.

These principles have been neglected in the past and are discussed at length: (a) using multiple, not just single, sources of evidence; (b) creating a case study database; and (c) maintaining a chain of evidence. The principles are extremely important for doing high-quality case studies, are relevant to all six types of sources of evidence, and should be followed whenever possible. In particular, the principles, as noted in Chapter 2 (see Figure 2.5), will help deal with the problems of construct validity and reliability.

SIX SOURCES OF EVIDENCE

The sources of evidence discussed here are documentation, archival records, interviews, direct observations, participant-observation, and physical artifacts. However, you should be aware that a complete list of sources can be quite extensive—including films, photographs, and videotapes; projective techniques and psychological testing; proxemics; kinesics; "street" ethnography; and life histories (Marshall & Rossman, 1989).

A useful overview of the six major sources considers their comparative strengths and weaknesses (see Figure 4.1). You should immediately note that

Source of Evidence	Strengths	Weaknesses
Documentation	• stable—can be reviewed repeatedly • unobtrusive—not created as a result of the case study • exact—contains exact names, references, and details of an event • broad coverage—long span of time, many events, and many settings	• retrievability—can be low • biased selectivity, if collection is incomplete • reporting bias—reflects (unknown) bias of author • access—may be deliberately blocked
Archival Records	• [Same as above for documentation] • precise and quantitative	• [Same as above for documentation] • accessibility due to privacy reasons
Interviews	• targeted—focuses directly on case study topic • insightful—provides perceived causal inferences	• bias due to poorly constructed questions • response bias • inaccuracies due to poor recall • reflexivity—interviewee gives what interviewer wants to hear
Direct Observations	• reality—covers events in real time • contextual—covers context of event	• time-consuming • selectivity—unless broad coverage • reflexivity—event may proceed differently because it is being observed • cost—hours needed by human observers
Participant-Observation	• [Same as above for direct observations] • insightful into interpersonal behavior and motives	• [Same as above for direct observations] • bias due to investigator's manipulation of events
Physical Artifacts	• insightful into cultural features • insightful into technical operations	• selectivity • availability

Figure 4.1. Six Sources of Evidence: Strengths and Weaknesses

no single source has a complete advantage over all the others. In fact, the various sources are highly complementary, and a good case study will therefore want to use as many sources as possible (see the later discussion in this chapter on "multiple sources of evidence").

Documentation

Except for studies of preliterate societies, documentary information is likely to be relevant to every case study topic. This type of information can take many forms and should be the object of explicit data collection plans. For instance, consider the following variety of documents:

- Letters, memoranda, and other communiques
- Agendas, announcements and minutes of meetings, and other written reports of events
- Administrative documents—proposals, progress reports, and other internal documents
- Formal studies or evaluations of the same "site" under study
- Newspaper clippings and other articles appearing in the mass media

The usefulness of these and other types of documents is not based on their necessary accuracy or lack of bias. In fact, documents must be carefully used and should not be accepted as literal recordings of events that have taken place. Few people realize, for instance, that even the "transcripts" of official U.S. congressional hearings are deliberately edited—by the congressional staff and others who may have testified—before being printed in final form. In another field, historians working with primary documents also must be concerned with the validity of a document.

For case studies, the most important use of documents is to corroborate and augment evidence from other sources. First, documents are helpful in verifying the correct spellings and titles or names of organizations that might have been mentioned in an interview. Second, documents can provide other specific details to corroborate information from other sources. If the documentary evidence is contradictory rather than corroboratory, the case study investigator has specific reason to inquire further into the topic. Third, inferences can be made from documents. For example, by observing the distribution list for a specific document, you may find new questions about communications and networking within an organization. However, these inferences should be treated only as clues worthy of further investigation rather than as definitive findings, because the inferences could later turn out to be false leads.

Because of their overall value, documents play an explicit role in any data collection in doing case studies. Systematic searches for relevant documents are important in any data collection plan. For example, during field visits, you should allot time for using local libraries and other reference centers. You

---

BOX 15
Using Documents in Case Study Research

Sometimes a case study can be about an exemplary "project"—such as a research effort or a federally funded activity. In this type of case study, much documentation is likely to be relevant.

This type of case study was conducted by Moore and Yin (1983), who examined nine separate R&D projects, most of them in university settings. For each project, the investigators collected such documents as project proposals, interim reports and working papers, completed manuscripts and reprints, correspondence between the research team and its sponsors, and agendas and summaries of advisory committee meetings. Attention was paid even to various drafts of the same document, as subtle changes often reflected key substantive developments in the project.

These documents were used in conjunction with other sources of information, such as interviews of the research team and observations of the research project's activities and work. Only when all of the evidence produced a consistent picture was the research team satisfied that a particular event had actually occurred in a certain manner.

---

should also arrange access to examine the files of any organizations being studied, including a review of documents that may have been put into cold storage. The scheduling of such retrieval activities is usually a flexible matter, independent of other data collection activities, and the search usually can be conducted at your convenience. For this reason, there is little excuse for omitting a thorough review of documentary evidence (see BOX 15).

At the same time, many people have been critical of the potential overreliance on documents in case study research. This is probably because the casual investigator may mistake certain kinds of documents—such as proposals for projects or programs—for those containing the unmitigated truth. In fact, it is important in reviewing any document to understand that it was written for some specific purpose and some specific audience *other than* those of the case study being done. In this sense, the case study investigator is a vicarious observer, and the documentary evidence reflects a communication among other parties attempting to achieve some other objectives. By constantly trying to identify these conditions, you are less likely to be misled by documentary evidence and more likely to be correctly critical in interpreting the contents of such evidence.[1]

BOX 16
Use of Archival Sources for Both
Quantitative and Qualitative Evidence

Archival sources can produce both quantitative and qualitative information. Numerical data (quantitative information) are often relevant and available for a case study, as are nonnumerical data (qualitative information).

Seventeen *Case Studies of Medical Technologies* were commissioned by the U.S. Office of Technology Assessment between 1979 and 1981 and illustrate the integration of quantitative and qualitative information, derived mainly from archival evidence of a unique sort: reports of scientific experiments. Each case covers a specific technology, whose development and implementation are reported in qualitative fashion. Each case also presents quantitative information, from numerous prior experiments, on the apparent costs and benefits of the technologies. In this manner, the case studies arrive at a "technology assessment," intended to aid decision makers in the health care field.

Archival Records

For many case studies, archival records—often in computerized form—also may be relevant. These can be as follows:

- *Service records*, such as those showing the number of clients served over a given period of time
- *Organizational records*, such as organizational charts and budgets over a period of time
- *Maps and charts* of the geographic characteristics of a place
- *Lists* of names and other relevant commodities
- *Survey data*, such as census records or data previously collected about a "site"
- *Personal records*, such as diaries, calendars, and telephone listings

These and other archival records can be used in conjunction with other sources of information in producing a case study (see BOX 16). However, unlike documentary evidence, the usefulness of these archival records will vary from case study to case study. For some studies, the records can be so important that they can become the object of extensive retrieval and analysis. In other studies, they may be of only passing relevance.

When archival evidence has been deemed relevant, an investigator must be careful to ascertain the conditions under which it was produced as well as its accuracy. Sometimes, the archival records can be highly quantitative, but numbers alone should not automatically be considered a sign of accuracy. Nearly every social scientist, for instance, is aware of the pitfalls of using the FBI's Uniform Crime Reports—or any other archival records based on crimes reported by law enforcement agencies. The same general word of caution therefore applies to the interpretation of documentary evidence: Most archival records were produced for a specific purpose and a specific audience (other than the case study investigation), and these conditions must be fully appreciated in order to interpret the usefulness of any archival records.

Interviews

One of the most important sources of case study information is the interview. Such a conclusion may be surprising, because of the usual association between interviews and the survey method. However, interviews are also essential sources of case study information.

The interviews may take several forms. Most commonly, case study interviews are of an *open-ended nature*, in which you can ask key respondents for the facts of a matter as well as for the respondents' opinions about events. In some situations, you may even ask the respondent to propose his or her own insights into certain occurrences and may use such propositions as the basis for further inquiry.

The more that a respondent assists in this latter manner, the more that the role may be considered one of an "informant" rather than a respondent. Key informants are often critical to the success of a case study. Such persons not only provide the case study investigator with insights into a matter but also can suggest sources of corroboratory evidence—and initiate the access to such sources. Such a person, named "Doc," played an essential role in the conduct of the famous case study presented in *Street Corner Society* (Whyte, 1943/1955), and similar informants have been noted in other case studies. Of course, you need to be cautious about becoming overly dependent on a key informant, especially because of the interpersonal influence—frequently undefinable—that the informant may have over you. A reasonable way of dealing with this pitfall again is to rely on other sources of evidence to corroborate any insight by such informants and to search for contrary evidence as carefully as possible.

A second type of interview is a *focused* interview (Merton et al., 1990), in which a respondent is interviewed for a short period of time—an hour, for example. In such cases, the interviews may still remain open-ended and assume a conversational manner, but you are more likely to be following a certain set of questions derived from the case study protocol.

For example, a major purpose of such an interview might be simply to corroborate certain facts that you already think have been established (but not to ask about other topics of a broader, open-ended nature). In this situation, the specific questions must be carefully worded, so that you appear genuinely naive about the topic and allow the respondent to provide a fresh commentary about it; in contrast, if you ask leading questions, the corroboratory purpose of the interview will not have been served. Even so, you need to exercise caution when interviewees appear to be echoing the same thoughts—corroborating each other but in a conspiratorial way. Further probing is needed. One way is similar to that used by good journalists, who will typically establish the sequence of events by deliberating checking with persons known to hold different perspectives. If one of the interviewees fails to comment, even though the others tend to corroborate one another's versions of what took place, the good journalist will even indicate this result by citing the fact that a person was asked but declined to comment.[2]

Yet a third type of interview entails more structured questions, along the lines of a formal *survey*. Such a survey could be designed as part of a case study. This situation would be relevant, for instance, if you were doing a case study of a neighborhood and surveyed the residents or shopkeepers as part of the case study. This type of survey would involve both the sampling procedures and the instruments used in regular surveys, and it would subsequently be analyzed in a similar manner. The difference would be the survey's role in relation to other sources of evidence; for example, the residents' perceptions of neighborhood decline or improvement would not necessarily be taken as a measure of actual decline or improvement but would be considered only one component of the overall assessment of the neighborhood. (See BOX 17 for another example showing how surveys can be used in conjunction with, rather than as parts of, case studies.)

Overall, interviews are an essential source of case study evidence because most case studies are about human affairs. These human affairs should be reported and interpreted through the eyes of specific interviewees, and well-informed respondents can provide important insights into a situation. They also can provide shortcuts to the prior history of the situation, helping you to identify other relevant sources of evidence. However, the interviews should always be considered *verbal reports* only. As such, they are subject to the common problems of bias, poor recall, and poor or inaccurate articulation. Again, a reasonable approach is to corroborate interview data with information from other sources.

BOX 17
Integrating Case Study and Survey Evidence

Certain studies may benefit when the same questions are posed for two pools of "sites"—a smaller pool that is the subject of case studies and a larger pool that is the subject of a survey. The answers can be compared for consistency, but the case study sites can allow some insight into the causal processes, whereas the survey sites can provide some indication of the prevalence of the phenomenon.

This approach was used in a study of organizational innovations by Robert K. Yin (*Changing Urban Bureaucracies*, 1979). For certain key questions, the evidence from 19 case study sites was tabulated alongside the evidence from 90 telephone sites. The comparison showed that the results did not differ and provided added confidence that the two sets of sites were pointing toward a consistent pattern of innovation behavior. In addition to the parallel tabulations, the analysis deliberately compared the findings from the case studies with those from the survey sites, again to determine the degree of convergence of the two sources of data.

A common question about recording interviews has to do with the use of tape recorders. Whether to use such devices is in part a matter of personal preference. The tapes certainly provide a more accurate rendition of any interview than any other method. However, a tape recorder should not be used when (a) an interviewee refuses permission or appears uncomfortable in its presence, (b) there is no specific plan for transcribing or systematically listening to the contents of the tapes, (c) the investigator is clumsy enough with mechanical devices so that the tape recorder creates a distraction during the interview itself, or (d) the investigator thinks that the tape recorder is a substitute for "listening" closely throughout the course of an interview.

Direct Observation

By making a field visit to the case study "site," you are creating the opportunity for direct observations. Assuming that the phenomena of interest have not been purely historical, some relevant behaviors or environmental conditions will be available for observation. Such observations serve as yet another source of evidence in a case study.

The observations can range from formal to casual data collection activities. Most formally, observational protocols can be developed as part of the case study protocol, and the fieldworker may be asked to measure the incidence of certain types of behaviors during certain periods of time in the field. This can involve observations of meetings, sidewalk activities, factory work, classrooms, and the like. Less formally, direct observations might be made throughout a field visit, including those occasions during which other evidence, such as that from interviews, is being collected. For instance, the condition of buildings or work spaces will indicate something about the climate or impoverishment of an organization; similarly, the location or the furnishings of a respondent's office may be one indicator of the status of the respondent within an organization.

Observational evidence is often useful in providing additional information about the topic being studied. If a case study is about, for instance, a new technology, observations of the technology at work are invaluable aids to any further understanding of the limits or problems with the technology. Similarly, observations of a neighborhood or of an organizational unit add new dimensions for understanding either the context or the phenomenon being studied. The observations can be so valuable that you may even consider taking photographs at the case study site. At a minimum, these photographs will help to convey important case characteristics to outside observers (see Dabbs, 1982). Note, however, that in some situations—such as photographing students in public schools—you will need written permission before proceeding.

To increase the reliability of observational evidence, a common procedure is to have more than a single observer making an observation—whether of the formal or the casual variety. Thus, when resources permit, a case study investigation should allow for the use of multiple observers.

Participant-Observation

Participant-observation is a special mode of observation in which you are not merely a passive observer. Instead, you may assume a variety of roles within a case study situation and may actually participate in the events being studied. In urban neighborhoods, for instance, these roles may range from having casual social interactions with various residents to undertaking specific functional activities within the neighborhood (see Yin, 1982a). The roles for different illustrative studies in neighborhoods and organizations have included:

- Being a resident in a neighborhood that is the subject of a case study (see Gans, 1962, and BOX 18)
- Taking some other functional role in a neighborhood, such as serving as a storekeeper's assistant
- Serving as a staff member in an organizational setting
- Being a key decision maker in an organizational setting (see Mechling, 1974)

BOX 18
Participant-Observation in a Neighborhood
Near "Street Corner Society"

Participant-observation was a method used frequently to study urban neighborhoods during the 1960s. One such study of subsequent fame was conducted by Herbert Gans, who wrote *The Urban Villagers* (1962), a study about "group and class in the life of Italian-Americans."

Gans's methodology is documented in a separate chapter of his book, titled "On the Methods Used in This Study." He notes that his evidence was based on six approaches: the use of the neighborhood's facilities, attendance at meetings, informal visiting with neighbors and friends, formal and informal interviewing, the use of informants, and direct observation. Of all these sources, the "participation role turned out to be most productive" (pp. 339-340). This role was based on Gans's being an actual resident, along with his wife, of the neighborhood he was studying. The result is a classical statement of neighborhood life undergoing urban renewal and change and a stark contrast to the stability found nearby, in Whyte's (1943/1955) *Street Corner Society*, some 20 years earlier.

The participant-observation technique has been most frequently used in anthropological studies of different cultural or subcultural groups. The technique also can be used in more everyday settings, such as an organization or other small group (see BOX 19).

Participant-observation provides certain unusual opportunities for collecting case study data, but it also involves major problems. The most distinctive opportunity is related to your ability to gain access to events or groups that are otherwise inaccessible to scientific investigation. In other words, for some topics, there may be no other way of collecting evidence than through participant-observation. Another distinctive opportunity is the ability to perceive reality from the viewpoint of someone "inside" the case study rather than external to it. Many have argued that such a perspective is invaluable in producing an "accurate" portrayal of a case study phenomenon. Finally, other opportunities arise because you may have the ability to manipulate minor events—such as calling a meeting of a group of persons in the case study. Only through participant-observation can such manipulation occur, as the use of documents, archival records, and interviews, for instance, all assume a passive investigator. The manipulations will not be as precise as those in

---

BOX 19
A Participant-Observer Study
in an "Everyday" Setting

Eric Redman provides an insider's account of how Congress works in his well-regarded case study, *The Dance of Legislation* (1973). The case study traces the introduction and passage of the legislation that created the National Health Service Corps during the 91st Congress in 1970.

Redman's account, from the vantage point of an author who was also on the staff of one of the bill's main supporters, Senator Warren G. Magnuson, is not simply well written and easy to read. The account also provides the reader with great insight into the daily operations of Congress—from the introduction of a bill to its eventual passage, including the politics of a lame-duck session when Richard Nixon was president.

The account is an excellent example of participant-observation in a contemporary setting. It contains information about insiders' roles that few persons have been privileged to share. The subtle legislative strategies, the overlooked role of committee clerks and lobbyists, and the interaction between the legislative and executive branches of government are all re-created by the case study, and all add to the reader's general understanding of the legislative process.

---

experiments, but they can produce a greater variety of situations for the purposes of collecting data.

The major problems related to participant-observation have to do with the potential biases produced (see Becker, 1958). First, the investigator has less ability to work as an external observer and may, at times, have to assume positions or advocacy roles contrary to the interests of good scientific practices. Second, the participant-observer is likely to follow a commonly known phenomenon and become a supporter of the group or organization being studied, if such support did not already exist. Third, the participant role may simply require too much attention relative to the observer role. The participant-observer may not have sufficient time to take notes or to raise questions about events from different perspectives, as a good observer might.

These trade-offs between the opportunities and the problems have to be considered seriously in undertaking any participant-observation study. Under some circumstances, this approach to case study evidence may be just the right approach; under other circumstances, the credibility of a whole case study project can be threatened.

Physical Artifacts

A final source of evidence is a physical or cultural artifact—a technological device, a tool or instrument, a work of art, or some other physical evidence. Such artifacts may be collected or observed as part of a field visit and have been used extensively in anthropological research.

Physical artifacts have less potential relevance in the most typical kind of case study. However, when relevant, the artifacts can be an important component in the overall case. For example, one case study of the use of microcomputers in the classroom needed to ascertain the nature of the actual use of the machines. Although use could be directly observed, an artifact—the computer printout—was also available. Students displayed these printouts as the finished products of their work and maintained notebooks of the printouts. Each printout showed not only the type of schoolwork that had been done but also the date and amount of computer time used to do the work. By examining the printouts, the case study investigators were able to develop a broader perspective concerning all of the classroom applications, beyond that which could be directly observed in a short period of time.

Summary

This section has reviewed six common sources of case study evidence. The procedures for collecting each type of evidence must be developed and mastered independently to ensure that each source is properly used. Not all sources will be relevant for all case studies. However, the trained case study investigator should be acquainted with each approach—or have colleagues who have the needed expertise and who can work as members of the case study team.

THREE PRINCIPLES OF DATA COLLECTION

The benefits from these six sources of evidence can be maximized if you follow three principles. These principles are relevant to all six sources and, when used properly, can help to deal with the problems of establishing the construct validity and reliability of a case study. The three are as follows.

Principle 1: Use Multiple Sources of Evidence

Any of the preceding sources of evidence can and have been the sole basis for entire studies. For example, some studies have relied only on participant-

---

BOX 20
Using Multiple Sources of Evidence in a Case Study

Case studies need not be limited to a single source of evidence. In fact, most of the better case studies rely on a wide variety of sources.

One example of a case study that used such a variety is a book by Gross et al., *Implementing Organization Innovations* (1971), covering events in a single school. The case study included a structured survey of a larger number of teachers, open-ended interviews with a smaller number of key persons, an observational protocol for measuring the time that students spent on various tasks, and a review of organizational documents. Both the survey and the observational procedures led to quantitative information about attitudes and behavior in the school, whereas the open-ended interviews and documentary evidence led to qualitative information.

All sources of evidence were reviewed and analyzed together, so that the case study's findings were based on the convergence of information from different sources, not quantitative or qualitative data alone.

---

observation but have not examined a single document; similarly, there are numerous studies that have relied on archival records but that have not involved a single interview.

This isolated use of sources may be a function of the independent way that sources have typically been conceived—as if an investigator should choose the single most appropriate source or the one with which he or she is most familiar. Thus, on many an occasion, investigators have announced the design of a new study by identifying both the problem to be studied and the selection of a *single* source of evidence—such as "interviews"—as the focus of the data collection effort.

Triangulation: Rationale for using multiple sources of evidence. An approach to the individual sources of evidence such as the one discussed above is not, however, recommended for conducting case studies. On the contrary, a major strength of case study data collection is the opportunity to use many different sources of evidence (see BOX 20 for an example of one such study). Further, the need to use multiple sources of evidence far exceeds that in other research strategies, such as experiments, surveys, or histories. Experiments, for instance, are largely limited to the measurement and recording of actual behavior in the laboratory and generally do not include the systematic use of survey or verbal information. Surveys tend to be the opposite, emphasizing verbal information but not the measurement or recording of actual behavior. Finally, histories are limited to events in the "dead" past and therefore seldom have any contemporary sources of evidence, such as direct observations of a phenomenon or interviews with key actors.

Of course, each of these strategies can be modified, creating hybrid strategies in which multiple sources of evidence are more likely to be relevant. An example of this is the evolution of "oral history" studies in the past few decades. Nevertheless, such a modification of the traditional strategies does not alter the fact that the case study inherently deals with a wide variety of evidence, whereas the other strategies do not.

The use of multiple sources of evidence in case studies allows an investigator to address a broader range of historical, attitudinal, and behavioral issues. However, the most important advantage presented by using multiple sources of evidence is the development of *converging lines of inquiry*, a process of triangulation mentioned repeatedly in the previous section of this chapter. Thus any finding or conclusion in a case study is likely to be much more convincing and accurate if it is based on several different sources of information, following a corroboratory mode.

Patton (1987) discusses four types of triangulation in doing evaluations— that is, the triangulation

1. of data sources (data triangulation),
2. among different evaluators (investigator triangulation),
3. of perspectives on the same data set (theory triangulation), and
4. of methods (methodological triangulation).

The present discussion pertains only to the first of these four types, encouraging you to collect information from multiple sources but aimed at corroborating the same fact or phenomenon. Figure 4.2 distinguishes between two conditions—when you have really triangulated (upper portion) and when you have multiple sources that nevertheless address *different* facts (lower portion).

With triangulation, the potential problems of *construct validity* also can be addressed, because the multiple sources of evidence essentially provide multiple measures of the same phenomenon. Not surprisingly, one analysis of case study methods found that those case studies using multiple sources of evidence were rated more highly, in terms of their overall quality, than those that relied only on single sources of information (see Yin, Bateman, & Moore, 1983).

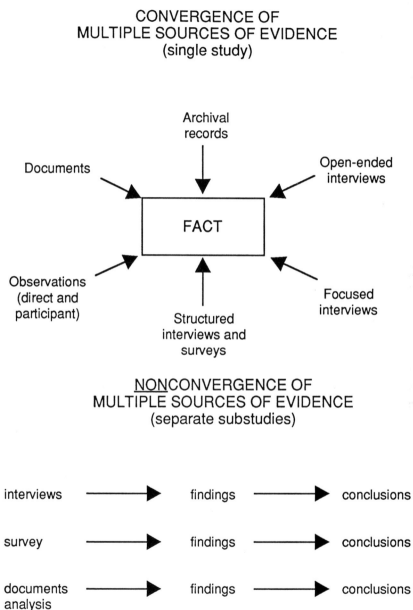

Figure 4.2. Convergence and Nonconvergence of Multiple Sources of Evidence
SOURCE: COSMOS Corporation.

Prerequisites for using multiple sources of evidence. At the same time, the use of multiple sources of evidence imposes a great burden, hinted at earlier, on yourself and any other case study investigator. First is that the collection of data from multiple sources is more expensive than if data were only collected from a single source (Denzin, 1978, p. 61). Second and more important, each investigator needs to know how to carry out the full variety of data collection techniques. For example, a case study investigator may have to collect and analyze documentary evidence as in history, to retrieve and analyze archival records as in economics or operations research, and to design and conduct surveys as in survey research. If any of these techniques is used improperly, the opportunity to address a broader array of issues, or to establish converging lines of inquiry, may be lost. This requirement for mastering multiple data collection techniques therefore raises important questions regarding the training and expertise of the case study investigator.

Unfortunately, many graduate training programs emphasize one type of data collection activity over all others, and the successful student is not likely to have a chance to master the others. To overcome such conditions, you should seek other ways of obtaining the needed training and practice. One such way is to work in a multidisciplinary research organization rather than being limited to a single academic department. Another way is to analyze the methodological writings of a variety of social scientists (see Hammond, 1968) and to learn of the strengths and weaknesses of different data collection techniques as they have been practiced by experienced scholars. Yet a third way is to design different pilot studies that will provide an opportunity for practicing different techniques.

No matter how the experience is gained, every case study investigator should be well versed in a variety of data collection techniques so that a case study can use multiple sources of evidence. Without such multiple sources, an invaluable advantage of the case study strategy will have been lost.

Principle 2: Create a Case Study Database

A second principle has to do with the way of organizing and documenting the data collected for case studies. Here, the case study strategy has much to learn from the practices used with other strategies, in which documentation generally consists of two *separate* collections:

1. the data or evidentiary base and
2. the report of the investigator, whether in article, report, or book form.

With the advent of computerized files, the distinction between these two collections has been made even more clear. For example, investigators in psychological, survey, and economic research may exchange data tapes and other documentation that contain only the actual database—for example, behavioral responses or test scores in psychology, itemized responses to various survey questions, or economic indicators. The database can then be the subject of separate, secondary analysis, independent of any reports by the original investigator.

However, with case studies, the distinction between a separate database and the case study report has *not yet* become an institutionalized practice. Too often, the case study data are synonymous with the evidence presented in the case study report, and a critical reader has no recourse if he or she wants to inspect the database that led to the case study conclusions. A major exception to this has been the Human Relations Area Files at Yale University, which store the "data" for numerous ethnographic studies of different cultural groups, making these data available to new research investigators. However, independent of the need for a central repository, the main point here is that every case study project should strive to develop a formal, presentable database, so that, in principle, other investigators can review the evidence directly and not be limited to the written reports. In this manner, a case study database markedly increases the *reliability* of the entire case study.

The lack of a formal database for most case study efforts is a major shortcoming of case study research and needs to be corrected in the future. There are numerous ways of accomplishing the task, as long as you and other investigators are aware of the need and are willing to commit the additional resources required to build the database. At the same time, the existence of an adequate database does not preclude the need to present sufficient evidence within the case study report itself (to be discussed further in Chapter 6). Every report should still contain enough data so that the reader of the report can draw independent conclusions about the case study.

Nevertheless, the initial problem of establishing a case study database has not been recognized by most of the books on "field methods." The subsections below represent an extension of the current state of the art. The problem of developing the database is described in terms of four components: notes, documents, tabular materials, and narratives.

Case study notes. For case studies, notes are likely to be the most common component of a database. These notes take a variety of forms. The notes may be a result of an investigator's interviews, observations, or document analysis. The notes may be handwritten, typed, on audiotapes, or on microcomputer diskettes, and they may be assembled in the form of a diary, on index cards, or in some less organized fashion.

Regardless of their form or content, these case study notes must be stored in such a manner that other persons, including the investigator, can retrieve them efficiently at some later date. Most commonly, the notes can be divided into the major subjects—as outlined in the case study protocol—covered by a case study; however, any classificatory system will do, as long as the system is evident to an outside party. Only in this manner will the notes be available as part of the case study database.

This identification of the notes as part of the case study database does not mean, however, that the investigator needs to spend excessive amounts of time in rewriting interviews or making extensive editorial changes to make the notes presentable. Such a building of a case record, including the editing and rewriting of interview notes, is recommended by at least one author (Patton, 1980, p. 303) but results in a misplaced priority. Any such editing effort should be directed at the case study report itself, not at the notes. The only essential characteristics of the notes are that they be organized, categorized, complete, and available for later access.

Case study documents. Many documents relevant to a case study will be collected during the course of a study. Chapter 3 indicated that the disposition of these documents should be covered in the case study protocol and suggested that one helpful way is to have an annotated bibliography of these documents. Such annotations would again facilitate storage and retrieval, so that later investigators can inspect or share the database.

The single, unique characteristic of these documents is that they are likely to require a large amount of physical storage space. In addition, the documents may be of varying importance to the database, and the investigator may want to establish a primary file and a secondary file for such documents. The main objective, again, is to make the documents readily retrievable for later inspection or perusal. In those instances in which the documents have been relevant to specific interviews, one additional cross-reference is to have the interview notes itemize the document.

Tabular materials. The data base may consist of tabular materials, either collected from the site being studied or created by the research team. Such materials also need to be organized and stored to allow for later retrieval.

The materials may include survey and other quantitative data. For example, a survey may have been conducted at one or more of the case study sites as part of the overall study. In such situations, the tabular materials may even be stored in computerized files. As another example, in dealing with archival

---

BOX 21
Narratives in the Case Study Database

A series of 12 case studies was done on microcomputer use in schools (Yin & White, 1984). Each case study was based on open-ended answers to about 50 protocol questions concerning matters such as the number and location of the microcomputers (an inventory question requiring tabular and narrative responses), the relationship between the microcomputer units and other computational systems within the school district, and the training and coordination provided by the district.

The case study investigator's first responsibility was to answer these 50 questions as completely as possible, citing specific sources of evidence in footnotes. These answers were unedited but served as the basis for both the individual case reports and the cross-case analysis. The availability of the database meant that other members of the case study team could determine the events at each site, even before the case study reports were completed. These files remain a rich source of evidence that could be used again, even as part of another study.

---

or observational evidence, a case study may have called for "counts" of various phenomena (see Miles, 1979). The documentation of these counts, done by the case study team, also should be organized and stored as part of the database. In brief, any tabular materials, whether based on surveys, observational counts, or archival data, can be treated in a manner similar to the way they are handled in other research strategies.

Narratives. Certain forms of narrative also may be considered a formal part of the database and not part of the final case study report. This is reflected by a special practice that should be used more frequently: to have the case study investigators compose *open-ended answers to the questions in the case study protocol.* This practice has been used on several occasions in multiple-case studies designed by the author (see BOX 21). The questions and answers, in modified form, can even serve directly as the basis for the final case study report, as described further in Chapter 6.

In such a situation, each answer represents an attempt to integrate the available evidence and to converge upon the facts of the matter or their tentative interpretation. The process is actually an analytic one and is an integral part of the case study analysis. The format for the answers may be considered analogous to that of a comprehensive "take-home" exam, used in graduate degree programs. The investigator is the respondent, and his or her goal is to cite the relevant evidence—whether from interviews, documents, observations, or archival evidence—in composing an adequate answer. The main purpose of the open-ended answer is to document the connection between specific pieces of evidence and various issues in the case study, using footnotes and citations generously.

The entire set of answers can be considered part of the case study database. The investigator, along with any other interested party, can then use this database to compose the actual case study report. Or, if no reports are composed concerning the individual cases (see Chapter 6 for such situations), the answers can serve as the database for the subsequent cross-case analysis. Again, because the answers are part of the database and not the final report, the investigators should not spend much time trying to make the answers presentable. In other words, they need not perform the standard editing and copyediting chores (and the answers may even remain handwritten and not typed). The most important attribute of good answers is that they indeed connect specific evidence—through adequate citation—to the pertinent case study issues.

Principle 3: Maintain a Chain of Evidence

Another principle to be followed, to increase the *reliability* of the information in a case study, is to maintain a chain of evidence. Such a principle is based on a notion similar to that used in criminological investigations.

The principle is to allow an external observer—the reader of the case study, for example—to follow the derivation of any evidence from initial research questions to ultimate case study conclusions. Moreover, this external observer should be able to trace the steps in either direction (from conclusions back to initial research questions or from questions to conclusions). As with criminological evidence, the process should be tight enough that evidence presented in "court"—the case study report—is assuredly the same evidence that was collected at the scene of the "crime" during the data collection process; conversely, no original evidence should have been lost, through carelessness or bias, and therefore fail to receive appropriate attention in considering the "facts" of a case. If these objectives are achieved, a case study also will have addressed the methodological problem of determining construct validity, thereby increasing the overall quality of the case.

Imagine the following scenario. You have read the conclusions in a case study report, want to know more about the derivation of this conclusion, and are tracing the research process backward.

First, the report itself should have made sufficient citation to the relevant portions of the case study database—for example, by citing specific docu-

---

BOX 22
Descriptive Cases in Need of Evidence

A descriptive case study is usually considered less demanding than an explanatory one. Little theory is said to be needed, causal links do not have to be made, and analysis is minimal. The case study investigator is simply supposed to be free to "tell it like it is."

Sara Lightfoot's three "Portraits of Exemplary Secondary Schools," published in *Daedalus* (1981), are examples of such descriptive case studies. Each case covers a distinguished secondary school, its staff and curriculum, some critical events, and snatches of everyday school life. The "portraits," like works of art, are idiosyncratic to each school and do not follow any common theoretical framework.

However, even under these conditions, the relevant evidence needs to be cited. A major shortcoming of these case studies is that none of them has a single footnote—citing specific interviews, documents, or observations. The reader cannot tell what sources the author used and therefore cannot independently judge the reliability of the information. Such a problem can undermine the credibility of an entire case study.

---

ments, interviews, or observations (see BOX 22 for a contrary example). Second, the database, upon inspection, should reveal the actual evidence and also indicate the circumstances under which the evidence was collected— for example, the time and place of an interview. Third, these circumstances should be consistent with the specific procedures and questions contained in the case study protocol, to show that the data collection followed the procedures stipulated in the protocol. Finally, a reading of the protocol should indicate the link between the content of the protocol and the initial study questions.

In the aggregate, you have therefore been able to move from one portion of the case study to another, with clear cross-referencing to methodological procedures and to the resulting evidence. This is the ultimate "chain of evidence" that is desired.

SUMMARY

This chapter has reviewed six types of case study evidence, how they can be collected, and three important principles regarding the data collection process.

The data collection process for case studies is more complex than the processes used in other research strategies. The case study investigator must have a methodological versatility not necessarily required for using other strategies and must follow certain formal procedures to ensure *quality control* during the data collection process. The three principles described above are steps in this direction. They are not intended to straitjacket the inventive and insightful investigator. They are intended to make the process as explicit as possible, so that the final results—the data that have been collected—reflect a concern for construct validity and for reliability, thereby becoming worthy of further analysis. How such analysis can be carried out is the subject of the next chapter.

EXERCISES

1. *Using evidence.* Select one of the case studies cited in the BOXES of this book. Go through the case study and identify five "facts" important to the case study. For each fact, indicate the source or sources of evidence, if any, used to define the fact. In how many instances was there more than a single source of evidence?

2. *Identifying illustrative types of evidence.* Name a case study topic you would like to study. For some aspect of this topic, identify the specific type of evidence that would be relevant—for example, if a document, what kind of document? If an interview, what respondent and what questions? If an archival record, what records and what variables?

3. *Seeking converging evidence.* Name a particular incident that occurred recently in your everyday life. How would you go about establishing the "facts" of this incident, if you wanted to demonstrate what had happened? Would you interview any important persons (including yourself)? Would there have been any artifacts or documentation to rely upon?

4. *Practicing the development of a database.* For the topic you covered in the preceding question, write a short report (no more than two typewritten pages). Start this report with the major question you were attempting to answer, and then provide the answer, citing the evidence you had used (your format should include footnotes). Envisage how this question-and-answer sequence might be one of many in your total case study "database."

5. *Establishing a chain of evidence.* State a hypothetical conclusion that might emerge from a case study you are going to do. Now work backward and identify the specific data or evidence that would have supported such a conclusion. Similarly, work backward and define the protocol question that would

have led to the collection of this evidence, and then the study question that in turn would have led to the design of the protocol question. Do you understand how this chain of evidence has been formed, and how one can move forward or backward in tracing the chain?

NOTES

1. Excellent suggestions regarding the ways of verifying documentary evidence, including the nontrivial problem of determining the actual author of a document, are offered by Barzun and Graff (1985, pp. 109-133).

2. This practice was illustrated most effectively in Bernstein and Woodward's best-selling book (1974) on the Watergate coverup. The authors' fieldwork, reflected in the ways in which individual articles were written for presentation in *The Washington Post*, continually included opportunities for all participants to express their own views or to deny the statements of others. When key persons did not wish to comment, this occurrence also was noted in the articles.

5

Analyzing Case Study Evidence

Data analysis consists of examining, categorizing, tabulating, or otherwise recombining the evidence to address the initial propositions of a study. Analyzing case study evidence is especially difficult because the strategies and techniques have not been well defined in the past. Nevertheless, every investigation should start with a general analytic strategy—yielding priorities for what to analyze and why.

Within such a strategy, four dominant analytic techniques should be used: pattern-matching, explanation-building, time-series analysis, and program logic models. Each is applicable whether a study involves a single- or a multiple-case design, and every case study should consider these techniques. Other types of analytic techniques also are possible but deal with special situations— namely, in which a case study has embedded units of analysis or in which there are a large number of case studies to be analyzed. These other techniques should therefore be used in conjunction with the four dominant techniques, and not alone.

GENERAL ANALYTIC STRATEGIES

Need for an Analytic Strategy

The analysis of case study evidence is one of the least developed and most difficult aspects of doing case studies. Too many times, investigators start case studies without having the foggiest notion about how the evidence is to be analyzed (despite Chapter 3's recommendation that the analytic approaches be developed as part of the case study protocol). Such investigations easily become stalled at the analytic stage; this author has known colleagues who have simply ignored their case study data for month after month, not knowing what to do with the evidence.

Because of this problem, the experienced case study investigator is likely to have great advantages over the novice at the analytic stage. Unlike statistical analysis, there are few fixed formulas or cookbook recipes to guide the novice (one of the few texts to attempt this is Miles & Huberman, 1984). Instead, much depends on an investigator's own style of rigorous thinking, along with the sufficient presentation of evidence and careful consideration of alternative interpretations.

Such an observation has led some to suggest that one approach to successful analysis is to make case study data conducive to statistical analysis—by coding events into numerical form, for example. Such "quantitative" case studies (Pelz, 1981) may be possible when one has an embedded unit of analysis within a case study, but this approach still fails to address the needs of doing analysis at the level of the whole case, in which there may be only a single or a few cases.

A second suggested approach has been to use various analytic *techniques* (see Miles & Huberman, 1984), such as:

- Putting information into different arrays
- Making a matrix of categories and placing the evidence within such categories
- Creating data displays—flowcharts and other devices—for examining the data
- Tabulating the frequency of different events
- Examining the complexity of such tabulations and their relationships by calculating second-order numbers such as means and variances
- Putting information in chronological order or using some other temporal scheme

These are indeed useful and important techniques and they should be used to put the evidence in some order prior to actual analysis. Moreover, such preliminary data manipulations are one way of overcoming the stalling problem mentioned above. At the same time, the manipulations must be done carefully to avoid biasing the results.

However, more important than these two approaches is to have a general analytic strategy in the first place. The ultimate goal is to treat the evidence fairly, to produce compelling analytic conclusions, and to rule out alternative interpretations. The role of the general strategy is to help an investigator to choose among different techniques and to complete the analytic phase of the research successfully. Two such types of strategies are described below, after which specific ways of conducting case study analysis are reviewed.

Two General Strategies

Relying on theoretical propositions. The first and more preferred strategy is to follow the theoretical propositions that led to the case study. The original objectives and design of the case study presumably were based on such propositions, which in turn reflected a set of research questions, reviews of the literature, and new insights.

The propositions would have shaped the data collection plan and therefore would have given priorities to the relevant analytic strategies. One example, from a study of intergovernmental relationships, followed the proposition that federal funds not only had redistributive dollar effects but also created new organizational changes at the local level (Yin, 1980). The basic proposition—the creation of a "counterpart" bureaucracy in the form of local planning organizations, citizen action groups, and other new offices within a local government itself, but all attuned to specific federal programs—was traced in case studies of several cities. For each city, the purpose of the case study was to show how the formation and modification in local organizations occurred *after* changes in related federal programs and to show how these local organizations acted on behalf of the federal programs even though they might have been components of local government.

This proposition is an example of a theoretical orientation guiding the case study analysis. Clearly, the proposition helps to focus attention on certain data and to ignore other data. (A good test is to decide what data you might cite if you had only 5 minutes to defend a proposition in your case study.) The proposition also helps to organize the entire case study and to define alternative explanations to be examined. Theoretical propositions about causal relations—answers to "how" and "why" questions—can be very useful in guiding case study analysis in this manner.

Developing a case description. A second general analytic strategy is to develop a descriptive framework for organizing the case study. This strategy is less preferable than the use of theoretical propositions but serves as an alternative when theoretical propositions are absent.

Sometimes, the original purpose of the case study may have been a descriptive one. This was the objective of the famous sociological study *Middletown* (Lynd & Lynd, 1929), which was a case study of a small midwestern city. What is interesting about *Middletown*, aside from its classic value as a rich and historic case, is its structure, reflected by its chapters:

- Chapter I: Getting a Living
- Chapter II: Making a Home
- Chapter III: Training the Young
- Chapter IV: Using Leisure
- Chapter V: Engaging in Religious Practices
- Chapter VI: Engaging in Community Activities

These chapters cover a range of topics relevant to community life in the early twentieth century, when Middletown was studied. The descriptive

---

BOX 23
Quantifying the Descriptive Elements of a Case Study

Pressman and Wildavsky's book, *Implementation: How Great Expectations in Washington Are Dashed in Oakland* (1973), is regarded as one of the foremost contributions to the study of implementation. This is the process whereby some programmatic activity—an economic development project, a new curriculum in a school, or a crime prevention program, for example—is installed in a specific organization. The process is complex and involves numerous individuals, organizational rules, social norms, and mixtures of good and bad intentions.

Can such a complex process also be the subject of quantitative inquiry and analysis? Pressman and Wildavsky offer one innovative solution. To the extent that successful implementation can be *described* as a sequence of decisions, an analyst can focus part of the case study on the number and types of such decisions or elements.

Thus, in their chapter titled "The Complexity of Joint Action," the authors analyze the difficulties in Oakland: To implement one public works program required a total of 70 sequential decisions—project approvals, negotiation of leases, letting of contracts, and so on. The analysis examined the level of agreement and the time needed to reach agreement at each of the 70 decision points. Given the normal diversity of opinion and slippage in time, the analysis illustrates—in a quantitative manner—the low probability of implementation success.

---

framework also organizes the case study analysis. (As an aside, a useful exercise is to note the structure of existing exemplary case studies—some cited in the BOXES throughout this book—by examining their tables of contents, as an implicit clue to different analytic approaches.)

In other situations, the original objective of the case study may not have been a descriptive one, but a descriptive approach may help to identify the appropriate causal links to be analyzed—even quantitatively. BOX 23 gives an example of a case study that was concerned with the complexity of implementing local economic development programs. Such complexity, the investigators realized, could be *described* in terms of the multiplicity of decisions that had to occur in order for implementation to succeed. This descriptive insight later led to the enumeration, tabulation, and hence quantification of the various decisions. In this sense, the descriptive approach was used to identify (a) a type of event that could be quantified and (b) an overall pattern of complexity that ultimately was used in a causal sense to "explain" why implementation had failed.

Summary. The best preparation for conducting case study analysis is to have a general analytic strategy. Two have been described, one relying on theoretical propositions and the other beginning with a descriptive approach to the case. These two general strategies underlie the specific analytic procedures to be described below. Without such strategies (or alternatives to them), case study analysis will proceed with difficulty. One way of overcoming such difficulty is to "play with the data," using some techniques that have been enumerated. However, if the general strategies are absent, and if one is not facile at playing with the data, the entire case study is likely to be in jeopardy.

The remainder of this chapter covers specific analytic techniques, to be used as part of a general strategy. The sections are divided into two sets. The first, "Dominant Modes of Analysis," contains four important techniques (pattern-matching, explanation-building, time-series analysis, and program logic models). This first set is especially intended to deal with the previously noted problems of developing *internal validity* and *external validity* in doing case studies (see Chapter 2). The second, "Lesser Modes of Analysis," contains techniques that usually need to be used in conjunction with one of the dominant modes.

DOMINANT MODES OF ANALYSIS

Pattern-Matching

For case study analysis, one of the most desirable strategies is to use a pattern-matching logic. Such a logic (Trochim, 1989) compares an empirically based pattern with a predicted one (or with several alternative predictions). If the patterns coincide, the results can help a case study strengthen its *internal validity*.

If the case study is an explanatory one, the patterns may be related to the dependent or the independent variables of study (or both). If the case study is a descriptive one, pattern-matching is still relevant, as long as the predicted pattern of specific variables is defined prior to data collection.

Nonequivalent dependent variables as a pattern. The dependent-variables pattern may be derived from one of the more potent quasi-experimental research designs, labeled a "nonequivalent, dependent variables design" (Cook & Campbell, 1979, p. 118). According to this design, an experiment or quasi-experiment may have multiple dependent variables—that is, a variety of outcomes. If, for each outcome, the initially predicted values have been found, and at the same time alternative "patterns" of predicted values (including those deriving from methodological artifacts, or "threats" to validity) have not been found, strong causal inferences can be made.

For example, consider a single case in which you are studying the effects of a newly installed office automation system. Your major proposition is that, because such a system is decentralized—that is, each automated piece of equipment, such as a word processor, can work independently of any central computer—a certain pattern of organizational changes and stresses will be produced. Among these changes and stresses, you specify the following, based on propositions derived from previous decentralization theory:

- employees will create new *applications* for the office equipment, and these applications will be idiosyncratic to each employee;
- traditional *supervisory links* will be threatened, as management control over work tasks and the use of central sources of information will be diminished;
- *organizational conflicts* will increase, due to competition for resources between the new system and the existing, mainframe computer system that the organization has had; but, nevertheless,
- *productivity* will increase over the levels prior to the installation of the new system.

In this example, these four outcomes each represent different dependent variables, and you would assess each with different measures and instruments. To this extent, you have a study that has specified *nonequivalent* dependent variables. You also have predicted an overall pattern of outcomes covering each of these variables. If the results are as predicted, you can draw a solid conclusion about the effects of decentralization in office automation. However, if the results fail to show the entire pattern as predicted—that is, even if one variable does not behave as predicted—your initial proposition would have to be questioned.

This first case could then be augmented by a second one, in which another office automation system has been installed, but of a centralized nature—that is, the equipment at all of the individual workstations was linked to the same network, and the entire network was controlled by a central computing unit (a "shared-logic" system). Now you would predict a different pattern of outcomes, using the same four dependent variables enumerated above. And now, if the results show that the decentralized system (Case 1) had actually produced the predicted pattern, and that this first pattern was different than that predicted and produced by the centralized system (Case 2), you would be able to draw an even stronger conclusion about the effects of decentralization. In this situation, you have made a *theoretical replication* across cases.

(In other situations, you might have sought a *literal replication* by finding two or more cases of decentralized systems.)

Finally, you might be aware of the existence of certain threats to the validity of this logic (see Cook & Campbell, 1979, for a full list of these threats). For example, a new corporate executive might have assumed office in Case 1, leaving room for a counterargument: that the apparent effects of decentralization were actually attributable to this executive's appointment and not to the newly installed office automation system. To deal with this threat, you would have to identify some subset of the initial dependent variables and show that the pattern would have been different (in Case 1) if the corporate executive had been the actual reason for the effects. If you only had a single-case study, this type of procedure would be essential; you would be using the same data to rule out arguments based on a potential threat to validity. Given the existence of a second case, as in our hypothetical example, you also could show that the argument about the corporate executive would not explain certain parts of the pattern found in Case 2 (in which the absence of the corporate executive should have been associated with certain opposing outcomes). In essence, your goal is to identify all reasonable threats to validity and to conduct repeated comparisons, showing how such threats cannot account for the dual patterns in both of the hypothetical cases.

Rival explanations as patterns. A second type of pattern-matching is that for independent variables. In such a situation (for an example, see BOX 24), several cases may be known to have had a certain type of outcome, and the investigation has focused on how and why this outcome occurred in each case.

This analysis requires the development of rival theoretical propositions, articulated in operational terms. The important characteristic of these rival explanations is that each involves a pattern of independent variables that is mutually exclusive: If one explanation is to be valid, the others cannot be. This means that the presence of certain independent variables (predicted by one explanation) precludes the presence of other independent variables (predicted by a rival explanation). The independent variables may involve several or many different types of characteristics or events, each assessed with different measures and instruments. The concern of the case study analysis, however, is with the overall pattern of results and the degree to which a pattern matches the predicted one.

This type of pattern-matching of independent variables also can be done either with a single case or with multiple cases. With a single case, the successful matching of the pattern to one of the rival explanations would be evidence for concluding that this explanation was the correct one (and that

---

BOX 24
Pattern-Matching for Rival Explanations

A common policy problem is to understand the conditions under which R&D can be made useful to society. Too often, people think that research serves only itself and does not meet practical needs.

This topic was the subject of several case studies in which an R&D project's results were known to have been used. The case studies investigated how and why this outcome had occurred, entertaining several rival explanations based on three prevailing models of research use: (a) the research, development, and diffusion model; (b) the problem-solving model; and (c) the social interaction model (Yin & Moore, 1984). The events of each case were compared with those predicted by each model, in a pattern-matching mode. For instance, the problem-solving model requires the prior existence of a problem, as prelude to the initiation of an R&D project, but this is not a condition recognized by the other two models. This is therefore an example of how different theoretical models can predict mutually exclusive events, facilitating effective comparisons.

For all of the cases that were studied (N = 9), the events turned out to match at best a combination of the second and third models. The investigators had therefore used rival explanations to analyze the data within each case and a replication logic across cases.

---

the other explanations were incorrect). Again, even with a single case, threats to validity—basically constituting another group of rival explanations—should be identified and ruled out. In addition, if this identical result were obtained over multiple cases, *literal replication* of the single cases would have been accomplished, and the cross-case results might be stated even more assertively. Then, if this same result also failed to occur in a second group of cases, due to predictably different circumstances, *theoretical replication* would have been accomplished, and the initial result would stand yet more robustly.

Simpler patterns. This same logic can be applied to simpler patterns, having a minimal variety of either dependent or independent variables. In the simplest case, in which there may be only two different dependent (or independent) variables, pattern-matching is possible as long as a different pattern has been stipulated for these two variables.

The fewer the variables, of course, the more dramatic the different patterns will have to be to allow any comparisons of their differences. Nevertheless, there are some situations in which the simpler patterns are both relevant and compelling. The role of the general analytic strategy would be to determine the best ways of contrasting any differences as sharply as possible and to develop theoretically significant explanations for the different outcomes.

Precision of pattern-matching. At this point in the state of the art, the actual pattern-matching procedure involves no precise comparisons. Whether one is predicting a pattern of nonequivalent dependent variables, a pattern based on rival explanations, or a simple pattern, the fundamental comparison between the predicted and the actual pattern may involve no quantitative or statistical criteria. (Available statistical techniques are likely to be irrelevant because none of the variables in the pattern will have a "variance," each essentially representing a single data point.)

This lack of precision can allow for some interpretive discretion on the part of the investigator, who may be overly restrictive in claiming a pattern to have been violated or overly lenient in deciding that a pattern has been matched. Major improvements in future case study research could be made therefore by developing more precise techniques. Until such improvements occur, investigators are cautioned not to postulate very subtle patterns. One wants to do case studies in which the outcomes are likely to lead to gross matches or mismatches and in which even an "eyeballing" technique is sufficiently convincing to draw a conclusion.

Explanation-Building

A second analytic strategy is in fact a special type of pattern-matching, but the procedure is more difficult and therefore deserves separate attention. Here, the goal is to analyze the case study data by building an explanation about the case (Yin, 1982b).

As used in this chapter, the procedure is mainly relevant to explanatory case studies. A similar procedure, for exploratory case studies, has been commonly cited as part of a hypothesis-generating process (see Glaser & Strauss, 1967); however, its goal is not to conclude a study but to develop ideas for further study.

Elements of explanations. To "explain" a phenomenon is to stipulate a set of causal links about it. These causal links are similar to the independent variables in the previously described use of rival explanations. In most studies, the links may be complex and difficult to measure in any precise manner.

In most existing case studies, explanation-building has occurred in narrative form. Because such narratives cannot be precise, the better case studies are the ones in which the explanations have reflected some theoretically significant propositions. For example, the causal links may reflect critical insights into public policy process or into social science theory. The public policy propositions, if correct, can lead to recommendations for future policy actions (see BOX 25, part A, for an example); the social science propositions, if correct, can lead to major contributions to theory-building (see BOX 25, part B, for an example).

Iterative nature of explanation-building. The explanation-building process, for explanatory case studies, has not been well documented in operational terms. However, one important characteristic is that the final explanation is a result of a series of iterations:

- Making an initial theoretical statement or an initial proposition about policy or social behavior
- Comparing the findings of *an initial case* against such a statement or proposition
- Revising the statement or proposition
- Comparing other details of the case against the revision
- Again revising the statement or proposition
- Comparing the revision to the facts of *a second, third, or more cases*
- Repeating this process as many times as is needed

In this sense, the final explanation may not have been fully stipulated at the beginning of a study and therefore differs in this respect from the pattern-matching approaches previously described. Rather, the case study evidence is examined, theoretical positions are revised, and the evidence is examined once again from a new perspective, in this iterative mode.

The gradual building of an explanation is similar to the process of refining a set of ideas, in which an important aspect is again to entertain other *plausible or rival explanations*. As before, the objective is to show how these explanations cannot be built, given the actual set of case study events. If this approach is applied to multiple-case studies (as in BOX 25), the result of the explanation-building process is also the creation of a cross-case analysis, not simply an analysis of each individual case.

Potential problems in explanation-building. Any investigator should be forewarned that this approach to case study analysis is fraught with dangers. Much intelligence is demanded of the explanation-builder. As the iterative process progresses, for instance, an investigator may slowly begin to drift away from the original topic of interest. Constant reference to the original purpose of the inquiry and the possible alternative explanations may help to

---

BOX 25
A. Explanation-Building in Multiple-Case Studies

In a multiple-case study, one goal is to build a general explanation that fits each of the individual cases, even though the cases will vary in their details. The objective is analogous to multiple experiments.

Martha Derthick's *New Towns In-Town: Why a Federal Program Failed* (1972) is a book about a housing program created by President Lyndon Johnson. The federal government was to give its surplus land—located in choice inner-city areas—to local governments for housing developments. But after 4 years, little progress had been made at the seven sites—San Antonio, New Bedford (Massachusetts), San Francisco, Washington, D.C., Atlanta, Louisville, and Clinton Township (Michigan)—and the program was considered a failure.

Derthick's account first analyzes the events at each of the seven sites. Then, a general explanation—that the projects failed to generate sufficient local support—is found unsatisfactory because the condition was not dominant at all of the sites. According to Derthick, although local support did exist, "federal officials had nevertheless stated such ambitious objectives that some degree of failure was certain" (p. 91). Instead, Derthick builds a modified explanation and concludes that "the surplus lands program failed both because the federal government had limited influence at the local level and because it set impossibly high objectives" (p. 93).

B. Explanation-Building in Multiple-Case Studies:
An Example From Another Field

A design similar to Derthick's is used by Barrington Moore in his history titled *Social Origins of Dictatorship and Democracy* (1966). The book serves as another illustration of explanation-building in multiple-case studies, even though the cases are actually historical examples.

Moore's book covers the transformation from agrarian to industrial societies in six different countries—England, France, the United States, China, Japan, and India—and the general explanation of the role of the upper classes and the peasantry is a basic theme that emerges. This explanation represents a significant contribution to the field of history.

---

reduce this potential problem. Other safeguards have already been covered by Chapters 3 and 4—that is, the use of a case study protocol (indicating what data were to be collected), the establishment of a case study database for each case (formally storing the entire array of data that were collected, available for inspection by a third party), and the following of a chain of evidence.

Time-Series Analysis

A third analytic strategy is to conduct a time-series analysis, directly analogous to the time-series analysis conducted in experiments and quasi-experiments. Such analysis can follow many intricate patterns, which have been the subject of several major textbooks in experimental and clinical psychology (see Kratochwill, 1978); the interested reader is referred to such works for further detailed guidance. The more intricate and precise the pattern, the more that the time-series analysis also will lay a firm foundation for the conclusions of the case study.

Especially relevant to case studies is an intriguing, methodological analysis of qualitative research by Louise Kidder (1981), who demonstrated that certain types of participant-observer studies followed time-series designs, unbeknownst to the original investigators. For example, one study was concerned with the course of events that led to marijuana use, the hypothesis being that a sequence or "time-series" of at least three conditions was necessary (Becker, 1963): initially smoking marijuana, later feeling its effects, and subsequently enjoying those effects. If a person experienced only one or two of these three steps but not all three, the hypothesis was that regular marijuana use would not follow. This type of insightful postanalysis, on Kidder's part, needs to be repeated in the future to help reveal such implicit analytic techniques.

Simple time-series. Compared with the more general pattern-matching analysis, a time-series design can be much simpler in one sense: In time series, there may only be a single dependent or independent variable. In these circumstances, when a large number of data points are relevant and available, statistical tests can even be used to analyze the data (see Kratochwill, 1978).

However, the pattern can be more complicated in another sense, because the multiple changes in this single variable, over time, may have no clear starting or ending points. Despite this problem, the ability to trace changes over time is a major strength of case studies—which are not limited to cross-sectional or static assessments of a particular situation. If the events over time have been traced in detail and with precision, some type of time-series analysis always may be possible, even if the case study analysis involves some other techniques as well.

BOX 26
A Simple Time-Series
Analysis and Pattern-Matching

One example of a time-series analysis is the classic article by Donald Campbell, "Reforms as Experiments" (1969). Although the author does not consider his study to be a case study, his analysis actually illustrates the use of pattern-matching with a simple set of data over time—a technique that is widely applicable to all sorts of case studies.

Campbell was trying to compare two theoretical propositions. In the first, the 1955 reduction in Connecticut's speed limit was claimed to have reduced the annual number of fatalities. In the second, the speed limit was claimed to have had no real effect. The facts of the case indicated that, although the number of fatalities declined the year following the new speed limit, further observation of the fatalities over a 10-year period showed that this apparent decline was well within the range of normal fluctuation for the whole period of time. Campbell therefore concluded that the speed limit did not have any effect.

What Campbell had done was to collect a single time series (the annual fatalities over time) and to match the data against two alternative explanations—an "effects" explanation and a "random fluctuation" explanation (see Figure 2.1 in Chapter 2). The results are clear to the naked eye, and no statistical comparison was needed (or conducted) to confirm the results.

The essential logic underlying a time-series design is the match between a trend of data points compared with (a) a theoretically significant trend specified before the onset of the investigation, versus (b) some rival trend, also specified earlier, versus (c) any trend based on some artifact or threat to internal validity. Within the same single-case study, for instance, two different patterns of events may have been hypothesized over time. This is what Campbell did in his now famous study of the Connecticut speed limit law (see BOX 26; also see Chapter 2, Figure 2.2). One time-series pattern was based on the proposition that the new law (an "interruption" in the time series) had substantially reduced the number of fatalities, whereas the other time-series pattern was based on the proposition that no such effect had occurred. The examination of the actual data points—that is, the annual number of fatalities over a period of years—was then made to determine which of the proposed time series best matched the empirical evidence. Such comparison of "interrupted time series" within the same case can be applied to many different settings.

Across single cases, the same logic can be used, with different time-series patterns postulated for different cases. For instance, a case study about economic development in cities may have postulated the reasons that manufacturing-based cities would have more negative employment trends than those of service-based cities. The pertinent outcome data might have consisted of annual employment figures over a limited period of time, such as 10 years. In the manufacturing-based cities, the data might have been examined for a declining employment trend, whereas in the service-based cities, they might have been examined for a rising employment trend. Similar analyses can be imagined with regard to the examination of crime trends over time within individual cities, changes in school enrollment and presumed neighborhood change, and many other urban indicators.

Complex time series. Time-series designs can be more complex when the trends within a given case are postulated to be more complex. One can postulate, for instance, not merely rising or declining trends, but some rise followed by some decline within the same case. This type of dual pattern, across time, would be the beginning of a more complex time series. As always, the strength of the case study strategy would not merely be in assessing this type of time series but also in having developed a rich explanation for the complex pattern of outcomes and in comparing the explanation with the outcomes.

Even greater complexities arise in those instances in which a set of multiple variables—not just a single one—are relevant to a case study and in which each variable is predicted to have a different pattern over time. A study of neighborhood change often assumes this characteristic. Typical neighborhood change theories, for instance, suggest that different time lags exist in the turnover rates among (a) the residential population, (b) commercial vendors and merchants, (c) local service institutions such as churches and public services, and (d) the housing stock. When a neighborhood is undergoing racial change, upgrading, or other types of common transitions, all of these turnover rates may have to be studied over a 10- or 20-year period. The resulting curves, according to neighborhood change theories, will vary in predictable ways. For example, certain population changes (such as a subtle shift from small to larger families) are said to be followed first by certain changes in municipal services (such as school enrollment as well as increases in the need for street services) but only later by turnover in commercial stores; furthermore, the types of churches may not change at all throughout this process.

Such a study frequently requires the collection of neighborhood indicators that in themselves are difficult to obtain (see BOX 27), much less to analyze.

BOX 27
Changes in Neighborhood Indicators Over Time

Concern over neighborhood and urban change reached new heights during the 1960s and 1970s, when urban places appeared to be suffering from inordinate decay and decline. Many observers speculated that the American central city was, in fact, on the verge of disappearing as a functional form.

This type of concern led to numerous efforts to catalog and trace changes in various indicators on a city-by-city basis. One study (Yin, 1972, reprinted in Yin, 1982a) even focused on the occurrence of fire alarms and the potentially different social phenomena reflected by alarms for real fires as opposed to false alarms. The alarm patterns were compared with numerous other social indicators, including crime trends, shifts in the residential location of households on welfare, and changes in urban services. This type of approach to urban and neighborhood change represents one example of a multiple time-series design and analysis.

However, if adequate time and effort have been set aside to conduct the necessary data collection and analysis, the result may be a compelling analysis—as in one study in which an "interrupted time-series design" was used to examine the long-term community effects of natural hazards. In this latter study, extensive data collection efforts were made in each of four communities, just to obtain the needed time-series data; the multiple-case results are described in BOX 28.

In general, although a more complex time series creates greater problems for data collection, it also leads to a more elaborate trend (or set of trends), making analysis more definitive. Any match of a predicted with an actual time series, when both are complex, will produce strong evidence for an initial theoretical proposition.

Chronologies. The analysis of chronological events is a frequent technique in case studies and may be considered a special form of time-series analysis. The chronological sequence again focuses directly on the major strength of case studies cited earlier—that case studies allow an investigator to trace events over time.

The arraying of events into a chronology permits the investigator to determine causal events over time, because the basic sequence of a cause and its effect cannot be temporally inverted. However, unlike the more general time-series approaches, the chronology is likely to cover many different types

---

BOX 28
Case Studies Using Complex Time-Series Analyses

A natural disaster—such as a hurricane, tornado, or flood—can be considered a major disruptive event for a community. Sales and business patterns, crimes, and other population trends might all be expected to change as a result of such a disaster.

Paul Friesema and his colleagues (1979) studied such changes in four communities that had suffered from major disasters: Yuba City, California, 1955; Galveston, Texas, 1961; Conway, Arkansas, 1965; and Topeka, Kansas, 1966. In each of these case studies, the investigators collected extensive time-series data for various economic and social indicators. Their analysis showed that the disastrous event, though having a short-term effect—that is, within a 12-month period—had few, if any, long-term effects. This analysis represents an excellent application of a complex time-series technique as the basis for a multiple-case study.

---

of variables and not be limited to a single independent or dependent variable. The analytic goal is to compare the chronology with that predicted by some explanatory theory—in which the theory has specified one or more of the following kinds of conditions:

- Some events must always occur before other events, with the reverse *sequence* being impossible.
- Some events must always be followed by other events, on a *contingency* basis.
- Some events can only follow other events after a prespecified *passage of time*.
- Certain *time periods* in a case study may be marked by classes of events that differ substantially from those of other time periods.

If the actual events of a case study, as carefully documented and determined by an investigator, have followed one predicted sequence of events and not those of a compelling, rival sequence, the single-case study can again become the initial basis for causal inferences. Comparison with other cases, as well as the explicit consideration of threats to internal validity, will further bolster this inference.

Summary conditions for time-series analysis. Whatever the stipulated nature of the time series, the important case study objective is to examine some relevant "how" and "why" questions about the relationship of events over time, not merely to observe the time trends alone. An interruption in a time series will be the occasion for postulating causal relationships; similarly, a chronological sequence should contain causal postulates. In contrast, if a study is limited to the analysis of time trends alone, as in a descriptive mode in which causal inferences are unimportant, a non-case study strategy is probably more relevant—for example, the economic analysis of consumer price trends over time.

On those occasions when the use of time-series analysis is relevant to a case study, an essential feature is to identify the specific indicator(s) to be traced over time as well as the specific time intervals to be covered. Only as a result of such prior specification are the relevant data likely to be collected in the first place, much less analyzed properly.

Program Logic Models

This fourth strategy is in fact a combination of pattern-matching and time-series analysis. The pattern being matched is the key cause-effect pattern between independent and dependent variables (Peterson & Bickman, 1992; Rog & Huebner, 1992). However, the analysis deliberately stipulates a complex chain of events (pattern) over time (time series), covering these independent and dependent variables. The strategy is useful for explanatory, exploratory, and case studies than for descriptive case studies.

Joseph Wholey (1979), then of the Urban Institute, first promoted the idea of a "program logic model." He applied this concept to the tracing of events when a public policy intervention was intended to produce a certain outcome. The intervention could initially produce activities with their own immediate outcomes; these immediate outcomes could in turn produce some intermediate outcome and in turn produce final or ultimate outcomes.

For example, a school intervention could have been initially based on a newly organized school program—one trying to deal with the "America 2000" school reform goals currently prevalent in the education field. One result of this new program was to create a new set of classroom activities during an extra hour in the school day. These activities provided time for students to work with their parents on joint exercises (immediate outcome). The result of this immediate outcome was a report of increased understanding of and satisfaction with the educational process on the part of students, parents, and teachers (intermediate outcome). Eventually, the exercises and the satisfaction led to increased learning of certain concepts by students and parents (ultimate outcome).

In this example, the case study analysis would provide the empirical data in support of (or to challenge) this logic model. The analysis would have to entertain rival chains of events as well as the potential importance of spurious external events. If the data were supportive of the initial chain, and no rivals could be substantiated, the analysis could claim a causal effect between the initial school reform intervention and the later increased learning. For an exploratory case study, the conclusion might be reached that the specified series of events was illogical—for instance, that the intervention was not aimed at the learning outcome of interest in the first place.

This program logic model strategy can be used in a variety of circumstances, not just those in which a public policy intervention has occurred. A key ingredient is the claimed existence of repeated cause-and-effect sequences of events, all linked together. The more complex the link, the more definitively the case study data can be analyzed to determine whether a pattern match has been made with these events over time.

LESSER MODES OF ANALYSIS

Three "lesser" modes of analysis also may be used in case studies: (a) analysis of embedded units of analysis, (b) repeated observations, and (c) the case survey approach. However, this second set consists of incomplete analytic approaches. They must be used in combination with one of the dominant modes in order to produce a compelling and full case study analysis, the reasons for which are given below.

Analyzing Embedded Units

When a case study design includes an embedded unit of analysis—that is, a lesser unit than the case itself, for which numerous data points have been collected (see Chapter 2)—the relevant analytic approaches can cover nearly any of the techniques in the social sciences.

For example, the embedded unit may have been a set of responses to a survey—if a survey of officials or of residents was conducted as part of a single-case study. Alternatively, the embedded unit may have been some archival indicator—if, for example, housing or market data had been collected as part of a single-case study. Finally, the embedded unit may have been some service outcome, such as the number of clients served by an organizational unit that had been the subject of a single-case study.

In each of these examples, the pertinent analytic strategy would reflect the propositions to be examined for the embedded unit. These propositions would be related to but different from the propositions for the larger case. The actual analytic techniques could involve survey analysis, economic analysis, historical analysis, or even operations research. What distinguishes this type of analysis, in each situation, from a regular survey, economic, historical, or operations research study is that the unit of analysis is clearly embedded within a larger case, and the larger case is the *major* interest of the study. If the embedded unit is itself the main focus of attention (or is allowed to become so), and if the larger case is only a minor contextual matter, the effort should not be considered a case study, and some other research strategy should be used.

This distinction appears most clearly in multiple, embedded case studies. In such instances, the appropriate analysis of the embedded unit of analysis should first be conducted *within each case*. The results should be interpreted at the single-case level and may be treated as but one of several factors in a pattern-matching or explanation-building analysis at the single-case level. The patterns or explanations for each single case may then be compared across cases, following the replication mode for multiple cases. Finally, the conclusions drawn for the multiple cases can become the conclusions for the overall study.

In contrast, a study that is not in fact a case study would follow a different analytic sequence, even given the same data. In such instances, the appropriate analysis of the embedded unit is first conducted *across cases*, with all of the data pooled across cases. The results of this analysis may be augmented by discussions of the individual cases as a context for these pooled data, but no formal attempt is made to relate the within-case data to individual case contexts, and no replication logic is applied across cases. In this type of study (such as a survey or an economic study of the inflation rates across cities), the primary conclusions deal with the pooled, embedded units, and the individual cases are of peripheral importance. This type of study is not a case study.

In short, where a genuine case study is involved, any analysis of the embedded units is done within each case (and not pooled). In addition, this analysis cannot be the sole analysis but must be augmented by some other analytic technique at the level of the "whole" case, such as pattern-matching, explanation-building, time-series, or program logic models.

Making Repeated Observations

Repeated observations are another, lesser mode of analysis. When such observations are made over time, this type of analysis may be considered a special type of time-series analysis. However, the repeated observations also may be made on a cross-sectional basis—for example, at repeated "sites" or for other embedded units of analysis within the same case. For this reason, the use of repeated observations is considered an analytic approach separate from time-series analysis.

For example, an evaluation of a large-scale, national reporting system (a single-case study) called attention to the problem that the system requested student test information from schools in the fall, and again in the spring. The assumption was that these pre-and-post data would serve to highlight the changes, if any, that had resulted from compensatory educational efforts made during the school year (Linn et al., 1982). However, the evaluation found that the sharp gains from fall to spring were contaminated by the fact that students normally make progress during this time period; as a result, the evaluation recommended that a fairer measure would compare students' performance on an annual basis. The study showed that for every elementary school grade during one illustrative year—that is, for repeated trials across grades—the fall-spring comparisons were artifactually more favorable than the annual comparisons (see Figure 5.1).

If a case study can pursue this type of analysis, it is following a repeated-observations analysis, whether the repetition is across different classrooms, schools, students, or other units of analysis. What makes the use of repeated observations a lesser mode of analysis is that the analysis is not likely to reflect all of a case study's concerns. As in the illustrative example, in which the major focus of the case was the compensatory educational effort and not simply the spring-fall testing sequence, the repeated observations are likely to be augmented by other analyses of the "whole" case.

Doing a Case Survey:
Secondary Analysis Across Cases

A final alternative is limited to those situations when numerous case studies are available for analysis. For example, a secondary analysis of certain topics—such as citizen participation in urban services (Yin & Yates, 1975) or innovations in urban services (Yin, Heald, & Vogel, 1977)—may be based on upward of 200 or 300 case studies. These cases are not the result of a single study but represent a "literature" of numerous studies.

The case survey approach calls for the development of a closed-ended coding instrument, which is then applied to each case study. The coder, or reader-analyst, uses each case as the basis for responding to the instrument, and the collective data are tallied and analyzed in much the same way as those of a regular survey (Lucas, 1974; Yin, Bingham, & Heald, 1976; Yin & Heald, 1975). As with a regular survey, the coding can be cross-checked and its reliability assessed, and the case survey results will be mainly quantitative in

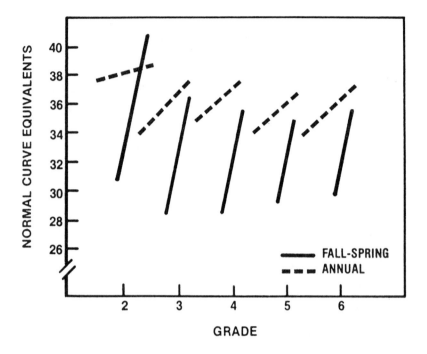

Figure 5.1. Illustrations of Repeated Observations
SOURCE: Linn et al. (1982).

nature. If the number of cases is large enough, different interactive propositions can be statistically examined; where categorical codes have been used,
innovative log-linear and discrete variable-analytic techniques (see Bishop,
Fienberg, & Holland, 1975; Goodman, 1978) should be used.

This approach to case study analysis, however, should not be confused with
two other approaches. First, the case survey is an approach to *cross*-case
analysis and is not the same as the quantitative analysis that might be conducted of an embedded unit *within* the same case. Second, and more important,
as in a cross-case technique, the case survey has severe limitations in relation
to the multiple-case analysis previously described.

This is because the case survey is unlikely to achieve either theoretical or
statistical generalization. Theoretical generalization is precluded because the
selection of the individual cases, unlike in a true multiple-case design, is
beyond the control of the investigator (being a secondary analysis) and is
therefore not based on any replication logic (the exception would be the rare

situation in which hundreds of individual cases were designed and conducted specifically as part of the same investigation, and in which the case survey was a primary and not a secondary analytic technique). Similarly, statistical generalization is precluded because the selection of the individual cases, again beyond the control of the investigator, is not based on any sampling logic.

However, this problem of generalization is not always relevant when doing a case survey. The survey may simply have been undertaken to synthesize the existing case studies on a topic, and in this situation neither theoretical nor statistical generalization would be of concern. Thus, the case survey is a relevant technique when the research objective is explicitly that of a secondary analysis—for example, to determine "what the existing literature says" about a certain topic. In such situations, the case survey is in fact preferred over other modes of "reviewing the literature," which generally reflect subjective judgments in the selection of the relevant studies and the amount of attention given to each. The case survey technique can minimize these biases and is the desired technique if it is applicable. However, the case survey should not be considered a dominant mode of analysis for designing and doing a fresh set of case studies.

PRESSING FOR A
HIGH-QUALITY ANALYSIS

No matter what specific analytic strategy is chosen, you must do everything to make sure that your analysis is of the highest quality. At least four principles appear to underlie all good social science (Yin, 1994) and require your attention.

First, your analysis should show that it relied on *all the relevant evidence*. Your analytic strategies, including the development of rival hypotheses, must be exhaustive. Your analysis should show how it sought as much evidence as was available, and your interpretations should account for all of this evidence and leave no loose ends.

Second, your analysis should include *all major rival interpretations*. If someone else has an alternative explanation for one or more of your findings, make this alternative into a rival. Is there evidence to address this rival? If so, what are the results? If not, how can the rival be restated as a loose end to be investigated in future studies?

Third, your analysis should address *the most significant aspect of your case study*. Whether it is a single- or multiple-case study, you will have demon-

---

BOX 29
Analytic Quality in a Multiple-Case Study of
International Trade Competition

The quality of a case study analysis is not dependent solely on the techniques used, although they are important. Equally important is that the investigator demonstrate expertise in carrying out the analysis. This expertise was reflected in Magaziner and Patinkin's book, *The Silent War: Inside the Global Business Battles Shaping America's Future* (1989).

Although the authors were management consultants and not academic social scientists, their nine cases were organized excellently. Across cases, major themes regarding America's competitive advantages (and disadvantages) were covered in a replication design. Within each case, the authors provided extensive interview and other documentation, showing the sources for their findings. (To keep the narrative reading smoothly, much of the data—in word tables, footnotes, and quantitative data—were relegated to footnotes and appendixes.) In addition, the authors showed that they had extensive personal exposure to the issues being studied, as a result of numerous domestic and overseas visits.

Technically, a more explicit "methodology" would have been helpful. However, the careful and detailed work in the absence of such a methodology helps to illustrate what more academically oriented investigators should strive to achieve as they apply more formal methodologies.

---

strated your best analytic skills if the analysis is on the biggest target. Why go to the effort of doing a case study unless you can address the largest issue?

Fourth, you should bring your own *prior, expert knowledge* to your case study. The strong preference here is for you to have analyzed similar issues in the past and to be aware of current thinking and debates about the case study topic. If you know your subject matter as a result of previous investigations and publications, so much the better.

The case study in BOX 29 was done by a management consultant, not an academic social scientist. Nevertheless, because several steps were taken, the author demonstrated a care for the empirical investigation whose spirit is worth consideration by all case study investigators. Remarkably, the care is reflected in the presentation of the cases themselves, and not just because of the existence of a stringent "methodology" section. If you can emulate these and other strategies in your analysis, your case study analysis also will be given appropriate respect and recognition.

SUMMARY

This chapter has presented several important strategies for analyzing case studies. First, the potential analytic difficulties can be reduced if an investigator has a general strategy for analyzing the data—whether such a strategy is based on theoretical propositions or a basic descriptive framework. In the absence of such a strategy, the investigator is encouraged to "play with the data" in a preliminary sense, as a prelude to developing a systematic sense of what is worth analyzing and how it should be analyzed.

Second, given a general strategy, several specific analytic strategies can be used. Of these, four strategies (pattern-matching, explanation-building, time-series analysis, and program logic models) are effective ways of laying the groundwork for high-quality case studies. For all four, a similar replication logic should be applied if the study involves multiple cases (thereby gaining external validity), but important comparisons to rival propositions and threats to internal validity should be made within each individual case.

Three other strategies (analyzing embedded units, making repeated observations, and doing case surveys) are incomplete ways of doing case study analysis. In general, these latter procedures must be used in conjunction with one of the other techniques in order to have an effective analysis.

None of these strategies is easy to use. None can be applied mechanically, following any simple cookbook procedure. Not surprisingly, case study analysis is the most difficult stage of doing case studies, and novice investigators are especially likely to have a troublesome experience. Again, one recommendation to the novice is to begin a case study career with a simple and straightforward case study, even if the research questions are not as sophisticated or innovative as might be desired. As experience is gained in completing such simpler case studies, the novice will become capable of tackling the more difficult research.

EXERCISES

1. *Analyzing the analytic process.* Select one of the case studies described in the BOXES of this book. Find one of the chapters (usually in the middle of the study) in which evidence is presented but conclusions also are being made. Describe how this linkage—from cited evidence to conclusions—occurs. Are data displayed in tables or other formats? Are comparisons being made?

2. *Merging quantitative and qualitative data.* Name some topic within a case study you might be conducting for which both qualitative and quantitative data might be relevant. Identify the two types of data, assume they have been

collected successfully, and discuss the ways in which they would be combined or compared. What is the value of having each type of data?

3. *Matching patterns.* Name a case study that used a pattern-matching technique in its analysis. What peculiar advantages and disadvantages does it have to offer? How can the technique produce a compelling analysis even when applied only to a single case?

4. *Constructing an explanation.* Identify some observable changes that have been occurring in your neighborhood (or the neighborhood around your campus). Develop an explanation for these changes, and indicate the critical set of evidence you would collect to support or challenge this explanation. If such evidence were available, would your explanation be complete? Compelling? Useful for investigating similar changes in another neighborhood?

5. *Analyzing time-series trends.* Identify a simple time series—for example, the number of students enrolled in your university for each of the past 20 years. How would you compare one period of time with another within the 20-year period? If the university admissions policies had changed during this time, how would you compare the effects of such policies? How might this analysis be considered part of a broader case study of your university?

6

Composing the Case Study "Report"

The reporting of a case study can take written or oral forms. Regardless of the form, however, similar steps need to be followed in the compositional process: identifying the audience for the report, developing the compositional structure, and following certain procedures (such as having the report reviewed by informed persons who have been the subject of the case study).

The reporting phase is one of the most difficult to carry out in doing case studies. The best general advice is to compose portions of the case study early (e.g., the bibliography) and to keep drafting various pieces of the report (e.g., the methodological section) rather than waiting until the end of the data analysis process. As for compositional structures, six alternatives are suggested: linear-analytic, comparative, chronological, theory-building, "suspense," and unsequenced structures.

As a general rule, the compositional phase puts the greatest demands on a case study investigator. The case study "report" does not follow any stereotypical form, such as a journal article in psychology. Moreover, the "report" need not be in written form only. Because of this uncertain nature, researchers who do not like to compose probably should not do case studies.

Of course, most investigators can eventually learn to compose easily and well, and inexperience in composing should not be a deterrent to doing case studies. However, much practice will be needed. Furthermore, you should want to become good at composing—and not merely put up with it. One indicator of whether you are likely to succeed at this phase of the craft is whether term papers were easy or difficult to do in high school or college. The more difficult they were, the more difficult it will be to compose a case study report. Another indicator is whether composing is viewed as an opportunity or as a burden. The successful investigator usually perceives the compositional phase as an opportunity—to make a significant contribution to knowledge or practice.

Unfortunately, few people are forewarned about this problem that lies at the end of designing and doing a case study. However, the smart investigator will begin to compose the case study report even before data collection and analysis have been completed. In general, whether the "report" takes a written, oral, or pictorial form (the quotation marks are used to remind you that a report can take all of these forms, not just the written form), the compositional phase is so important that it should be given explicit attention throughout the earlier phases of a case study.

Despite this advice, most investigators typically ignore the compositional phase until the very end of their case studies. Under these circumstances, all sorts of "writer's cramps" may appear, and the case study report may become impossible to compose. Thus, a prelude to any case study research may be to consult a textbook covering the writing of research reports more generally (see Barzun & Graff, 1985). Such texts offer invaluable reminders for taking notes, making outlines, using plain words, writing clear sentences, establishing a schedule for composing, and combatting the common urge not to compose.

The purpose of this chapter is not to repeat these general lessons, although they are applicable to case studies. Most of the lessons are important to all forms of research composition, and to describe them here would defeat the purpose of providing information specific to case studies. Instead, the main purpose of this chapter is to highlight those aspects of composition and reporting that are directly related to case studies. These include the following topics, each covered in a separate section:

- Audiences for case studies
- Varieties of case study compositions
- Illustrative structures for case study compositions
- Procedures to be followed in doing a case study report
- And, in conclusion, speculations on the characteristics of an exemplary case study (extending beyond the report itself and covering the design and content of the case)

One reminder from Chapter 4 is that the case study report should not be the main way of recording or storing the evidentiary base of the case study. Rather, Chapter 4 advocated the use of a case study database for this purpose (see Chapter 4, Principle 2), and the compositional efforts described in this chapter are primarily intended to serve reportorial, and not documentation, objectives.

BOX 30
Famous Case Study Reprinted

For many years, Philip Selznick's *TVA and the Grass Roots* (1949) has stood as a classic about public organizations. The case has been cited in many subsequent studies of federal agencies, political behavior, and organizational decentralization.

Fully 30 years after its original publication, this case was reprinted in 1980 as part of the Library Reprint Series by the University of California Press, the original publisher. This type of reissuance allows numerous other researchers to have access to this famous case study and reflects its substantial contribution to the field.

AUDIENCES FOR CASE STUDIES

Range of Possible Audiences

Case studies have a more diverse set of possible audiences than do most other types of research. These audiences include: (a) colleagues in the same field; (b) policymakers, practitioners, community leaders, and other professionals who do not specialize in case study methodology; (c) special groups such as a student's dissertation or thesis committee; and (d) funders of research.[1]

With most research reports, such as experiments, the second audience is not typically relevant, as few would expect the results of a laboratory experiment to be directed to nonspecialists. However, for case studies, this second audience may be a frequent target of the case study report. As another contrast, the third audience would rarely be relevant for some types of research—such as evaluations—because evaluations are not usually suitable as theses or dissertations. However, for case studies, this third audience also is a frequent consumer of the case study report, due to the large number of theses and dissertations in the social sciences that rely on case studies.

Because case studies have more potential audiences than other types of research, an essential task in designing the overall case study report is to identify the specific audiences for the report. Each audience has different needs, and no single report will serve all audiences simultaneously.

For *colleagues*, the relationships among the case study, its findings, and previous theory or research are likely to be most important. If a case study

---

BOX 31
Two Versions of the Same Case Study

The city planning office of Broward County, Florida, implemented an office automation system beginning in 1982 ("The Politics of Automating a Planning Office," Standerfer & Rider, 1983). The implementation strategies were innovative and significant—especially in relation to tensions with the county government's computer department. As a result, the case study is interesting and informative, and a popularized version—appearing in a practitioner journal—is fun and easy to read.

Because this type of implementation also covers complex technical issues, the authors made supplementary information available to the interested reader. The popularized version provided a name, address, and telephone number, so that such a reader could obtain the additional information. This type of dual availability of case study reports is but one example of how different reports of the *same* case study may be useful for communicating with different audiences.

---

succeeds in conveying these relationships, it may be widely read for a long period of time (see BOX 30 for an example). For *nonspecialists*, the descriptive elements in portraying some real-life situation, as well as the implications for action, are likely to be more important. For a *thesis committee*, mastery of the methodology and the theoretical issues of a case study topic, an indication of the care with which the research was conducted, and evidence that the student has successfully negotiated all phases of the research process are important. Finally, for *research funders*, the significance of the case study findings, whether cast in academic or practical terms, is probably as important as the rigor with which the research was conducted. Because of these differences among audiences, successful communication with more than one audience may mean the need for more than one version of a case study report. Investigators should seriously consider catering to such a need (see BOX 31).

Communicating With Case Studies

One additional difference between the case study and other types of research is that the case study report can itself be a significant communication device. For many nonspecialists, the description and analysis of a single case often conveys information about a more general phenomenon.

BOX 32
Making a Good Case Study
Available to a Wider Audience

Neustadt and Fineberg's excellent analysis of a mass immunization campaign was issued originally as a government report in 1978, *The Swine Flu Affair: Decision-Making on a Slippery Disease*. This case study was thereafter cited, among public policy circles, as an example of a thorough and high-quality case study, and the case also was used frequently for teaching purposes.

The original form of the case study, however, was difficult to obtain, having been published by the U.S. Government Printing Office, which, according to the authors, "has many virtues, . . . but . . . filling orders which do not have exact change and precise stock numbers is not one of them" (1983, p. xxiv). As a result, a revised version of the original case study—adding new material to the original case—was later published as *The Epidemic That Never Was: Policy-Making and the Swine Flu Affair* (1983). This commercial issuance of such a highly regarded case study is a rare example of what can be done to improve the dissemination of case studies.

A related situation, often overlooked, occurs when testimony is made before a committee of the U.S. Congress. If an elderly person, for instance, testifies about his or her health services before such a committee, its members may assume that they have acquired an understanding of health care for the elderly more generally—based on this "case." Only then might the committee be able to interpret broader statistics about the prevalence of similar cases. Later, the committee may inquire about the representative nature of the initial case, before proposing new legislation. However, throughout this entire process, the initial "case"—represented by a witness—may have been the essential ingredient in calling attention to the health care issue in the first place.

In these and other ways, case studies can communicate research-based information about a phenomenon to a variety of nonspecialists. In this manner, the usefulness of case studies goes far beyond the role of the typical research report, which is generally addressed to colleagues rather than nonspecialists (see BOX 32). Obviously, descriptive as well as explanatory case studies can be important in this role, and the smart investigator should not overlook the potential descriptive impact of a well-presented case study.[2]

Orienting the Case Study Report
to an Audience's Needs

Overall, the presumed preferences of the potential audience should dictate the form of a case study report. Although the research procedures and methodology should have followed other guidelines, suggested in Chapters 1 through 5, the report itself should reflect emphases, detail, compositional forms, and even a length suitable to the needs of the potential audience. You should formally collect information about what the audiences need and their preferred types of communication (Morris, Fitz-Gibbon, & Freeman, 1987, p. 13). Along these lines, this author has frequently called the attention of thesis or dissertation students to the fact that the thesis or dissertation committee may be their *only* audience. The ultimate report, under these conditions, should attempt to communicate directly with this committee. A recommended tactic is to integrate the committee members' previous research into the thesis or dissertation, thereby increasing its potential communicability.

Whatever the audience, the greatest error an investigator can make is to compose a report from an egocentric perspective. This error will occur if a report is completed without identifying a specific audience or without understanding the specific needs of such an audience. To avoid this error, one suggestion is to identify the audience, as previously noted. A second and equally important suggestion is to examine previous case study reports that have successfully communicated with this audience. Such prior reports may offer helpful clues for composing a new report. For instance, consider again the thesis or dissertation student. The student should consult previous dissertations and theses that have passed the academic regimen successfully—or are known to have been exemplary documents. The inspection of such documents may yield sound information regarding the departmental norms (and reviewers' likely preferences) for the design of the new thesis or dissertation.

VARIETIES OF
CASE STUDY COMPOSITIONS

Written Versus Nonwritten "Reports"

A case study "report" need not take written form only. The information and data from a case can be reported in other ways—as an oral presentation or even a set of pictures or videotapes. Even though most case studies do ultimately appear as written products, a deliberate task is to select the most relevant and effective mode for any given "report." The choice will clearly interact with that of identifying the case study audience.

However, written products do offer several important advantages. More precise information can be conveyed and communicated than through oral or pictorial forms. Although the maxim about the picture being worth "a thousand words" is often true, most case studies are about abstract concepts—such as organizational structure, implementation, public programs, and social group interactions—not readily converted into pictorial form. Individual pictures can often enhance a written text (see Dabbs, 1982), but the text will be difficult to replace in its entirety. This author knows of one situation in which pictures did play a critical role in conveying information about neighborhood organizations to policymakers who had never visited such organizations. However, even though the photographs improved the communication of the case study information, they did not replace the need for other types of evidence, which in turn gave more credibility to the findings and conclusions.

The written product also has the advantage of familiarity, both for the writer and for the reader. Most of us have practiced composing or reviewing written reports and are aware of the general problems of expressing—in an unbiased but compact manner—data and ideas through sentences, tables, and chapters. In contrast, these relationships are less well understood with other modes of communication. For instance, in another situation known to the author, a thesis student selected a videotape as the medium of communication. However, neither the student nor the reviewers could explain how the rules used to edit the tape—reflecting the "artistry" of the author—in fact affected the evidence and presentation of the case. Consequently, an unknown bias was introduced through the editing process.

Nevertheless, innovative forms of presentation should still be sought. And written materials should be readily complemented by attractive visuals and graphics (Morris, Fitz-Gibbon, & Freeman, 1987, p. 37). The most desirable innovations should deal with a major disadvantage of the written case study—its bulkiness and length. In such a form, case study information is being stored in an inefficient and cumbersome manner. Imagine a comparison between the review of some survey data and of some case study data. For the former, a computer tape or disk would contain a large amount of survey information and be susceptible to intensive and precise probes; for the latter, a similar amount of information is likely to require a huge amount of text, an inefficient retrieval procedure, and substantial time for review.[3]

Varieties of Written Reports

Among written forms of case studies, there are at least four important varieties. The first is the classic single-case study. A single narrative is used to describe and analyze the case. Furthermore, the narrative information may be augmented with tabular as well as graphic and pictorial displays. Depending upon the depth of the case study, these classic single cases are likely to appear as books, as journals cannot accommodate the needed space. (Some sociologists also claim that journals discriminate against case study research—Feagin, Orum, & Sjoberg, 1991—however, case studies are the second largest and fastest growing category of empirical studies in the leading journal in public administration—Perry & Kraemer, 1986.) As a word of advice, if you know ahead of time that your case study will fall into this category, and that you can produce only a book-length manuscript, you should be establishing some early contact with a publisher.

A second type of written product is the multiple-case version of this classic single case. This type of multiple-case report will contain multiple narratives, usually presented as separate chapters or sections, about each of the cases singly. In addition to these individual case narratives, the report also will contain a chapter or section covering the cross-case analysis and results. Some situations may even call for several cross-case chapters or sections (see BOX 33), and the cross-case portion of the final text may justify a volume separate from the individual case narratives. In these situations, a frequent form of presentation is to have the bulk of the main report contain the cross-case analysis, with the individual cases presented as part of a long appendix to that basic volume.

A third type of written product covers either a multiple- or a single-case study but does not contain the traditional narrative. Instead, the composition for each case follows a series of questions and answers, based on the questions and answers in the case study database (see Chapter 4). For reporting purposes, the content of the database is shortened and edited for readability, with the final product still assuming the format, analogously, of a comprehensive examination. (In contrast, the traditional case study narrative may be considered similar to the format of a term paper.) This question-and-answer format may not reflect the full, creative talent of an investigator, but the format is helpful in avoiding the problems of writer's cramps. This is because an investigator can proceed immediately to answer the required set of questions. (Again, the comprehensive exam has a similar advantage over a term paper.)

BOX 33
A Multiple-Case Report

Multiple-case studies often contain both the individual case studies and some cross-case chapters. The composition of such a multiple-case study also may be shared among several authors.

This type of arrangement was used in one study of rural school districts by Herriott and Gross, *The Dynamics of Planned Educational Change* (1979). The final report, a book, contained 10 chapters. Five of them were the individual case narratives. Five more covered significant cross-case issues. Moreover, as a reflection of the actual division of labor in conducting the research, each of the chapters was written by a different person.

If this question-and-answer format has been used for multiple-case studies, the advantages are potentially enormous: A reader need only examine the answers to the same question or questions within each case study to begin making cross-case comparisons. Because each reader may be interested in different questions, the entire format facilitates the development of a cross-case analysis tailored to the specific interests of its readers (see BOX 34).

The fourth and last type of written product applies to multiple-case studies only. In this situation, there may be *no* separate chapters or sections devoted to the individual cases. Rather, the entire report may consist of the cross-case analysis, whether purely descriptive or also covering explanatory topics. In such a report, each chapter or section would be devoted to a separate cross-case issue, and the information from the individual cases would be dispersed throughout each chapter or section. With this format, summary information about the individual cases, if not ignored altogether (see BOX 35), might be presented in abbreviated vignettes.

As a final note, the specific type of case study composition, involving a choice among at least these four alternatives, should be identified during the *design* of the case study. The initial choice can always be altered, as unexpected conditions may arise, and a different type of composition may become more relevant than the one originally selected. However, early selection will facilitate both the design and the conduct of the case study. Such an initial selection should be part of the case study protocol, alerting the case study investigator(s) to the likely nature of the final composition and its requirements.

BOX 34
A Question-and-Answer Format:
Case Studies Without the Traditional Narrative

Case study evidence does not need to be presented in the traditional narrative form. An alternative format for presenting the same evidence is to write the narrative in question-and-answer form. A series of questions can be posed, with the answers taking some reasonable length—for example, three or four paragraphs each. Each answer can contain all the relevant evidence and can even be augmented with tabular presentations.

This alternative was followed in 40 case studies of community organizations produced by the U.S. National Commission on Neighborhoods, *People, Building Neighborhoods* (1979). The same question-and-answer format was used in each case, so that the interested reader could do his or her own cross-case analysis by following the same question across all of the cases. The format allowed hurried readers to find exactly the relevant portions of each case. For people offended by the absence of the traditional narrative, each case also called for a summary, unconstrained in its form (but no longer than three pages), allowing the author to exercise his or her more literary talents.

ILLUSTRATIVE STRUCTURES
FOR CASE STUDY COMPOSITIONS

The chapters, sections, subtopics, and other components of a report must be organized in some way, and this constitutes the report's structure. Attending to such structure has been a topic of increasing attention with other methodologies. For instance, Kidder and Judd (1986, pp. 430-431) write of the "hourglass" shape of a report for quantitative studies. Similarly, in ethnography, John Van Maanen (1988) has developed the concept of "tales" for reporting fieldwork results. He has identified several different types of tales: realist tales, confessional tales, impressionist tales, critical tales, formal tales, literary tales, and jointly told tales. These different types may be used in different combinations in the same report.

Alternatives also exist for structuring case study reports. The purpose of this section is to suggest some illustrative structures, which may be used with any of the types of case study composition just described. Six structures are suggested, with the hope that they will reduce an investigator's compositional problems:

BOX 35
A. Writing a Multiple-Case Report:
An Example in Which No Single Cases
Are Presented

In a multiple-case study, the individual case studies need not always be presented in the final manuscript. The individual cases, in a sense, serve only as the evidentiary base for the study and may be used solely in the cross-case analysis.

This approach was used in a book about six federal bureau chiefs, by Herbert Kaufman, *The Administrative Behavior of Federal Bureau Chiefs* (1981). Kaufman spent intensive periods of time with each chief to understand his day-to-day routine. He interviewed the chiefs, listened in on their phone calls, attended meetings, and was present during staff discussions in the chiefs' offices.

The book's purpose, however, was not to portray any single one of these chiefs. Rather, the book synthesizes the lessons from all of them and is organized around such topics as how chiefs decide things, how they receive and review information, and how they motivate their staffs. Under each topic, Kaufman draws appropriate examples from the six cases, but none of the six is presented as a single-case study.

B. Writing a Multiple-Case Report:
An Example (from Another Field) in Which
No Single Cases Are Presented

A design similar to Kaufman's is used in another field—history—in a famous book by Crane Brinton, *The Anatomy of a Revolution* (1938). Brinton's book is based on four revolutions: the English, American, French, and Russian revolutions. The book is an analysis and theory of revolutionary periods, with pertinent examples drawn from each of the four "cases"; however, as in Kaufman's book, there is no attempt to present the single revolutions as individual case studies.

---

1. linear-analytic structures,
2. comparative structures,
3. chronological structures,
4. theory-building structures,

Type of Structure	Purpose of Case Study (single- or multiple-case)		
	Explanatory	Descriptive	Exploratory
1. Linear-analytic	X	X	X
2. Comparative	X	X	X
3. Chronological	X	X	X
4. Theory-building	X		X
5. "Suspense"	X		
6. Unsequenced		X	

Figure 6.1. Application of Six Structures to Different Purposes of Case Studies

5. "suspense" structures, and
6. unsequenced structures.

The illustrations are described mainly in relation to the composition of a single-case study, although the principles are readily translatable into multiple-case reports. As a further note, the first three are all applicable to descriptive, exploratory, and explanatory case studies. The fourth is applicable mainly to exploratory and explanatory case studies; the fifth, to explanatory cases; and the sixth, to descriptive cases (see Figure 6.1).

Linear-Analytic Structures

This is a standard approach for composing research reports. The sequence of subtopics involves the issue or problem being studied, a review of the relevant prior literature, the methods used, the findings from the data collected and analyzed, and the conclusions and implications from the findings.

Most journal articles in experimental science reflect this type of structure, as do many case studies. The structure is comfortable to most investigators and probably is the most advantageous when research colleagues or a thesis or dissertation committee constitutes the main audience for a case study. Note that the structure is applicable to explanatory, descriptive, or exploratory case studies. For example, an exploratory case may cover the issue or problem being explored, the methods of exploration, the findings from the exploration, and the conclusions (for further research).

Comparative Structures

A comparative structure repeats the same case study two or more times, comparing alternative descriptions or explanations of the same case. This is best exemplified in Graham Allison's noted case study on the Cuban missile crisis (1971). In this book, the author repeats the "facts" of the case study three times, each time in conjunction with a different conceptual model of how bureaucracy operates (see Chapter 1, BOX 2). The purpose of the repetition is to show the degree to which the facts fit each model, and the repetitions actually illustrate a pattern-matching technique at work.

A similar approach can be used even if a case study is serving descriptive, and not explanatory, purposes. The same case can be described repeatedly, from different points of view or with different descriptive models, to understand how the case might best be categorized for descriptive purposes—as in arriving at the correct diagnosis for a clinical patient in psychology. Of course, other variants of the comparative approach are possible, but the main feature is that the entire case study (or the results of the cross-case analysis) is repeated two or more times in an overtly comparative mode.

Chronological Structures

Because case studies generally cover events over time, a third type of approach is to present the case study evidence in chronological order. Here, the sequence of chapters or sections might follow the early, middle, and late phases of a case history. This approach can serve an important purpose in doing explanatory case studies, because causal sequences must occur linearly over time. If a presumed cause of an event occurs after the event has occurred, one would have reason to question the initial causal proposition.

Whether for explanatory or descriptive purposes, a chronological approach has one pitfall to be avoided: Disproportionate attention is usually given to the early events and insufficient attention to the later ones. Most commonly, an investigator will expend too much effort in composing the introduction to a case, including its early history and background, and leave insufficient time to write about the current status of the case. To avoid this situation, one recommendation, when using a chronological structure, is to *draft* the case study *backward*. Those chapters or sections that are about the current status of the case should be drafted first, and only after these drafts have been completed should the background to the case study be drafted. Once all drafts have been completed, you can then return to the normal chronological sequence in composing the final version of the case.

Theory-Building Structures

In this approach, the sequence of chapters or sections will follow some theory-building logic. The logic will depend on the specific topic and theory, but each chapter or section should unravel a new part of the theoretical argument being made. If structured well, the entire sequence produces a compelling statement that can be most impressive.

The approach is relevant to both explanatory and exploratory case studies, both of which can be concerned with theory-building. Explanatory cases will be examining the various facets of a causal argument; exploratory cases will be debating the value of further investigating various hypotheses or propositions.

Suspense Structures

This structure inverts the analytic approach. The direct "answer" or outcome of a case study is, paradoxically, presented in the initial chapter or section. The remainder of the case study—and its most suspenseful parts—is then devoted to the development of an explanation of this outcome, with alternative explanations considered in the ensuing chapters or sections.

This type of approach is relevant mainly to explanatory case studies, as a descriptive case study has no especially important outcome. When used well, the suspense approach is often an engaging compositional structure.

Unsequenced Structures

An unsequenced structure is one in which the sequence of sections or chapters assumes no particular importance. This structure is often sufficient for descriptive case studies, as in the example of *Middletown* (Lynd & Lynd, 1929), cited in Chapter 5. Basically, one could change the order of the chapters in that book and not alter its descriptive value.

Descriptive case studies of organizations often exhibit the same characteristic. Such case studies cover an organization's genesis and history, its ownership and employees, its product lines, its formal lines of organization, and its financial status, in separate chapters or sections. The particular order in which these chapters or sections is presented is not critical and may therefore be regarded as an unsequenced approach (also see BOX 36 for another example).

BOX 36
Unsequenced Chapters, But in a Best-Selling Book

A best-selling book, appealing to both popular and academic audiences, was Peters and Waterman's *In Search of Excellence* (1982). Although the book is based on more than 60 case studies of America's most successful large businesses, the text contains only the cross-case analysis, each chapter covering an insightful set of general characteristics associated with organizational excellence. However, the particular sequence of these chapters is alterable. The book would make a significant contribution even if the chapters were in some other order.

If an unsequenced structure is used, the investigator does need to attend to one other problem: a test of completeness. Thus, even though the order of the chapters or sections may not matter, the overall collection does. If certain key topics are left uncovered, the description may be regarded as incomplete. An investigator must know a topic well enough—or have related models of case studies to reference—to avoid such a shortcoming. If a case study fails, without excuse, to present a complete description, the investigator can be accused of being biased—even though the case study was only descriptive.

PROCEDURES IN DOING A
CASE STUDY REPORT

Every person should have a well-developed set of procedures for analyzing social science data and for composing the report. Numerous texts offer good advice on how you can develop your own customized procedures, including the benefits and pitfalls of using word processing software—which will not necessarily save time (Becker, 1986, p. 160). One common warning is that writing means rewriting—a function not commonly practiced by students and therefore underestimated during the early years of research careers (Becker, 1986, pp. 43-47). The more the rewriting, especially in response to others' comments, the better the report is likely to be. In this respect, the case study report is not much different from other reports.

However, three important procedures pertain specifically to case studies and deserve further mention. The first deals with a general tactic for starting a composition, the second covers the problem of whether to leave the case identities anonymous, and the third describes a review procedure for increasing the *construct validity* of a case study.

When and How to Start Composing

The first procedure is to start composing early in the analytic process. One guide in fact admonishes that "you cannot begin writing early enough" (Wolcott, 1990, p. 20). From nearly the beginning of an investigation, certain sections of the report will always be draftable, and this drafting should proceed even before data collection and analysis have been completed.

For instance, after the literature has been reviewed and the case study has been designed, two sections of a case study report can be drafted: the bibliography and the methodological sections. The *bibliography* can always be augmented later with new citations if necessary, but by and large the major citations will have been covered in relation to the literature review. This is therefore the time to formalize the citations, to be sure that they are complete, and to construct a draft bibliography. If some citations are incomplete, the remaining details can be tracked down while the rest of the case study proceeds. This will avoid the usual practice among researchers, who do the bibliography last and who therefore spend much clerical time at the very end of their research, rather than attending to the more important (and pleasurable!) tasks of writing, rewriting, and editing.

The *methodological section* also can be drafted at this stage because the major procedures for data collection and analysis should have become part of the case study design. This section may not even become a formal part of the final narrative but may be designated as an appendix. Whether part of the text or an appendix, however, the methodological section can and should be drafted at this early stage. You will remember your methodological procedures with greater precision at this juncture.

After data collection but before analysis begins, another section that can be composed covers the *descriptive data about the cases being studied*. Whereas the methodological section should have included the issues regarding the selection of the case(s), the descriptive data should cover qualitative and quantitative information about the case(s). At this stage in the research process, you may not have finalized your ideas about the type of composition to be used and the type of structure to be followed. If this is true, the descriptive sections may still be drafted in abbreviated form, and the drafting itself may stimulate your thinking about an overall compositional structure.

If you can draft these three sections before analysis has been completed, you will have made a major advance. Further, these sections can call for substantial documentation, and the best time to assemble such documentation is at this stage of the research. You also will be at an advantage if all details—citations, references, organizational titles, and spellings of people's names—have been accurately recorded during data collection and are integrated into the text at this time (Wolcott, 1990, p. 41).

If these sections are drafted properly, more attention can then be devoted to the analysis itself as well as to the findings and conclusions. To begin composing early also serves another important, psychological function: You may get accustomed to the compositional process and have a chance to practice it before the task becomes truly awesome. Thus, if you are doing a case study and can identify other sections that can be drafted at these early stages, you should draft them as well.

Case Identities: Real or Anonymous?

Nearly every case study presents an investigator with a choice regarding the anonymity of the case. Should the case study and its informants be accurately identified, or should the names of the entire case and its participants be disguised? Note that the anonymity issue can be raised at two levels: that of the entire case (or cases) and that of an individual person within a case (or cases).

The most desirable option is to disclose the identities of both the case and the individuals. Disclosure produces two helpful outcomes. First, the reader is able to recall any other previous information he or she may have learned about the same case—from previous research or other sources—in reading and interpreting the case report. This ability to integrate a new case study with prior research is invaluable, similar to the ability to recollect previous experimental results when reading about a new set of experiments. Second, the entire case can be reviewed more readily, so that footnotes and citations can be checked, if necessary, and appropriate criticisms can be raised about the published case.

Nevertheless, there are some occasions when anonymity is necessary. The most common rationale is that, when the case study has been on a controversial topic, anonymity serves to protect the real case and its real participants. A second reason is that the issuance of the final case report may affect the subsequent actions of those that were studied. This rationale was used in Whyte's famous case study, *Street Corner Society* (which was about an anonymous neighborhood, "Cornerville").[4] As a third illustrative situation, the purpose of the case study may be to portray an "ideal type," and there may be no reason for disclosing true identities in such a case. This rationale was used by the Lynds in their study *Middletown*, in which the names of the small town, its residents, and its industries all were disguised.

On such occasions when anonymity may appear justifiable, however, other compromises should still be sought. First, you should determine whether the anonymity of the individuals alone might be sufficient, thereby leaving the case itself to be identified accurately.

A second compromise would be to name the individuals but to avoid attributing any particular point of view or comment to a single individual, again allowing the case itself to be identified accurately. This second alternative is most relevant when you want to protect the confidentiality of specific individuals. However, the lack of attribution may not always be completely protective—you also may have to disguise the comments so that no one involved in the case can infer the likely source.

For multiple-case studies, a third compromise would be to avoid composing any single-case reports and to compose only a cross-case analysis. This last situation would be roughly parallel to the procedure used in surveys, in which the individual responses are not disclosed and in which the only published report is about the aggregate evidence.

Only if these compromises are impossible to use should an investigator consider making the entire case study and its informants anonymous. However, anonymity is not to be considered a desirable outcome. Not only does it eliminate some important background information about the case, but it also makes the mechanics of composing the case difficult. The case and its components must be systematically converted from their real identities to fictitious ones, and you must undergo considerable effort to keep track of the conversions. The cost of undertaking such a procedure should not be underestimated.

The Review of the Draft Case Study: A Validating Procedure

A third procedure to be followed in doing the case study report is related to the overall quality of the study. The procedure is to have the draft report reviewed, not just by peers (as would be done for any academic endeavor) but also by the participants and informants in the case. If the comments are exceptionally helpful, the investigator may even want to publish them as part of the entire case study (see BOX 37).

Such review is more than a matter of professional courtesy. The procedure has been correctly identified—but only rarely—as a way of corroborating the essential facts and evidence presented in the case report (Schatzman &

BOX 37
Reviewing Case Studies—
and Printing the Comments

A major way of improving the quality of case studies and ensuring their construct validity is to have the draft cases reviewed by those who have been the subjects of study. This procedure was followed to an exemplary degree in a set of five case studies by Marvin Alkin et al. (1979).

Each case study was about a school district and the way that district used evaluative information about its students' performance. As part of the analytic and reporting procedure, the draft for each case was reviewed by the informants from the relevant district. The comments were obtained in part as a result of an open-ended questionnaire devised by the investigators for just this purpose. In some instances, the responses were so insightful and helpful that the investigators not only modified their original material but also printed the responses as part of their book.

With such presentation of supplementary evidence and comments, any reader can reach his or her own conclusions about the adequacy of the cases—an opportunity that has occurred, unfortunately, all too seldom in traditional case study research.

Strauss, 1973, p. 134). The informants and participants may still disagree with an investigator's conclusions and interpretations, but these reviewers should not disagree over the actual facts of the case. If such disagreement emerges during the review process, an investigator knows that the case study report is not finished and that such disagreements must be settled through a search for further evidence. Often, the opportunity to review the draft also produces further evidence, as the informants and participants may remember new materials that they had forgotten during the initial data collection period.

This type of review should be followed even if the case study or some of its components are to remain anonymous. Under this condition, some recognizable version of the draft must be shared with the case study informants or participants. After they have reviewed this draft, and after any differences in facts have been settled, the investigator can disguise the identities so that only the informants or participants will know the true identities. Even 40 years ago, when Whyte first completed *Street Corner Society*, he followed this procedure by sharing drafts of his book with "Doc," his major informant. He notes,

---

BOX 38
Formal Reviews of Case Studies

As with any other research product, the review process plays an important role in enhancing and ensuring the quality of the final results. For case studies, such a review process should involve, at a minimum, a review of the draft case study.

One set of case studies that followed this procedure, to an exemplary degree, was sponsored by the U.S. Office of Technology Assessment (1980-1981). Each of 17 case studies, which were about medical technologies, was "seen by at least 20, and some by 40 or more, outside reviewers." Furthermore, the reviewers reflected different perspectives, including those of government agencies, professional societies, consumer and public interest groups, medical practice, academic medicine, and economics and decision sciences.

In one of the case studies, a contrary view of the case—put forth by one of the reviewers—was included as part of the final published version of the case, as well as a response by the case study authors. This type of open printed interchange adds to the reader's ability to interpret the case study's conclusions and therefore to the overall quality of the case study evidence.

As I wrote, I showed the various parts to Doc and went over them with him in detail. His criticisms were invaluable in my revision. (Whyte, 1943/1955, p. 341)

From a methodological viewpoint, the corrections made through this process will enhance the accuracy of the case study, hence increasing the *construct validity* of the study. The likelihood of falsely reporting an event should be reduced. In addition, where no objective truth may exist—as when different participants indeed have different renditions of the same event—the procedure should help to identify the various perspectives, which then can be represented in the case study report.

The review of the draft case study by its informants will clearly extend the period of time needed to complete the case study report. Informants, unlike academic reviewers, may use the review cycles as an opportunity to begin a fresh dialogue about various facets of the case, thereby extending the review period. You must anticipate these delays and not use them as an excuse to avoid the review process altogether. When the process has been given careful attention, the potential result is the production of a high-quality case study (see BOX 38).

WHAT MAKES AN
EXEMPLARY CASE STUDY?

In all of case study research, one of the most challenging tasks is to define an exemplary case study. Although no direct evidence is available, some speculations seem an appropriate way of concluding this book.[5]

The exemplary case study goes beyond the methodological procedures already highlighted throughout this book. Even if you, as a case study investigator, have followed most of the basic techniques—using a case study protocol, maintaining a chain of evidence, establishing a case study database, and so on—you still may not have produced an *exemplary* case study. The mastering of these techniques makes you a good technician but not necessarily an esteemed scientist. To take but one analogy, consider the difference between a chronicler and a historian: The former is technically correct but does not produce the insights into human or social processes provided by the latter.

Five general characteristics of an exemplary case study are described below; they are intended to help you to be more than a mere chronicler and to assume the role of a historian.

The Case Study Must Be Significant

The first general characteristic may be beyond the control of many investigators. If an investigator has access to only a few "sites," or if resources are extremely limited, the ensuing case study may have to be on a topic of only marginal significance. This situation is not likely to produce an exemplary case study. However, where choice exists, the exemplary case study is likely to be one in which:

- The individual case or cases are unusual and of general public interest.
- The underlying issues are nationally important, either in theoretical terms or in policy or practical terms.
- Or they are both of the preceding.

Sometimes, for instance, a single-case study may have been chosen because it was a revelatory case—that is, one reflecting some real-life situation that social scientists had not been able to study in the past. This revelatory case is in itself likely to be regarded as a discovery and to provide an opportunity for doing an exemplary case study. Alternatively, a critical case may have been chosen because of the desire to compare two rival propositions; if the propositions are at the core of a well-known theory—or reflect major strands of thought in a discipline—the case study is likely to be significant. Finally, imagine the situation in which both discovery and theory development are found within the same case study, as in a multiple-case study in which each individual case reveals a discovery but in which the replication across cases also adds up to a significant theoretical breakthrough. This situation truly lends itself to the production of an exemplary case study.

In contrast to these promising situations, many students select nondistinctive cases or stale theoretical issues as the topics for their case studies. This situation can be avoided, in part, by doing better homework with regard to the existing body of research. Prior to selecting a case study, you should describe, in detail, the contribution to be made, assuming that the intended case study were to be completed successfully. If no satisfactory answer is forthcoming, you might reconsider doing the case study.

The Case Study Must Be "Complete"

This characteristic is extremely difficult to describe operationally. However, a sense of completeness is as important in doing a case study as it is in defining a complete set of laboratory experiments (or in completing a symphony or drawing a mural). All have the problem of defining the boundaries of the effort, but few guidelines are available.

For case studies, completeness can be characterized in at least three ways. First, the complete case is one in which the boundaries of the case—that is, the distinction between the phenomenon being studied and its context—are given explicit attention. If this is done only mechanically—for example, by declaring at the outset that only certain time intervals or spatial boundaries will be considered—a nonexemplary case study is likely to result. The best way is to show, through either logical argument or the presentation of evidence, that as the analytic periphery is reached the information is of decreasing relevance to the case study. Such testing of the boundaries can occur throughout the analytic and reporting steps in doing case studies.

A second way involves the collection of evidence. The complete case study should demonstrate convincingly that the investigator expended exhaustive effort in collecting the relevant evidence. The documentation of such evidence need not be placed in the text of the case, thereby dulling its content. Footnotes, appendixes, and the like will do. The overall goal, nevertheless, is to convince the reader that very little relevant evidence remained untouched by the investigator, given the boundaries of the case study. This does not mean that the investigator should literally collect all available evidence—an impossible task—but that the critical pieces have been given "complete" attention. Such critical pieces, for instance, would be those representing rival propositions.

A third way concerns the absence of certain artifactual conditions. A case study is not likely to be complete if the study ended only because resources were exhausted, because the investigator ran out of time (when the semester ended), or because he or she faced other, nonresearch constraints. When a time or resource constraint is known at the outset of a study, the responsible investigator should design a case study that can be completed within such constraints rather than reaching and possibly exceeding his or her limits. This type of design requires much experience and some good fortune. Nevertheless, these are the conditions under which an exemplary case study is likely to be produced. Unfortunately, if in contrast a severe time or resource constraint suddenly emerges in the middle of a case study, it is unlikely that the case study will become exemplary.

The Case Study Must Consider Alternative Perspectives

For explanatory case studies, one valuable approach is the consideration of rival propositions and the analysis of the evidence in terms of such rivals (see Chapter 5). However, even in doing an exploratory or a descriptive case study, the examination of the evidence from different perspectives will increase the chances that a case study will be exemplary.

For instance, a descriptive case study that fails to account for different perspectives may raise a critical reader's suspicions. The investigator may not have collected all the relevant evidence and may have attended only to the evidence supporting a single point of view. Even if the investigator was not purposefully biased, different descriptive interpretations were not entertained, thereby rendering a one-sided case. In the 1960s, this type of problem was demonstrated vividly in debates over the "culture of poverty," in which middle-class investigators were accused of failing to appreciate the true dimensions of lower-class cultures (see Valentine, 1968).

To represent different perspectives adequately, an investigator must seek those alternatives that most seriously challenge the design of the case study. These perspectives may be found in alternative cultural views, different theories, variations among the people or decision makers who are part of the case study, or some similar contrasts. A major prerequisite for all teaching case studies, for instance, is that they be able to present the point of view of all the major actors in the case (Stein, 1952).

Many times, if an investigator describes a case study to a critical listener, the listener will immediately offer an alternative interpretation of the facts of the case. Under such circumstances, the investigator is likely to become defensive and to argue that the original interpretation was the only relevant or correct one. In fact, the exemplary case study anticipates these "obvious" alternatives, even advocates their positions as forcefully as possible, and shows—empirically—the basis upon which such alternatives can be rejected.

The Case Study Must Display Sufficient Evidence

Although Chapter 4 encouraged investigators to create a case study database, the critical pieces of evidence for a case study must still be contained within the case study report. The exemplary case study is one that judiciously and effectively presents the most compelling evidence, so that a reader can reach an independent judgment regarding the merits of the analysis.

This selectiveness does not mean that the evidence should be cited in a biased manner—for example, by including only the evidence that supports an investigator's conclusions. On the contrary, the evidence should be presented neutrally, with both supporting and challenging data. The reader should then be able to conclude, independently, whether a particular interpretation is valid. The selectiveness is relevant in limiting the report to the most critical evidence and not cluttering the presentation with supportive but secondary information. Such selectiveness takes a lot of discipline among investigators, who usually want to display their entire evidentiary base, in the (false) hope that sheer volume or weight will sway the reader. (In fact, sheer volume or weight will bore the reader.)

Another goal is to present enough evidence to gain the reader's confidence that the investigator "knows" his or her subject. In doing a field study, for instance, the evidence presented should convince the reader that the investigator has indeed been in the field, has acted thoughtfully while there, and has become steeped in the issues about the case. A parallel goal exists in multiple-case studies; the investigator should show the reader that all of the single cases have been treated fairly and that the cross-case conclusions have not been biased by undue attention to one or a few of the entire array of cases.

Finally, the display of adequate evidence should be accompanied by some indication that the investigator attended to the validity of the evidence—in maintaining a chain of evidence, for example. This does not mean that all case studies need to be burdened with methodological treatises. A few judicious footnotes can do, some words in the preface of the case study can cover the critical validating steps, or the notes to a table or figure will help. As a negative example, a figure or table that presents evidence without citing its

---

BOX 39
High-Quality and Clear Writing
Can Go Together in a Case Study

A common complaint about case studies is that they are lengthy, cumbersome to read, and boring. This communication problem has been considered independent of whether the case study is of high quality.

Herbert Kaufman's *The Forest Ranger: A Study in Administrative Behavior* (1960) is an excellent exception to this observation. Kaufman's writing is lucid and clear. Moreover, no compromise has been made in the substance of the case, which stands as one of the most highly regarded cases in the field of public administration. Not surprisingly, this book had, by 1981, gone through *nine* printings—three in hardback and six in paperback. Every case study investigator should aspire to this type of record.

---

source is an indication of sloppy research and cautions the reader to be more critical of other aspects of the case study. This is not a situation that produces exemplary case studies.

The Case Study Must Be
Composed in an Engaging Manner

One last global characteristic has to do with the composition of the case study report. Regardless of the modality used (a written report, an oral presentation, or another form), the report should be engaging.

For written reports, this means a clear writing style, but one that constantly entices the reader to continue reading (see BOX 39). A good manuscript is one that "seduces" the eye. If you read such a manuscript, your eye will not want to leave the page but continue to read paragraph after paragraph, page after page, until exhaustion sets in. This type of seduction should be the goal in composing any case study report.

The production of this type of writing calls for talent and experience. The more often that someone has written for the same audience, the more likely that the communication will be effective. However, the clarity of writing also increases with rewriting, which is highly recommended. With the advent of personal computers and word processing software, an investigator has no excuse for shortcutting the rewriting process.

Engagement, enticement, and seduction—these are unusual characteristics of case studies. To produce such a case study requires an investigator
to be enthusiastic about the investigation and to want to communicate the
results widely. In fact, the good investigator might even think that the case
study contains earth-shattering conclusions. This sort of enthusiasm should
pervade the entire investigation and will indeed lead to an exemplary case
study.

EXERCISES

1. *Defining the audience.* Name the alternative types of audiences for a case study
you might compose. Indicate, for each audience, the features of the case study
composition that you should highlight or deemphasize. Would the same composition
serve the needs of all audiences, and why?

2. *Reducing the barriers to composition.* Everyone has difficulties in composing
reports, whether they are case studies or not. To succeed at composing, investigators
must take specific steps during the conduct of a study to reduce barriers to composition. Name five such steps that you would take—such as starting on a portion of the
composition at an early stage. Have you used these five steps in the past?

3. *Anticipating the difficulties of the review process.* Case study compositions,
whether in written or oral form, are likely to be improved by having some review by
informants—that is, those persons who were the subjects of the study. Discuss the
pros and cons of having such reviews. What specific advantage, for quality-control
purposes, is served? What disadvantages are there? On balance, are such reviews
worthwhile?

4. *Maintaining anonymity in case studies.* Identify a case study whose "case" has
been given a fictitious name (examples from the BOXES are community studies such
as Lynd and Lynd's *Middletown* and organizational studies such as Gross et al.'s
Implementing Organizational Innovations). What are the advantages and disadvantages of using such a technique? What approach would you use in reporting your own
case study, and why?

5. *Defining a good case study.* Select a case study that you believe is one of the
best you know (the selection can be from the BOXES in this book). What makes it a
good case study? Why are such characteristics so infrequently found in other case
studies? What specific efforts might you have to make in order to emulate such a good
case study?

NOTES

1. Ignored here is a frequent audience for case studies: students taking a course using case studies as curriculum material. Such use of case studies, as indicated in Chapter 1, is for teaching and not research purposes, and the entire case study strategy might be defined and pursued differently under these conditions.

2. Lois-Ellin Datta, formerly of the U.S. General Accounting Office, has another way of describing this role of case studies (U.S. General Accounting Office, 1990). According to her, the case report should be viewed as a substitute for an actual site visit; such a goal can provide the investigator with guidance in composing the report.

3. The author suffered directly from this problem in trying to have several independent reviewers examine and rate a large number of case studies (see Yin, Bateman, & Moore, 1983). Each reviewer eventually had to be sent boxfuls of case studies to peruse, and substantial time had to be allotted to the rating process.

4. Of course, even when an investigator makes the identity of a case or its participants anonymous, a few other colleagues—sharing the confidence of the investigator—will usually know the real identities. In the case of both *Street Corner Society* and *Middletown*, other sociologists, especially those working in the same academic departments as Whyte and the Lynds, were quite aware of the real identities.

5. The speculations also are based on some empirical findings. As part of an earlier investigation, 21 prominent social scientists were asked to name the best qualities of case studies (see Yin, Bateman, & Moore, 1983). Some of these qualities are reflected in this discussion of exemplary case studies.

References

Agranoff, R., & Radin, B. A. (1991). The comparative case study approach in public adminis-tration. *Research in Public Administration, 1,* 203-231.

Alkin, M., et al. (1979). *Using evaluations: Does evaluation make a difference?* Beverly Hills, CA: Sage.

Allison, G. T. (1971). *Essence of decision: Explaining the Cuban missile crisis.* Boston: Little, Brown.

Auger, D. A. (1979). The politics of revitalization in gentrifying neighborhoods: The case of Boston's South End. *Journal of the American Planning Association, 45,* 515-522.

Barzun, J., & Graff, H. (1985). *The modern researcher* (4th ed.). New York: Harcourt Brace Jovanovich.

Becker, H. S. (1958). Problems of inference and proof in participant observation. *American Sociological Review, 23,* 652-660.

Becker, H. S. (1963). Becoming a marijuana user. In H. S. Becker (Ed.), *The outsiders* (pp. 41-58). New York: Free Press.

Becker, H. S. (1967). Whose side are we on? *Social Problems, 14,* 239-247.

Becker, H. S. (1986). *Writing for social scientists: How to start and finish your thesis, book, or article.* Chicago: University of Chicago Press.

Bernstein, C., & Woodward, B. (1974). *All the president's men.* New York: Simon & Schuster.

Bickman, L. (1987). The functions of program theory. In L. Bickman (Ed.), *Using program theory in evaluation* (pp. 5-18). San Francisco: Jossey-Bass.

Bishop, Y. M., Fienberg, S. E., & Holland, P. W. (1975). *Discrete multivariate analysis.* Cam-bridge: MIT Press.

Blalock, H. M., Jr. (1961). *Causal inferences in nonexperimental research.* New York: Norton.

Blau, P. M. (1955). *The dynamics of bureaucracy.* Chicago: University of Chicago Press.

Bolgar, H. (1965). The case study method. In B. B. Wolman (Ed.), *The handbook of clinical psychology* (pp. 28-38). New York: McGraw-Hill.

Boruch, R. (forthcoming). *Conducting ramdomized experiments.* Thousand Oaks, CA: Sage.

Bouchard, T. J., Jr. (1976). Field research methods. In M. D. Dunnette (Ed.), *Industrial and organizational psychology* (pp. 363-413). Chicago: Rand McNally.

Brinton, C. (1938). *The anatomy of a revolution.* Englewood Cliffs, NJ: Prentice Hall.

Campbell, D. T. (1969). Reforms as experiments. *American Psychologist, 24,* 409-429.

Campbell, D. T. (1975). Degrees of freedom and the case study. *Comparative Political Studies, 8,* 178-193.

Campbell, D. T., & Stanley, J. (1966). *Experimental and quasi-experimental designs for research.* Chicago: Rand McNally.

Campbell, J. P., Daft, R. L., & Hulin, C. L. (1982). *What to study: Generating and developing research questions.* Beverly Hills, CA: Sage.

Carroll, J., & Johnson, E. (1992). Decision research: A field guide. *Journal of the Operational Research Society, 43,* 71-72.

Caulley, D. N., & Dowdy, I. (1987). Evaluation case histories as a parallel to legal case histories. *Evaluation and Program Planning, 10,* 359-372.

Cochran, W. G., & Cox, G. M. (1957). *Experimental designs* (2nd ed.). New York: John Wiley.

Cook, T. D., & Campbell, D. T. (1979). *Quasi-experimentation: Design and analysis issues for field settings.* Chicago: Rand McNally.

Cooper, H. M. (1984). *The integrative research review.* Beverly Hills, CA: Sage.

Cronbach, L. J., et al. (1980). *Toward reform of program evaluation: Aims, methods, and institutional arrangements.* San Francisco: Jossey-Bass.

Dabbs, J. M., Jr. (1982). Making things visible. In J. Van Maanen et al. (Eds.), *Varieties of qualitative research* (pp. 31-63). Beverly Hills, CA: Sage.

Denzin, N. K. (1978). The logic of naturalistic inquiry. In N. K. Denzin (Ed.), *Sociological methods: A sourcebook.* New York: McGraw-Hill.

Derthick, M. (1972). *New towns in-town: Why a federal program failed.* Washington, DC: Urban Institute.

Douglas, J. D. (1976). *Investigative social research: Individual and team field research.* Beverly Hills, CA: Sage.

Drucker, P. F. (1986). The changed world economy. In P. F. Drucker (Ed.), *The frontiers of management* (pp. 21-49). New York: E. P. Dutton.

Eckstein, H. (1975). Case study and theory in political science. In F. I. Greenstein & N. W. Polsby (Eds.), *Strategies of inquiry* (pp. 79-137). Reading, MA: Addison-Wesley.

Eisenhardt, K. M. (1989). Building theories from case study research. *Academy of Management Review, 14*(4), 532-550.

Feagin, J. R., Orum, A. M., & Sjoberg, G. (Eds.). (1991). *A case for the case study.* Chapel Hill: University of North Carolina Press.

Fetterman, D. (1989). *Ethnography: Step by step.* Newbury Park, CA: Sage.

Fiedler, J. (1978). *Field research: A manual for logistics and management of scientific studies in natural settings.* San Francisco: Jossey-Bass.

Fowler, F. J., Jr. (1988). *Survey research methods* (rev. ed.). Newbury Park, CA: Sage.

Friesema, P., et al. (1979). *Aftermath: Communities after natural disasters.* Beverly Hills, CA: Sage.

Gans, H. J. (1962). *The urban villagers: Group and class in the life of Italian-Americans.* New York: Free Press.

George, A. L. (1979). Case studies and theory development: The method of structured, focused comparison. In P. G. Lauren (Ed.), *Diplomacy: New approaches in history, theory, and policy* (pp. 43-68). New York: Free Press.

Glaser, B., & Strauss, A. (1967). *The discovery of grounded theory: Strategies for qualitative research.* Chicago: Aldine.

Goodman, L. (1978). *Analyzing quantitative categorical data.* Cambridge, MA: Abt Books.

Gottschalk, L. (1968). *Understanding history: A primer of historical method.* New York: Knopf.

Gross, N., et al. (1971). *Implementing organizational innovations.* New York: Basic Books.

Guba, E. G., & Lincoln, Y. S. (1981). *Effective evaluation.* San Francisco: Jossey-Bass.

Guba, E. G., & Lincoln, Y. S. (1989). *Fourth generation evaluation.* Newbury Park, CA: Sage.

Hamel, J. (Ed.). (1992, Spring). The case study method in sociology [Whole issue]. *Current Sociology, 40.*

Hammond, P. E. (1968). *Sociologists at work: Essays on the craft of social research.* Garden City, NY: Doubleday.

Harrison, M. I. (1987). *Diagnosing organizations.* Newbury Park, CA: Sage.

Hedrick, T., Bickman, L., & Rog, D. J. (1993). *Applied research design.* Newbury Park, CA: Sage.

Herriott, R. E., & Firestone, W. A. (1983). Multisite qualitative policy research: Optimizing description and generalizability. *Educational Researcher, 12,* 14-19.

Herriott, R. E., & Gross, N. (Eds.). (1979). *The dynamics of planned educational change.* Berkeley, CA: McCutchan.

Hersen, M., & Barlow, D. H. (1976). *Single-case experimental designs: Strategies for studying behavior.* New York: Pergamon.

Hoaglin, D. C., Light, R. J., McPeek, B., Mosteller, F., & Stoto, M. A. (1982). *Data for decisions: Information strategies for policymakers.* Cambridge, MA: Abt Books.

Hooks, G. (1990). The rise of the Pentagon and U.S. state building: The defense program as industrial policy. *American Journal of Sociology, 96,* 358-404.

Jacob, E. (1987). Qualitative research traditions: A review. *Review of Educational Research, 57,* 1-50.

Jacob, E. (1989). Qualitative research: A defense of traditions. *Review of Educational Research, 59,* 229-235.

Jacobs, G. (Ed.). (1970). *The participant observer: Encounters with social reality.* New York: George Braziller.

Jacobs, J. (1961). *The death and life of great American cities.* New York: Random House.

Johnson, J. (1976). *Doing field research.* New York: Free Press.

Jorgensen, D. (1989). *Participant observation: A methodology for human studies.* Newbury Park, CA: Sage.

Kaufman, H. (1960). *The forest ranger: A study in administrative behavior.* Baltimore: Johns Hopkins University Press.

Kaufman, H. (1981). *The administrative behavior of federal bureau chiefs.* Washington, DC: Brookings Institution.

Kennedy, M. M. (1976). Generalizing from single case studies. *Evaluation Quarterly, 3,* 661-678.

Kidder, L. (1981). Qualitative research and quasi-experimental frameworks. In M. Brewer & B. E. Collins (Eds.), *Scientific inquiry and the social sciences* (pp. 227-256). San Francisco: Jossey-Bass.

Kidder, L., & Judd, C. M. (1986). *Research methods in social relations* (5th ed.). New York: Holt, Rinehart & Winston.

Kidder, T. (1981). *The soul of a new machine.* Boston: Little, Brown.

King, J. A., Morris, L. L., & Fitz-Gibbon, C. T. (1987). *How to assess program implementation.* Newbury Park, CA: Sage.

Kratochwill, T. R. (1978). *Single subject research.* New York: Academic Press.

Larsen, J. (1982). *Use of knowledge in mental health services.* Palo Alto, CA: American Institutes for Research.

Latané, B., & Darley, J. M. (1969). Bystander apathy. *American Behavioral Scientist, 57,* 244-268.

Lavrakas, P. J. (1987). *Telephone survey methods.* Newbury Park, CA: Sage.

Liebow, E. (1967). *Tally's corner.* Boston: Little, Brown.

Lightfoot, S. L. (1981). Portraits of exemplary secondary schools. *Daedalus, 110,* 17-38, 59-80, 97-116.

Lijphart, A. (1975). The comparable-cases strategy in comparative research. *Comparative Political Studies, 8,* 158-177.

Lincoln, Y. S. (1991). The arts and sciences of program evaluation. *Evaluation Practice, 12,* 1-7.

Lincoln, Y. S., & Guba, E. G. (1985). But is it rigorous? Trustworthiness and authenticity in naturalistic evaluation. In D. D. Williams (Ed.), *Naturalistic evaluation.* San Francisco: Jossey-Bass.

Lincoln, Y. S., & Guba, E. G. (1986). *Naturalistic inquiry.* Beverly Hills, CA: Sage.

Linn, R. L., et al. (1982, April). The validity of the Title I evaluation and reporting system. In E. Reisner et al. (Eds.), *Assessment of the Title I evaluation and reporting system*. Washington, DC: U.S. Department of Education.

Lipset, S. M., Trow, M., & Coleman, J. (1956). *Union democracy: The inside politics of the International Typographical Union*. New York: Free Press.

Llewellyn, K. N. (1948). Case method. In E. Seligman & A. Johnson (Eds.), *Encyclopedia of the social sciences*. New York: Macmillan.

Lofland, J. (1971). *Analyzing social settings: A guide to qualitative observation and analysis*. Belmont, CA: Wadsworth.

Lucas, W. A. (1974). *The case survey method*. Santa Monica, CA: RAND Corporation.

Lupo, A., et al. (1971). *Rites of way*. Boston: Little, Brown.

Lynd, R. S., & Lynd, H. M. (1929). *Middletown: A study in modern American culture*. New York: Harcourt Brace Jovanovich.

Magaziner, I. C., & Patinkin, M. (1989). *The silent war: Inside the global business battles shaping America's future*. New York: Random House.

Majchrzak, A. (1984). *Methods for policy research*. Beverly Hills, CA: Sage.

Markus, M. L. (1983). Power, politics, and MIS implementation. *Communications of the ACM, 26*, 430-444.

Marshall, C., & Rossman, G. B. (1989). *Designing qualitative research*. Newbury Park, CA: Sage.

McCall, G. J., & Simmons, J. L. (1969). *Issues in participant observation*. Reading, MA: Addison-Wesley.

McClintock, C. (1985). Process sampling: A method for case study research on administrative behavior. *Educational Administration Quarterly, 21*, 205-222.

Mechling, J. E. (1974). Successful innovation: Manpower scheduling. *Urban Analysis, 3*, 259-313.

Merton, R. K., Fiske, M., & Kendall, P. L. (1990). *The focused interview: A manual of problems and procedures* (2nd ed.). New York: Free Press.

Miles, M. B. (1979). Qualitative data as an attractive nuisance: The problem of analysis. *Administrative Science Quarterly, 24*, 590-601.

Miles, M. B., & Huberman, A. M. (1984). *Analyzing qualitative data: A source book for new methods*. Beverly Hills, CA: Sage.

Moore, B., Jr. (1966). *Social origins of dictatorship and democracy: Lord and peasant in the making of the modern world*. Boston: Beacon.

Moore, G. B., & Yin, R. K. (1983). *Innovations in earthquake and natural hazards research: Unreinforced masonry*. Washington, DC: COSMOS Corporation.

Morris, L. L., Fitz-Gibbon, C. T., & Freeman, M. E. (1987). *How to communicate evaluation findings*. Newbury Park, CA: Sage.

Murphy, J. T. (1980). *Getting the facts: A fieldwork guide for evaluators and policy analysts*. Santa Monica, CA: Goodyear.

Nachmias, D., & Nachmias, C. (1992). *Research methods in the social sciences*. New York: St. Martin.

Naroll, R., & Cohen, R. (Eds.). (1973). *A handbook of method in cultural anthropology*. New York: Columbia University Press.

Neustadt, R. E., & Fineberg, H. (1983). *The epidemic that never was: Policy-making and the swine flu affair*. New York: Vintage.

Patton, M. Q. (1980). *Qualitative evaluation methods*. Beverly Hills, CA: Sage.

Patton, M. Q. (1987). *How to use qualitative methods in evaluation*. Newbury Park, CA: Sage.

Pelto, P. J., & Pelto, G. H. (1978). *Anthropological research: The structure of inquiry.* Cambridge: Cambridge University Press.

Pelz, D. C. (1981). *Use of innovation in innovating processes by local governments.* Ann Arbor: University of Michigan, CRUSK, Institute for Social Research.

Perry, J. M., & Kraemer, K. L. (1986). Research methodology in the public administration review. *Public Administration Review, 46,* 215-226.

Peters, T. J., & Waterman, R. H., Jr. (1982). *In search of excellence.* New York: Harper & Row.

Peterson, K. A., & Bickman, L. (1992). Using program theory in quality assessments of children's mental health services. In H. T. Chen & P. Rossi (Eds.), *Using theory to improve program and policy evaluations* (pp. 165-176). Westport, CT: Greenwood.

Philliber, S. G., Schwab, M. R., & Samsloss, G. (1980). *Social research: Guides to a decision-making process.* Itasca, IL: Peacock.

Platt, J. (1992a). "Case study" in American methodological thought. *Current Sociology, 40,* 17-48.

Platt, J. (1992b). Cases of cases . . . of cases. In C. C. Ragin & H. S. Becker (Eds.), *What is a case? Exploring the foundations of social inquiry* (pp. 21-52). New York: Cambridge University Press.

Pressman, J. L., & Wildavsky, A. (1973). *Implementation: How great expectations in Washington are dashed in Oakland.* Berkeley: University of California Press.

Redman, E. (1973). *The dance of legislation.* New York: Simon & Schuster.

Rog, D. J., & Huebner, R. B. (1992). Using research and theory in developing innovative programs for homeless individuals. In H. T. Chen & P. Rossi (Eds.), *Using theory to improve program and policy evaluations* (pp. 129-144). Westport, CT: Greenwood.

Rosenthal, R. (1966). *Experimenter effects in behavioral research.* New York: Appleton-Century-Crofts.

Rothney, J. M. (1968). *Methods of studying the individual child: The psychological case study.* Waltham, MA: Blaisdell.

Schatzman, L., & Strauss, A. (1973). *Field research.* Englewood Cliffs, NJ: Prentice Hall.

Schramm, W. (1971, December). *Notes on case studies of instructional media projects.* Working paper, the Academy for Educational Development, Washington, DC.

Schwartz, H., & Jacobs, J. (1979). *Qualitative sociology: A method to the madness.* New York: Free Press.

Sechrest, L. (1991, October-November). *Roots: Back to our first generations.* Presidential remarks at the annual meeting of the American Evaluation Association, Chicago.

Selznick, P. (1980). *TVA and the grass roots: A study of politics and organization.* Berkeley: University of California Press. (Original work published 1949)

Sidowski, J. B. (Ed.). (1966). *Experimental methods and instrumentation in psychology.* New York: Holt, Rinehart & Winston.

Sieber, S. D. (1973). The integration of fieldwork and survey methods. *American Journal of Sociology, 78,* 1335-1359.

Smith, J. K., & Heshusius, L. (1986). Closing down the conversation: The end of the quantitative-qualitative debate among educational inquirers. *Educational Researcher, 15,* 4-12.

Smith, N. L. (1990). Cautions on the use of investigative case studies in meta-evaluation. *Evaluation and Program Planning, 13*(4), 373-378.

Spilerman, S. (1971). The causes of racial disturbances: Tests of an explanation. *American Sociological Review, 36,* 427-442.

Stake, R. E. (1983). The case study method in social inquiry. In G. F. Madaus, M. S. Scriven, & D. L. Stufflebeam (Eds.), *Evaluation models* (pp. 279-286). Boston: Kluwer-Nijhoff.

Stake, R. E. (1986). *Quieting reform: Social science and social action in an urban youth program.* Urbana: University of Illinois Press.

Stake, R. E. (1994). Case studies. In N. K. Denzin & Y. S. Lincoln (Eds.), *Handbook of qualitative research* (pp. 236-247). Thousand Oaks, CA: Sage.

Standerfer, N. R., & Rider, J. (1983). The politics of automating a planning office. *Planning, 49,* 18-21.

Stein, H. (1952). Case method and the analysis of public administration. In H. Stein (Ed.), *Public administration and policy development* (pp. xx-xxx). New York: Harcourt Brace Jovanovich.

Stoecker, R. (1991). Evaluating and rethinking the case study. *The Sociological Review, 39,* 88-112.

Strauss, A., & Corbin, J. (1990). *Basics of qualitative research: Grounded theory procedures and techniques.* Newbury Park, CA: Sage.

Sudman, S., & Bradburn, N. M. (1982). *Asking questions: A practical guide to questionnaire design.* San Francisco: Jossey-Bass.

Szanton, P. (1981). *Not well advised.* New York: Russell Sage Foundation and the Ford Foundation.

Towl, A. R. (1969). *To study administrations by cases.* Boston: Harvard University Business School.

Trochim, W. (1989). Outcome pattern matching and program theory. *Evaluation and Program Planning, 12,* 355-366.

U.S. General Accounting Office, Program Evaluation and Methodology Division. (1990). *Case study evaluations.* Washington, DC: Government Printing Office.

U.S. National Commission on Neighborhoods. (1979). *People, building neighborhoods.* Washington, DC: Government Printing Office.

U.S. Office of Technology Assessment. (1980-1981). *The implications of cost-effectiveness analysis of medical technology: Case studies of medical technologies.* Washington, DC: Government Printing Office.

Valentine, C. A. (1968). *Culture and poverty: Critique and counter-proposals.* Chicago: University of Chicago Press.

Van Maanen, J. (1988). *Tales of the field: On writing ethnography.* Chicago: University of Chicago Press.

Van Maanen, J., Dabbs, J. M., Jr., & Faulkner, R. R. (1982). *Varieties of qualitative research.* Beverly Hills, CA: Sage.

Wax, R. (1971). *Doing field work.* Chicago: University of Chicago Press.

Webb, E., Campbell, D. T., Schwartz, R. D., Sechrest, L., & Grove, J. B. (1981). *Nonreactive measures in the social sciences* (2nd ed.). Boston: Houghton Mifflin.

Webb, E., & Weick, K. E. (1979). Unobtrusive measures in organizational theory: A reminder. *Administrative Science Quarterly, 24,* 650-659.

Wholey, J. (1979). *Evaluation: Performance and promise.* Washington, DC: Urban Institute.

Whyte, W. F. (1955). *Street corner society: The social structure of an Italian slum.* Chicago: University of Chicago Press. (Original work published 1943)

Wilford, J. N. (1992). *The mysterious history of Columbus.* New York: Vintage.

Windsor, D., & Greanias, G. (1983). The public policy and management program for case/course development. *Public Administration Review, 26,* 370-378.

Wolcott, H. F. (1990). *Writing up qualitative research.* Newbury Park, CA: Sage.

Yin, R. K. (1970). Face recognition by brain-injured patients: A dissociable ability? *Neuropsychologia, 8,* 395-402.

Yin, R. K. (1972). *Participant-observation and the development of urban neighborhood policy.* New York: New York City-Rand Institute.

Yin, R. K. (1978). Face perception: A review of experiments with infants, normal adults, and brain-injured persons. In R. Held, H. W. Leibowitz, & H. Teuber (Eds.), *Handbook of sensory physiology: Vol. 8. Perception* (pp. 593-608). New York: Springer-Verlag.

Yin, R. K. (1979). *Changing urban bureaucracies: How new practices become routinized.* Lexington, MA: Lexington Books.

Yin, R. K. (1980). Creeping federalism: The federal impact on the structure and function of local government. In N. J. Glickman (Ed.), *The urban impacts of federal policies* (pp. 595-618). Baltimore: Johns Hopkins University Press.

Yin, R. K. (1981a). The case study as a serious research strategy. *Knowledge: Creation, Diffusion, Utilization, 3*, 97-114.

Yin, R. K. (1981b). The case study crisis: Some answers. *Administrative Science Quarterly, 26*, 58-65.

Yin, R. K. (1981c). Life histories of innovations: How new practices become routinized. *Public Administration Review, 41*, 21-28.

Yin, R. K. (1982a). *Conserving America's neighborhoods.* New York: Plenum.

Yin, R. K. (1982b). Studying the implementation of public programs. In W. Williams et al. (Eds.), *Studying implementation: Methodological and administrative issues* (pp. 36-72). Chatham, NJ: Chatham House.

Yin, R. K. (1982c). Studying phenomenon and context across sites. *American Behavioral Scientist, 26*, 84-100.

Yin, R. K. (1983). *The case study method: An annotated bibliography* (1983-1984 ed.). Washington, DC: COSMOS Corporation.

Yin, R. K. (1993). *Applications of case study research.* Newbury Park, CA: Sage.

Yin, R. K. (1994). Evaluation: A singular craft. In C. Reichardt & S. Rallis (Eds.), *New directions in program evaluation* (pp. 71-84). San Francisco: Jossey-Bass.

Yin, R. K., Bateman, P. G., & Moore, G. B. (1983, September). *Case studies and organizational innovation: Strengthening the connection.* Washington, DC: COSMOS Corporation.

Yin, R. K., Bingham, E., & Heald, K. A. (1976). The difference that quality makes. *Sociological Methods & Research, 5*, 139-156.

Yin, R. K., & Heald, K. A. (1975). Using the case survey method to analyze policy studies. *Administrative Science Quarterly, 20*, 371-381.

Yin, R. K., Heald, K. A., & Vogel, M. (1977). *Tinkering with the system: Technological innovations in state and local services.* Lexington, MA: Lexington Press.

Yin, R. K., & Moore, G. B. (1984). *The utilization of research: Lessons from a multi-disciplined field.* Washington, DC: COSMOS Corporation.

Yin, R. K., & White, J. L. (1984). *Microcomputer implementation in schools.* Washington, DC: COSMOS Corporation.

Yin, R. K., & Yates, D. (1975). *Street-level governments: Assessing decentralization and urban services.* Lexington, MA: Lexington Press.

Name Index

Subject Index

About the Author

Robert K. Yin is President of COSMOS Corporation, a research and management technology firm specializing in social policy problems. Within the firm, he is involved with individual projects, including those using the case study method. Most of the applications reported in this book derive from work done with COSMOS's projects. He is the author of numerous other books and articles. This book on the case study method, *Case Study Research: Design and Methods*, has had two editions (1984, eight printings; 1989, fifteen printings). Dr. Yin is a former member of the RAND Corporation (1970-1978) and a member of the Cosmos Club. He has also served as Visiting Scholar to the U.S. General Accounting Office during 1992-1993 (Program Evaluation and Methodology Division) and has served on the editorial boards of numerous journals, on peer review panels, and on committees of the National Academy of Sciences. He is known internationally for his presentations, seminars, and workshops on applied social research. A recent honor was his being invited to make a plenary presentation—"Evaluation: A Singular Craft"—at the American Evaluation Association (November 1992). He received his B.A. (magna cum laude) from Harvard College in 1962 (in history) and his Ph.D. in 1970 from the Department of Brain and Cognitive Sciences, Massachusetts Institute of Technology.